We Are All Chile

We Are All Chile

Representations of Difference in Contemporary Chilean Historical Fiction

KATHERINE KARR-CORNEJO

UNIVERSITY OF NEW MEXICO PRESS | ALBUQUERQUE

© 2025 by the University of New Mexico Press
All rights reserved. Published 2025
Printed in the United States of America

Library of Congress Cataloging-in-Publication Data

Names: Karr-Cornejo, Katherine Elizabeth Bunting, author.
Title: We are all Chile: representations of difference in
contemporary Chilean historical fiction / Katherine Karr-Cornejo.
Description: Albuquerque: University of New Mexico Press, 2025. |
Includes bibliographical references and index.
Identifiers: LCCN 2024039152 (print) | LCCN 2024039153 (ebook) |
ISBN 9780826367877 (cloth) | ISBN 9780826367884 (paperback) |
ISBN 9780826367891 (epub)
Subjects: LCSH: Chile—History. | Chile—History—Fiction. |
Chile—Civilization. | Chile—Social life and customs. | BISAC:
LITERARY CRITICISM / Caribbean & Latin American |
HISTORY / Latin America / General
Classification: LCC F3081 .K37 2025 (print) | LCC F3081 (ebook) |
DDC 983—dc23/eng/20241216
LC record available at https://lccn.loc.gov/2024039152
LC ebook record available at https://lccn.loc.gov/2024039153

Founded in 1889, the University of New Mexico sits on the
traditional homelands of the Pueblo of Sandia. The original peoples
of New Mexico—Pueblo, Navajo, and Apache—since time
immemorial have deep connections to the land and have made
significant contributions to the broader community statewide. We
honor the land itself and those who remain stewards of this land
throughout the generations and also acknowledge our committed
relationship to Indigenous peoples. We gratefully recognize our
history.

Cover illustration: *Tabula geographica regni Chile*. Studio et labore
P. procuratoris Chilensis Societatis Jesu, 1645.
Designed by Felicia Cedillos
Composed in Adobe Garamond Pro

CONTENTS

Acknowledgments   vii

Introduction. We Are All Chile   1
Chapter One. The Conquest of Chile   23
Chapter Two. The Viceregal Period   57
Chapter Three. Independence   93
Chapter Four. The Occupation of Araucanía   129
Chapter Five. Civil War   159
Conclusion. Chile Awakens?   189

Notes   195
Works Cited   213
Index   227

ACKNOWLEDGMENTS

The book in your hands (or on your screen) is a product of over two decades of friendships, study and research, and experiences. When I was a student in Santiago, back in the time of the old yellow micros, one of my daily joys was reading their *letreros* and looking up the places they indicated; those places went into my book of maps to create a mental atlas of the city for myself. That posture opened a world to me that continues to nourish my imagination and shape me personally and professionally. I am grateful to all of the people, known to me and not, who enabled those experiences and encouraged my curiosity. Among the known, I count the extended Cornejo family; the extended Faúndez family, especially Carmen and Marisol; Susana and Natalia Olmedo, Carolina Castro, Claudia Hormazábal, Elizabeth Grünholz, and the folks who were part of the Iglesia Providencia's young adult group. Gloria Favi, thank you for lending me books I wouldn't have otherwise read. I fondly remember Evelyn Vitagliano, Nora Martínez, Hilda Luna, José Cornejo, Filomena Morgado, and Inés Cox, qepd. Thank you all for your love and support, even when you weren't quite sure what I was doing.

The support that I have received from academic communities of which I have been a part has been a gift. I am grateful to the University of Virginia, Hampden–Sydney College, and Whitworth University for institutional support, as well as the Andrew W. Mellon Foundation's Dissertation Seminar in the humanities. The many folks who work in administrative support roles at these institutions enabled this work and I appreciate their help and patience. I also thank everyone at the University of New Mexico Press for their support of this work, especially Michael Millman, Anna Pohlod, and James Cruise.

I am indebted to those scholars with whom I had the privilege to study: Joseph Schraibman, Elzbieta Sklodowska, J. Andrew Brown, Ruth Hill, Daniel Chávez, Ricardo Padrón, David Gies, Joel Rini, Emily Scida, and the incomparable and much missed Donald L. Shaw. Thomas Klubock, Susan

Fraiman, Mrinalini Chakravorty, and Heather Warren brought wisdom and insight from their disciplines to bear on my thinking.

I had a wonderful model of scholarly generosity and kindness in María-Inés Lagos, who was always a delight to work with. My inner writing coach has your voice. Thank you for walking with me. I am so grateful.

Scholarship only thrives in community, and I am beyond appreciative of the communities of which I have been a part professionally. I have been influenced and learned from classmates throughout undergraduate and graduate school, especially the folks who read and discussed feminist theory with me. My gratitude also goes to conference attendees, panelists, and reviewers of my work throughout the years. I wish I had kept better records to thank everyone by name. I give my heartfelt gratitude to Leila Gómez, Rocío Quispe-Agnoli, Vilma Navarro-Daniels, Luis Cárcamo-Huechante, Cristian Opazo, Laura Demaria, María-Rosa Olivera Williams, Bernardita Llanos, Gloria Medina-Sancho, Ilana Luna, Cheyla Samuelson, Amanda Petersen, Rebecca Janzen, Sara Potter, Niamh Thornton, Emily Hind, Tamara Williams, Fernando Blanco, the folks of the Southern Cone Studies section of LASA, and the folks of the Asociación de Estudios de Género y Sexualidades.

Colleagues at Whitworth University who have participated in writing groups with me through the years have provided invaluable support: Jake Rapp, Bendi Schrambach, Dawn Keig, Amanda Clark, Casey Andrews, Marc Robinson, Stacy Keogh, Nicole Sheets, Megan Hershey, Tony Clark, Bert Emerson, Patricia Bruininks, Elise Leal, Elizabeth Abbey, Dale Soden. I also thank the students who have contributed in one way or another to the success of this project, including: Haley Baxley, Delaney From, Madeline Harris, Khristian Paul, Donna Schrock, Cilicia Stachowiak, Katie Tassan, Hannah Tweet, Kayden Vargas. Pamela Corpron Parker and Laura Bloxham were amazing mentors, and I wish I had had more years with them.

Natalie McManus Chu and Ashley Kerr Muhlenkamp, thank you for playing word bingo with me! Banji Iyun, Erica Salkin, Vange Mariet Ocasio, Danny and Janice Dean, thank you for being beloved friends who are family. Rosa Mirna Sánchez, Rafaela Acevedo-Field, Jennifer Brown, thank you for being beloved friends who are family who talk to me about literature and history and encourage me to be brave.

My much loved family, you are amazing and I am who I am because of you. Thank you for your support over the years: Bruce and Mary Karr, Nicholas Karr and Sofia Balters, Benjamin Tatham and Rebecca Karr who gets a special shout-out because she has always read my work and is also my indexer! Thanks, Becks!

The world can be better than it is, and that is what I want for the next generation, for whom I am grateful: Matias Karr, Carina Pérez, Coral Pérez, Ọmọlọlá Tirzah Iyùn, and Ọmọ́táyọ̀ Nathaniel Iyùn.

And because all cats are beautiful: gracias Violet, gracias Izkia.

INTRODUCTION
We Are All Chile

FOR NEARLY TWENTY-FIVE YEARS, the We Are All Chile International Committee (*Comité Internacional Chile Somos Todos*) has brought together Chilean citizens abroad to promote and defend their rights. The Ministry of Foreign Affairs has also used the same language, "Chile Somos Todos," in varied forms to highlight its portfolio of work, from websites to magazines that draw attention to consular services abroad, as well as initiatives and meetings of note. At the beginning of his second presidential term in 2018, Sebastián Piñera (1949–2024) declaimed from the balcony of La Moneda Palace:

> Chilenas y chilenos, queridos compatriotas: Chile somos todos, y por eso tenemos que soñarlo, dibujarlo y construirlo entre todos. . . . Queridos compatriotas: En las grandes tareas que tenemos por delante, les puedo asegurar que todos tendremos la oportunidad de aportar . . . no sólo todos tendremos un lugar para aportar, sino que también todos tendremos una justa participación en los beneficios que esta gran misión va a generar. Porque Chile somos todos, porque en Chile no sobra nadie, salvo el odio, la maldad, la intolerancia y la violencia. (Piñera)

By the end of the next year, however, the rhetoric of solidarity, collaboration, and benefit rang as hollow as the burned-out subway trains that stood as a testament to social unrest and dissatisfaction. While Piñera had presented a vision of a Chile again in transition, and in which each person had a role to play, the citizenry and residents en masse did not see or receive that promised fair distribution of capital.

One might take issue with "We Are All Chile," given that it is the language of a small advocacy group, a slogan in a government ministry, and a key phrase associated with a President who ended his final term with historically low approval ratings.[1] However, this shibboleth still communicates an ideal of community in which all people belong and flourish. When Gabriel Boric (b. 1986) officially announced Piñera's death in February 2024, he recognized that, despite his own political opposition, Piñera "buscó genuinamente lo que él creía que era lo mejor para el país" (Boric) and highlighted the key phrase from Piñera's second inaugural address as a sort of official epitaph: "Chile somos todos, y por eso tenemos que soñarlo, dibujarlo y construirlo entre todos." Everyone is called to dream, draw, and construct a Chile in which everyone belongs, despite the mechanisms of exclusion that have and continue to operate in Chilean society.

Many communities, admittedly, have considered themselves to be uniquely important or exemplary. The ideology of exceptionalism—that a particular community or nation is superior to others—impregnates all political rhetoric.[2] Chile does not deviate from this practice, as the myths of its unique democratic heritage in a region known for instability or its singular economic development show. Chile is and has been a model, inhabiting an affective place of privilege for non-Chileans across political, economic, and ideological spectrums. The idea of Chile—its history, cultures, and present—today embodies neoliberal reforms, which have their roots in the demise of the leftist project of the early 1970s. As a relatively small country, it occupies an outsized imaginary footprint. The politically motivated torture and killing that the military dictatorship of Augusto Pinochet (1973–1990) carried out dominates this footprint outside Chile's borders. These abuses have also contributed to the way in which mainstream Chilean society has dealt with varying forms of diversity after the end of the dictatorship. In a country in which 87.2% of individuals self-identify as white or nonindigenous (*Síntesis* 16) and the pay gap between men and women is growing, attention to the representations of socially disadvantaged groups, such as those who do not identify as nonindigenous and women of all ethnicities, can illuminate ideologies of difference that undergird continued inequality and discrimination. This study aims to address the expanses and limits of the idea that "we are all Chile." Normative *chilenidad* restricts belonging, though those borders shift periodically, and the distinction between the ideal community and reality bears noting. To that end, engaging with the representations of race, gender, and social class in historical fiction of the period after the return of democracy in 1990 allows us to understand the narratives that are woven throughout civic life and culture. Historical fiction reflects ideologies of the present even as it purports to tell a story of the past. I propose that history and geography, stories and maps, provide different frames for understanding such a world and that historical fiction, in particular, plays with the frameworks provided because it is a vehicle by which these categories of exclusion are constructed, changed, and challenged. Historical fiction written in the 1990s and 2000s in Chile uses previous Chilean history to reflect on the challenges of Chilean society during the democratic transition (1990–2010) in ways that differ from how these historical individuals and events were used prior to 1990. These differences illustrate hegemonic Chilean society's attitudes toward disadvantaged communities, particularly women and indigenous groups, and call into question how legacies of the dictatorial authoritarian state effect possibilities for diversity and unity in contemporary Chile.

The Shape of Chilean History

Chilean history rarely becomes a subject of study for those outside its national borders, unless those outsiders are somehow involved in Chilean affairs—as, for example, the United States has been in many parts of Latin America. Given that missing knowledge, I offer this brief summary of the shape of events in the territory today known as Chile between the arrival of Spanish occupiers in the early sixteenth century and the present day. I concentrate on the periods before 1891 and after 1973, despite a number of historical fictions that deal with twentieth-century events (such as the 1907 massacre of Santa María de Iquique)[3] because most Chilean historical novels written between 1990 and 2010 refer to the nineteenth-century and earlier.

Those unfamiliar with Chilean history should know that at the dawn of the sixteenth century, Chilean territory was inhabited by a variety of indigenous groups, and the Inka empire extended as far south as the Maule River.[4] South of the territory loosely associated with the Inkas, many Mapuche groups maintained independence, while even further south different indigenous groups populated Patagonia. With the establishment of Spanish control over the center of the Inka empire, Spanish expeditions went south to lay claim to the territories past the Atacama Desert. Pedro de Valdivia (1497–1553) led the first successful mission to establish Spanish settlements, departing Peru in 1540 accompanied by Inés Suárez (1507–1580), the subject of the first chapter. The conflicts that the European expeditioners initiated with the indigenous groups whose territory they wished to claim for Spain constitute what is known as the War of Arauco, a struggle between the Mapuche and Spanish occupiers that continued until the late nineteenth century, the vestiges of which continue to influence Chilean policy today. This war serves as the backdrop for Chilean colonial history, a kind of buzz that at times remains low-level and at others threatens to drown out other concerns. Power struggles influence the comings and goings of governors and church officials, as particular events shift influence along a civil-ecclesiastical axis. These shifts are particularly notable during the early seventeenth century and, taken alongside military developments, frame many of the issues that Catalina de los Ríos y Lisperguer (ca. 1604–1665), the main subject of the second chapter, negotiates.

Lacking many of the economic enticements to be found in other possessions of the Spanish crown, Chile remained marginal to the empire throughout the colonial period. The eighteenth century saw fewer direct armed conflicts with the indigenous groups in the south and greater development of trade between Chile and other parts of the Hispanic world. Destruction routinely threatened settlement in the form of uprisings, pirate attacks, or natural phenomena such as earthquakes and tsunamis. In general, however, the elite accumulated increased wealth throughout the century. The work of Joaquín Toesca (1752–1799), one subject of the third chapter, to improve the architecture and building practices of Santiago reflects this increased affluence. Moreover, the circumstances of his marriage to a woman whose family fortune had steadily decreased emphasizes the growing importance of commerce. In the early nineteenth century, *criollos*[5] reacted against Napoleon's invasion of Spain disparately, with various groups vying for power in the name of the deposed Spanish King or in the name of complete independence. After a series of conflicts, whether between different factions in Chile or external groups, Chile became an independent state in 1818. Javiera Carrera (1781–1862) and Rosario Puga (1796–1858), members of two of these factions, are, with Toesca, the main characters of the third chapter. While this overview grossly simplifies a number of complex situations and glosses over many interesting stories over the course of three centuries of Spanish rule, the main features of Chile's colonial history remain: its frontier situation remained dogged by armed conflict, its geographical isolation limited interaction with other areas until the eighteenth century, and internal power struggles shaped the outcomes of any number of conflicts.

Postindependence, Chile faced a series of internal and external challenges, illustrating Hilda Sabato's observation that the constitution of new polities in Latin America were "long, contested, and often contradictory process[es]" (1294). Political conflict and negotiation between liberals and conservatives shaped practices of civic life. Political crises and armed conflict from 1818–1830 gave way to the Portalian state, characterized by a strong and authoritarian executive center. Conservatives and Liberals vied to control this center over the next sixty years, with the first half under the domination of the Conservatives and the latter portion, up to the Civil War of 1891, under the control of Liberal leadership. Chile fought with and against neighbors in a series of wars that shifted political boundaries, benefitted various economic actors, and formed a foundation on which to construct edifices of belonging. However, armed conflict was not limited to wars against other nation-state actors. It was also in evidence at the conclusion of the War of Arauco: the Occupation of Araucanía (at times referred to euphemistically as the Pacification) came in the wake of a series of regional uprisings in the 1850s that resulted in the restriction of the indigenous Mapuche peoples to the Chilean equivalent of reservations. On these reservations, attempts at cultural annihilation prepared the way for a whiter European immigration to newly "available" land in southern Chile. A peculiar character in this tragedy, a French adventurer named Orélie-Antoine de Tounens, took the side of the Mapuche and is the subject of the fourth chapter.

The close of the nineteenth century saw Chile at war again, but this time among its own elite. Elected in 1886, the polemical figure José Manuel Balmaceda (1840–1891) assumed the presidency and found himself in conflict with the congress. This conflict culminated in a budgetary impasse that triggered both the January 1891 revolt of the Navy fleet in support of congress and Balmaceda's February 1891 closing of congress. The resulting civil war claimed four thousand lives—an unprecedented number for Chilean casualties against foreign powers—and the defeat of Balmaceda and his supporters. In defeat, Balmaceda sought refuge in the Argentine Embassy where he spent twenty days before committing suicide on 19 September 1891, the day after the conclusion of his official presidential period. The social class issues brought to bear by the war and Balmaceda's suicide evoke images of the 1970–1973 Popular Unity government and another Chilean President's suicide in 1973. As such, this armed conflict has provided authors with historical parallels to exploit for historiographical and artistic gain, several examples of which are the subject of the fifth chapter.

At the start of the period in which the authors I study are publishing their works, 1990, Chile was shifting away from dictatorship toward democracy. General Augusto Pinochet Ugarte (1915–2006) had risen within the armed forces to a privileged position during the Popular Unity government led by Salvador Allende (1908–1973) and was one of the four military men who established themselves as political leaders after the violent coup d'état on 11 September 1973. The military government argued that its seizure of power was required by the policies of the democratically elected Allende and the Popular Unity coalition. Pinochet quickly emerged as the leader of the military junta, notorious for its abuse of the human rights of those opposed to his regime. Internally, Pinochet's government enacted an economic program of neoliberalization while imposing conservative social programs and authoritarian governmental structures.[6] A new constitution, still in force,[7] was implemented in 1980 that required a plebiscite to be held on military rule in 1988. Pinochet lost the 1988 plebiscite, and in the following presidential elections, the right-wing candidate lost to Patricio Aylwin (1918–2016), the candidate from the prodemocracy coalition of parties known as the *Concertación de Partidos por la Democracia*, or *Concertación*. Aylwin was sworn in as president on 11 March 1990, becoming a public and political face for the formal political process of democratic transition. Although no longer president, Pinochet remained Commander-in-Chief of the Chilean armed forces until 1998, at which point he was sworn in as senator-for-life, a position that was abolished in 2005 as part of the limited constitutional reforms carried out during the presidency of Ricardo Lagos (b. 1938). Pinochet died at the end of 2006, and the *Concertación* lost the 2010 presidential elections, signaling the end of this transitional era. It is during this twenty-year period of attempted redefinition—of civil society, of relationships between different social actors, of recent history—that the authors I study here publish their historical fictions, which center on figures active during the Chilean colonial period and nineteenth century.

Democratic transition itself describes a political process, even though in the Chilean context it is not limited to political events and reforms; as an ideal, it signifies diversely in academic and popular culture. Although Chile enjoys a reputation as a nation with a long tradition of democratic governance, that notion is, in truth, a national myth. Research in history and the social sciences has also confirmed how misleading that reputation is by demonstrating the depth of authoritarian structures that have dominated Chilean political history and culture, even during democratic periods.[8] Indeed, an interdisciplinary consensus exists that the Chilean democratic transition was limited or even failed, as authoritarian and exclusionary societal structures and practices from that interval have not only survived but also remained firmly in place.[9] The shift from closed and censored public expression to rhetorical and societal spaces opened in democracy facilitated new manifestations of axes of difference—characteristics by which individuals are differentiated into groups and identities. Artistic texts have engaged extensively with these representations, and historical fiction in particular offers links between the present and various pasts.

Given the impact of the political trajectory of the Chilean state between the 1970s and 1990, the practices and ideologies of dictatorship have an outsized influence on the period immediately following the end of Pinochet's rule. As such, many pieces examining the period between 1990 and 2010 in Chile use the term "postdictatorship" as a descriptive label, particularly when focusing on themes related to violence, exile, and absence.[10] I have chosen instead to use "democratic transition," which is the term political science commonly employs. I recognize that my use of democratic transition echoes the preference of economic and political actors in Chile during this phase and invokes what Nelly Richard calls "el peso normativizador de su formalismo político-institucional" ("Introducción" 9). Dependent on the functions of the state over this twenty-year span, democratic transition is a label that affirmatively defines the processes that occur,[11] as opposed to "postdictatorship," which defines the period preceding it and necessarily differs, though perhaps less than what triumphalist popular culture might imply. Reading 1990–2010 as postdictatorial "attempt[s] to read in every document of culture the barbarism that made [dictatorship] possible" (Avelar 97). For some, defining 1990–2010 by its relationship to the dictatorship intimately links those events to the subjects of the authors of historical fiction. While these traces are present in some texts, as a rule historical fiction more clearly reflects the era in which it was written—the democratic transition—even as it reveals patterns in time.

Memory, History, Nation, Difference

Discussions of memory have recently dominated considerations of the relationship of subjects with the past. Memory can be profoundly individual; when present in cultural production, however, memory often attempts to bridge the gap between individuals to create a shared intelligibility. Memory is representative; it is "a narrative rather than a replica of an experience that can be retrieved and relived" (Sturken 7). Iwona Irwin-Zarecka locates collective memory—that which exceeds the limits of the individual subject—in the shared resources of a group of individuals (qtd. in Gómez-Barris 7), a setting that Andreas Huyssen reads as definitive of lived memory (28). Memory is not neutral, but rather a place in which "se enfrentan una pluralidad de memorias que corresponden a la más amplia diversidad de grupos y actores sociales" (Waldman "Cultura" 18). Scholars offer different metaphors to conceptualize the functions of memory in cultural productions, such as Michael Lazzara's lens of memory, Lauren Berlant's national symbolic, and Macarena Gómez-Barris's memory symbolic.[12] These critics attempt to bridge the cognitive divide between a sense of difference and a collective process. Marita Sturken asks:

> What does it mean for a *culture* to remember? The collective remembering of a specific culture can often appear similar to the memory of an individual—it provides cultural identity and gives a sense of the importance of the past. Yet the process of cultural memory is bound up in complex political stakes and meanings. It both defines a culture and is the means by which its divisions and conflicting agendas are revealed. To define a memory as cultural is, in effect, to enter into a debate about what that

memory means. This process does not efface the individual but rather involves the interaction of individuals in the creation of cultural meaning. Cultural memory is a field of cultural negotiation through which different stories vie for a place in history. (1)

The processes of meaning-making also afford "a mechanism to interpret how differences are produced and rationalized in and through power" (Dhamoon 13); that historical fiction participates in these cultural negotiations by offering interpretations of shared memories for popular consumption appears self-obvious.

Where memory evokes "subjective processes anchored in experiences and in symbolic and material markers" (Jelin xv), history has often been presented in popular culture as unchanging, objective, and consequently divorced from the personal. The lines between memory and history are therefore constituted by power and can be likened to the way in which difference can, per Dhamoon, be understood as meaning-making around the function and exercise of power. When Anthony Giddens argues that "'history' can be identified as a progressive appropriation of rational foundations of knowledge . . . [that] is expressed in the notion of 'overcoming': the formation of new understandings serves to identify what is of value, and what is not, in the cumulative stock of knowledge," he alludes to a dynamism in the construction of historical discourse that can be read as indicative of meaning itself (47). Emphasizing the conflation of the construction of a narrative of the past with objectivity, Keith Jenkins defines history as "a way of looking at the past in terms that assigned to contingent events and situations an objective significance by identifying their place and function within a general schema of historical development" (8). In simple terms, "history means both the facts of the matter and a narrative of those facts" (Trouillot 2). It is at the intersection of the facts and creative invention in fictional prose that historical fiction distinguishes itself. "Representations prove to be productive and nuanced sites for encountering individual, family, community and social responses that resist incorporation into hegemonic projects of memory and forgetting," that is, into the narrative that requires Jenkins's objective significance (Gómez-Barris 157).

Considering memory in collective terms prompts inquiry into how we define the group within which cultural and collective memories operate.

Political philosopher Seyla Benhabib identifies collective identity as one of the components of the social practice of citizenship that distinguishes analytically between citizenship and national identity because "political communities are not composed of nationally and ethnically homogeneous groups" (162). However, this difference between being a citizen—a member of a political group—and a national subject—a member of a "particular linguistic, ethnic, religious, and cultural group" (162)—challenges traditional group definitions that revolve around the concept of a nation, provisionally defined by Benedict Anderson as "an imagined political community—and imagined as both inherently limited and sovereign" (6). Anderson's definition recognizes the artificial nature of this grouping while also emphasizing the importance of community as a component of the nation because, "regardless of the actual inequality and exploitation that may prevail in each, the nation is always conceived as a deep, horizontal comradeship" (7).[13] The nation is often aspirational and inclusive in theory while perpetuating systemic disparities in practice; though we often speak in terms of a nation-state, what concerns me in this project is the idea of a nation identified as Chilean that may or may not correspond to the geopolitical boundaries of the political state and its constituent citizens.

The idea of the nation as a discrete unit for understanding group interactions has been challenged by the rise of globalization and cosmopolitanism in cultural understandings of the self. If nation functions as a synonym for society, Néstor García Canclini discards any conflation of an entire society as "one homogenous culture, with a corresponding single distinct and coherent identity. The transnationalization of the economy and symbols has eroded the verisimilitude of this mode of legitimizing identities" (138). However, in some arenas, a collective vocabulary of national identity remains that may or may not represent a culture that one can trace through diverse cultural productions such as school textbooks, television dramas, and popular novels. While globalization standardizes many aspects of cultural consumption, local productions nevertheless reflect specificities of the ideal group to which citizens aspire to belong. There has been a trend in recent literary studies in Spanish to argue that narrative is now postnational; while some works may still be read this way, they are but a slice of the cultural production of an entire region. As Gustavo Guerrero argues in a dossier of the *Revista de estudios hispánicos* entitled "Más allá de la nación en la literatura latinoamericana del siglo XXI"

> El horizonte nacional aún está lejos de desaparecer del todo—y parece bastante improbable que esto suceda ni a mediano ni a corto plazo. De hecho, ese horizonte sigue siendo un espacio de resistencia cultural para comunidades sometidas a Estados ajenos y que aspiran a constituir sus propios Estados, tanto en Europa como en las Américas. Sin embargo, lo que sí parece innegable es que ha disminuido su fuerza de coerción, y su monopolio emotivo sobre las consciencias, abriendo la posibilidad de que se le vea como un espacio de mediaciones identitarias. (80)

This notion of the nation as a space of mediation emphasizes its discursive construction; the flexibility of this discursivity allows for individuals who desire a sense of belonging to this collectivity to mold both themselves and the nation itself within this unified group identity. Although some cultural products seek to transcend concepts of nationality,[14] a large body of work remains grounded in the identity of a nation.

Cosmopolitanism—a concept that invokes the end or critical irrelevance of nationalism—and nationalism both aspire to a utopian sense of the universal. In the purported postnational world of the twenty-first century, the individual moves easily within an assumed shared culture unmoored from place or location. The invented homogeneity of this postnational culture papers over difference and excludes those who cannot or will not access multinational cultural markers.[15] This culture presents itself as value-neutral, invisibilized as normative global citizenship. Sociologist Craig Calhoun observes that

> Imagining a world without nationalism, a world in which ethnicity is simply a consumer taste, a world in which each individual simply and directly inhabits the whole, is like imagining the melting pot in which all immigrant ethnicities vanish into the formation of a new kind of individual. In each case this produces an ideology especially attractive to some. It neglects the reasons why many others need and reproduce ethnic or national distinctions. And, perhaps most importantly, it obscures the issues of inequality that make ethnically unmarked national identities

accessible mainly to elites and make being a comfortable citizen of the world contingent on having the right passports, credit cards, and cultural credentials. (286)

To be concerned with difference is to be concerned with inequality; to discard the structuring concepts through which inequality is effected and experienced is to minimize the lived experiences of those who do not belong to the elite. Bear in mind that "nations . . . structure subjects' ability to belong. In this light, the nation is a project that is always made, challenged, and remade through exclusionary practices as much as through inclusionary structures of meaning" (Gómez-Barris 14). Privilege allows the nation to matter no more because it implies the power to choose whether to belong and have that choice recognized as valid.

Power similarly drives my understanding of identity and difference in that questions of power organize identity/difference (Dhamoon 9) within an understanding of identity as a contested process. Within this project, however, this contested process is read in fiction rather than fact, in stories and relationships rather than lived experience, and in the connection between the past and its narration. Rita Dhamoon argues that "an identity is . . . a symbol of difference rather than a synonym for a person" (11); the focus on difference as symbol as opposed to an essentialized inherent characteristic emphasizes the importance of considering the representations of difference. Here, representations are taken to be engaged representation: "relational, local, and historically contingent" (Greenblatt 12). Representations of difference are representations that reflect the continual process of identity construction and, through that mimesis, reveal not only the mechanisms of power but also the inclusion and exclusion that operate in those mechanisms.

Fictionalizing the Past: Historical Fiction in Chile

Despite protestations to the contrary,[16] Chile has produced a quantity of historical fiction during the years after the Pinochet dictatorship that mirrors the themes and practices of contemporary historical fiction throughout the region, though the vast majority of literary production attends to local Chilean history, rather than moments in the past that are geographically centered as "away." Historical fiction participates in what Nelly Richard has described as

> An open process of reinterpretation that unties and reties its knots so that events and understandings can again be undertaken. Memory stirs up the static fact of the past with new unclosed meanings that put its recollections to work, causing both beginnings and endings to rewrite new hypotheses and conjectures and thereby dismantle the explanatory closures of totalities that are too sure of themselves. (*Cultural* 17)

In cultural productions such as written fiction, the creativity of the author participates in this stirring-up, contributing to the dynamic nature of this definition of memory. Despite this role in cultural meaning-making, the historical novel in Chile has not attracted the same level of critical interest as have other narrative forms during the democratic transition. Part of the difficulty of dealing with the historical novel in the Chilean context might also be attributed to the habit of study of narrative literary production according to "generations." Rodrigo Cánovas continues this critical tradition in his 1997 study of the *nueva narrativa chilena*, which admittedly treats a first moment of the postdictatorship narrative production in Chile. However, the volume of historical novels published during the period under study remains outside the categorizations Cánovas identifies as the main currents of the "new" narrative: "la reiteración de un género menor (la serie negra), los pronunciamientos de la mujer (las voces alternas), y el surgimiento de un nuevo héroe, señalado por un actuar paradójico" (10). In a longer enumeration of trends Cánovas observes in Chilean narrative of the 1990s, historical fiction does not appear alongside "folletín . . . serie negra, aventuras, melodrama, logo, vanguardia, parodia, grotesco; espionaje, ciencia-ficción, testimonio rosa, fotograma, pastiche, simulación, mascarada, retro, rito, manierismo, pop, popular" (66). Guillermo García-Corales also omits historical fiction from his inventory of trends in literary practice, even as he overlaps with several of Cánovas's identifications: "la experimentación neovanguardista, el melodrama, la novela neopolicial, el relato de aventuras y ciencia ficción, el reportaje mediático, el simulacro de la epopeya social y la crónica urbana" (6). Within the recent historical novel in Chile, the reader can observe these characteristics, though they remain outside the general study of the literature published between 1990 and 2010. On a regional level, however, considerations of the meanings and uses of historical fiction as part of contemporary literary production are more widespread.

Historians recover and methodically narrate past events with varying levels of awareness of the systems of narration implicit within their own work. By challenging the idea of scientific historiography inherited from the nineteenth century that affirmed the role of history as a singular truth, late twentieth-century philosophers of history such as Hayden White and Paul Ricoeur have allowed for a more explicit coming together of the work of historians in historiography and the work of writers in fictional narrative production. White examines historiography of the nineteenth century to conclude that the different schools of thought proposed by particular historical individuals are stylistic choices that can reveal certain perspectives about history.[17] White's work is perhaps the most widely cited with regard to narrative and history. Because of this, when considering fictional writing, the reader should recall that White's interest follows how literary discourse affects historiography rather than the other way around. The ambiguity of the distinction between literary and historiographical discourse remains a theme throughout the philosophy of history, with the emphasis and conclusions always returning to what Paul Ricoeur states most clearly, that "the relation between history and fiction is certainly more complex than we can ever say" (*Reality* 34). This fuzziness has been partially resolved in literary studies by considering the condition of the historical novel as a hybridized genre (LaCapra and Perkowska) or an oxymoron (Jitrik) and exploring the spaces of tension that the lack of definitional clarity creates.

While a unifying theory has yet to emerge about the ways in which history and fiction interact, a growing corpus of critical work scrutinizing the question now exists, particularly in the context of the historical novel in Latin America. That said, the existing definitions of "historical novel" and varying other terms that critics use to refer to the intersection of history and novelistic fiction remain unclear; some, such as María Cristina Pons, prefer it that way to allow for more flexibility in the study of these works.[18] Indeed, this move toward elasticity in our considerations of evidence of the past can be linked to some of Ricoeur's writings on memory. In one, he describes memory as the only "resource . . . concerning our reference to the past," which leads, in turn, to his understanding of a historian's sources as limited to a set of documents recognized and used as an archive (*Memory* 21). Ricoeur's explicit valuation of memory as a source of historiographical knowledge about the past can be correlated with the positions of critics such as Pons and Juan José Barrientos who advocate that the label "historical" should have application to recent events.

Literary historians agree that the historical novel can be traced to the work of Sir Walter Scott in the early nineteenth century; while the Scott-inspired view of the historical novel is rooted in literary romanticism, one may investigate historical novels written within virtually all major nineteenth-century literary movements.[19] The Hungarian critic György Lukács distinguishes differences in the historical novels before and after the establishment of bourgeois society in Europe;[20] he proposes that what underlies the historical novel does not differ from what underpins the novel in more general terms (241). The characteristics that a historical novel in Scott's mode may display include historical information, local color, exoticism; collective and representative emotion; and a fictional plot (Maigron qtd. in Alonso 55). Amado Alonso notes that "la novela histórica no puede ser histórica; la novela histórica lleva, congénito, el inevitable fracaso, porque no puede cumplir los fines que se propone . . . la novela histórica no vale como historia" (98). In an environment in which professors of history argue in favor of the usefulness of novels in teaching history to undergraduate students[21] and philosophers of history discuss the literary tropes used in the construction of historiographical narratives, current debates centered on the devaluation of the historical novel as history vis-à-vis the work of historians and historiography do not so simply resolve the limits between the two but focus, instead, on their shared techniques and differing motivations.[22]

In Spanish America, various critics have suggested different nexuses for the relative explosion in historical fiction beginning in the late 1970s, ranging from the 500th anniversary of Columbus's arrival in the Caribbean to a cynical view of the role of publishing houses in their production. Although no consensus exists as to the specific causal relationships between proposed theories and increased publication, the reader is faced with an ever-growing corpus of historical fiction written in Spanish about the past of the continent, which is distinguished from prior historical fiction both in quantity and quality. Seymour Menton's 1992 study of what he terms the New Historical novel has served as a benchmark within and against which scholars have worked while studying historical fiction written in Spanish America. The rigid lines of inclusion and exclusion that Menton demarcates allow him to make formal claims about the way in which the novels he identifies as New Historical are written. Fernando Aínsa, who, with Menton, is one of the most cited critics of the New Historical novel, proposes that many of the disquisitions on the past found in the historical novels of the most recent decades can be attributed to the utilization of the past as a way to understand the present, particularly in the cases of novels that look to the past for the possibility of reconciliation with a recently violent and oppressive political present. He also considers the theoretical truth-telling function of historiography with relationship to fiction. "Al releer 'críticamente' la historia, la literatura es capaz de plantear con franqueza y sentido crítico lo que no quiere o no puede hacer la historia que se pretende científica" (Aínsa 115). However, Aínsa's view of historiography appears to be based on the nineteenth-century ideal of objective and reasoned scientific history as opposed to more recent work in the philosophy of history that problematizes how we construct historical narrative. In contrast, Linda Hutcheon's historiographic metafiction "acknowledges the paradox of the *reality* of the past by its *textualized accessibility* to us today" in ways that function as a destabilizing force working on the spectrum of historiography and fiction (114).

The "past" is an ever-evolving term that refers to events centuries earlier or merely a few decades distant; indeed this moving line between current events and history is fraught with debates and exclusions. Seymour Menton and Enrique Anderson Imbert omit relatively recent events from their concept of historical fiction; however, other critics argue for their inclusion, claiming that "lo histórico se relaciona menos con el pasado que con la memoria y que por eso hay hechos en el presente que nos parecen históricos, es decir, dignos de recordarse" (Barrientos 22). The shifting borders for the historical part of historical fiction are also replicated in the fiction part of the term. To what extent does a text follow the conventions of a novel, a biography, or narrative nonfiction? These distinctions matter insofar as they influence the assumptions related to truth and interpretation that the text supports, as well as the expectations the reader has because of such assumptions. The definitional blurriness of the term "historical fiction" frustrates the human desire for clarity; its effect allows for historical fiction to mirror and connect more closely the historical narratives, fictional or not, with the other cultural concerns of the community they target.

Historical fiction written in Chile, and aimed toward a Chilean reading public, became more common and wide-ranging in the period after the return of democracy to the country in 1990. This pattern crosses generational lines, joining together many disparate writers who, when read together, allow for a nuanced vision of a literary reconciliation with knowledge of the past.

Although this study reads the Chilean case, a number of recent monographs have focused on a variety of regional manifestations. While some scholars, including Elisabeth Guerrero, define a corpus of historical fiction based on national divisions, others study Latin American historical fiction narrowed along thematic axes, as in the case of studies of the novel of the conquest, modeled in, for instance, Kimberle López's work. Guerrero herself defines historical fiction as "a work of fiction in which a substantial portion of the narrative takes place in the past in a historically identifiable moment or period" (5). She uses the image of the two angels of history, the *angelus novus* as described in Walter Benjamin's work and the Mexican Angel of Independence, as an entry point to understand historical fiction as an allegory for the present. This function of historical fiction silently undergirds many of the formulations that attempt to define it.

Why, then, is it so difficult to theorize the historical novel? José de Piérola posits that it is not a genre (much as Lukács does) but rather a mode of literary production that depends on a reaction and recognition of content from the reader to produce the destabilization of the boundaries between history and fiction. While he recognizes the useful work done by earlier critics, he prefers to leave lists of postmodern narrative techniques and definitions of the sufficiently "historical" behind in favor of featuring the reader's construction of the historical novel. His proposal privileges the concept of historical competence, defined as "the minimal knowledge necessary to identify history in the historical novel" (155). He continues:

In this context, 'history' is not the unproblematic record of the past, but

> rather what is most commonly accepted during the reader's time—the agreed-upon historical record. This 'historical competence' will allow a reader to understand the historical references in a historical novel—although not without some hesitation—and, at the same time, 'historical competence' will make the reader aware that he is reading a historical novel. (155)

Historical competence shares much with the idea of intertextuality; in fact, one might consider it to be a reader-response oriented intertextuality grounded in an archive that can include the historiographical record alongside memories, commemorations, and fictions. This concept allows for a more flexible idea of what constitutes historical fiction. To extend this notion, the reader will also recognize when a text resists or undermines the agreed-upon historical record. In a similar vein, Joseph Turner's methodological essay on historical fiction, though not specific to the case of Spanish America, stresses a method of thinking about historical fiction that is not bound by technical considerations, but rather influenced by reader-response criticism and Georg Wilhelm Friedrich Hegel's classes of historical consciousness. These categorizations, adapted by Fernando Moreno (*Novelar*) for use in writing on Chilean narrative, allow for a broad definition of historical fiction that avoids the limitations often criticized in older work on historical fiction in Spanish America. As has been noted, "all we can say in general about the genre [historical fiction] is that it resists generalization" (Turner 335).

In the context of Chilean historical fiction, Fernando Moreno adopts and adapts Turner's systematization by constructing groupings that impose limits on historical fiction produced in the past decades. He shares Turner's conception of the varying relationships between fictional text and historiographical referent, elaborating further on the relationship between the two with three categories: the archeological novel, in which a long temporal distance exists between the referent and the moment of writing; the cathartic novel, in which the focus is on the reactions to a temporally recent event; and a functional or systematic novel, in which the text highlights a particular piece of historiographical documentation from an ethical or political point of view. Moreno considers three different modes of writing in the subgenre: (1) the reconstruction of a historical era or process; (2) a novelized biography; and (3) metahistory (*De la Historia* 148). To this scheme, Moreno emphasizes the reading experience of these texts, identifying several different "intentionalities."[23] These different characterizations can be useful in terms of arriving at a systematization of a large body of work, as is evident in Antonia Viu's monograph on the recent Chilean historical novel.[24] Her study is one of very few that have been done on the genre in the Chilean context. Several notable exceptions to the general critical neglect of historical fiction are studies and essays by Moreno, Viu, and Eddie Morales Piña, as well as several essays on individual works of historical fiction. Those who write on Chilean historical fiction of the democratic transition participate in the same questioning work that Viu identifies as the shared interest of the novels in her study: "plantear el descentramiento, la crisis de la imagen armónica o totalizadora, favoreciendo en cambio la denuncia de la fractura, la contradicción, la mirada unívoca del discurso historiográfico y de los relatos integradores sobre la historia y la identidad nacional" (238).

We Are All Chile

The five chapters of this project attend to separate moments in Chilean history: the conquest in the sixteenth century; the viceregal period in the seventeenth century; independence from Spain in texts set during the late eighteenth and early nineteenth centuries; armed conflict in the second half of the nineteenth century; and the Civil War of 1891. Within this chronological structure, each chapter pairs a representative figure or event represented in fiction with relevant historiography so as to understand how narrative choices in both fiction and historiography portray difference and exclusion that nuance the claim that "We Are All Chile" in novels written since the end of the dictatorship. These novels are a diverse corpus, including selected relevant novels published prior to and after 1990 that reflect contrasting styles within the historical novel. The primary texts of this study range from bestsellers, such as those by Isabel Allende, to the lesser known —those by Juanita Gallardo, Virginia Vidal, and Gustavo Frías, among them. Others are best known for works outside of the genre, such as Jorge Edwards and Isidora Aguirre. The historical referent of the text determines its selection, which allows this project to look at the representation of difference in historical novels. All of these novels, however, utilize selected characteristics of the New Historical novel, particularly related to the ways in which Menton's descriptions overlap with Linda Hutcheon's concept of historiographical metafiction. The creation of these narratives are explored explicitly within the texts themselves, a shared practice that helps to make legible the relationships between the novels, the historiography on which they are often based, and how they reflect, reify, and undermine ideologies of inclusion and exclusion through their representations of difference.

The first chapter, "The Conquest of Chile," centers on the period of the Spanish conquest and the figure of the Spanish conquistador. Fictional narratives of the conquest follow the relationship between Pedro de Valdivia and Inés Suarez, telling the story of the conquest as a love story.[25] Suárez's role is commonly told in this mode in fiction, echoing the gender ideologies of the time in which each text is written. A number of texts have been published on Suárez since 1990, all of which engage in metafictional musings on narrative and history, particularly around women and, to a lesser extent, indigenous peoples. Isabel Allende's *Inés del alma mía* is a historical novel composed and published prior to her first significant break from the genre;[26] as a novelist who has sold over seventy-seven million copies of her works worldwide in many languages, one may safely affirm that her novel has been more widely read than any other piece of historical fiction on Inés Suárez, even as it mirrors the trends of the democratic transition historical narrative. Reading Allende's version of Suárez through postcolonial and feminist evaluations of the symbolic use of women's figures in revolutionary movements, I argue that Allende fashions a project to recuperate Inés Suárez as a foundational symbolic figure and, by her doing so, expands symbolic citizenship to majority-culture women.

The second chapter, "The Viceregal Period," focuses on the figure of Catalina de los Ríos y Lisperguer, alias Quintrala, and how her recent portrayals reflect and challenge her nineteenth-century myth that dominates Chilean popular culture. The embodied experiences of this mestiza continue to participate in a shared symbolic language while challenging some of the overtly negative characterizations as represented in fictional works by three authors in the democratic transition: Mercedes Valdivieso's *Maldita yo entre las mujeres* (1991), Virginia Vidal's *Oro veneno puñal* (2002), and the first two volumes of

Gustavo Frías's *Tres nombres para Catalina* (2001, 2003). The stories about Catalina de los Ríos address women's agency, racial mixing, property rights, and church-civil conflicts in the center of the Kingdom of Chile. A counterpoint to this narrative of the relative center can be found in Isidora Aguirre's posthumous *Guerreros del sur* (2011), which focuses on the Jesuit-educated Mapuche leader Lientur and set during the same period at the southern flashpoints of the Mapuche struggle against continued Spanish colonization. Read together, Catalina de los Ríos and Lientur draw particular attention to power differentials around gender and race in seventeenth-century Chile, emphasize the nuances in contemporary understanding of historical identity formations, and trouble the notion of a singular representation of the period.

"Independence," the third chapter, examines a series of texts that reflect stories about the build-up to the independence movement in the late eighteenth century and the nineteenth-century conflict with Spain itself. Although a number of texts about the independence movement appeared around the bicentennial celebrations in 2010, stories about Chilean independence have been and continue to be popular. This chapter studies a series of novels that play with traditional ideas of the nation and its symbols, as well as how that play opens space for greater inclusion; it examines Jorge Edwards's *El sueño de la historia* (2000), Virginia Vidal's *Javiera Carrera, madre de la patria* (2000), and Juanita Gallardo's *Déjame que te cuente* (1997). Through readings of these three novels, we can observe an adjustment in the construction of symbolic structures related to national inclusion and exclusion that aligns with the political processes of the twenty-year democratic transition. Postmodern narrative practices create literary space for inclusion that, while exploring the limits of difference in Chile, also run up against the limits of authoritarian societal structures.

The failure of the narrative imagination concerning indigenous inclusion permeates the fourth chapter, "Occupation of Araucanía." The Occupation is a less popular topic for historical fiction than the simultaneous War of the Pacific. Just as there are some who prefer a David McCullough book to *The 1619 Project*, so too the orientations of the stories of the Occupation and the War of the Pacific serve different purposes. The novels, biographies, and other texts about the history of southern Chile and the ongoing conflict in the nineteenth century between Chilean forces and indigenous residents reveal explicit and implicit racial attitudes. The eccentric character of Orélie-Antoine de Tounens receives the lion's share of fictional narrative attention, but confounds the reader who is left to figure out why a European man figures as the central character in a genocidal war against indigenous peoples. This chapter shows how this orientation makes the Occupation legible to a majority culture uncomfortable with an association with the villains of the story. Pedro Staiger's *La corona de Araucanía* (1998) emphasizes this dissonance by drawing connections between the failed efforts of Tounens to change the actions of the Chilean state and the structures of the democratic transition during which the novel was written.

The final chapter, "Civil War," examines texts written about the 1891 Chilean Civil War in light of their textual representation of internecine conflict—a war between brothers—as an attempt to understand the notion of who is included in the Chilean family and, by extension, the connection between this framing of conflict and Chilean social class. Historiographical reflections within the novels also prompt the reader to consider the ways these stories come to terms with the end of utopian dreams, as well as how the links between the events of 1891 and 1973 play in understanding the politics of inclusion in democratic Chile. Works such as Dario Oses's *El viaducto* (1994) and Isidora Aguirre's *Balmaceda: diálogos de amor y muerte* (2008) integrate multiple voices and perspectives into their narratives. The contrast between the way multiple voices and intertextuality work within each illustrates different coping mechanisms for mourning the tragedy of the Civil War. Reading sympathetic portrayals of Balmaceda's projects alongside a historiographic view that remonstrates against the political questions that led to the Civil War itself emphasizes the gifts and dangers of multiple narratives sharing space, if not how such sharing creates provocative juxtapositions that invite reimagining the Chilean social class system and the inclusion of difference in democratic Chile.

CHAPTER ONE
The Conquest of Chile

STREETS, PLAZAS, STATUES, STATIONS, and regions bear the names of the traditional protagonists of Chilean history. Those who conform to the triumphal narrative of conquest receive a special place of prominence. However, signs of challenge to that version of history can bubble up into public consciousness, as the world sometimes demonstrates: from the removal of statues of Cecil Rhodes in Zimbabwe to innumerable street renaming projects in Spain and throughout North America. In the massive protests in Chile at the end of 2019, crowds inhabited public space to repudiate those triumphal narratives in a gesture to make real the promise that *Chile somos todos*. While much of the story of those protests focused on events in the capital, the actions reclaiming a shared historical narrative occurred throughout the country and abroad. In one provincial city on 14 November 2019, a group of protesters pulled down a prominent statue of Pedro de Valdivia. Located in southern Chile, Concepción was founded by Valdivia in 1550 in a place densely populated by indigenous communities that resisted Spanish colonialism, fully destroying the settlement three times in its first decade of its existence ("Concepción colonial—Memoria Chilena"). A year after agents of the state murdered Mapuche activist Camilo Catrillanca (1994–2018), visible signs of the conquering narrative fell, literally.[1] Power continues to shape those who can tell their own story and those stories that are remembered, valued, and transmitted to new generations.

The stories of the European conquest of the Americas are much more diverse today than they were prior to the 1992 quincentennial observance of Christopher Columbus's arrival. As Michel-Rolph Trouillot observes, "celebrations are created, and this creation is part and parcel of the process of historical production . . . they impose a silence upon the events that they ignore, and they fill that silence with narratives of power about the event they celebrate" (118). The commemoration of Columbus's 12 October landing has drawn attention to the silences of what is ignored, which has shaped the frames within which we tell the origin story of a European-colonized America. Historical fiction of the conquest may not literally tear down statues, but it often imagines the silences in new ways. This generative imagination expands received narratives of conquest and foundation, most often through the recuperation of selected marginal (male) figures or the destabilization of canonical (male) figures.[2] Fiction of the conquest of Chile does not fall into that pattern. Pedro de Valdivia (1497–1553), the primary leader of the Spanish conquest of Chile, reappears in the contemporary historical novel in stories about Inés Suárez (1507–1580). Twenty-first-century readers bring with them prior knowledge that Inés Suárez was a woman born in Spain who immigrated to the Americas and travelled with Valdivia's expedition to Chile in 1540–41. She is commonly named as the first Spanish woman to establish residence in Chile and was respected in her society. Valdivia, the leader of the Spanish colonial force, was married to another woman in Spain, which resulted in a series of political complications stemming from his relationship with Suárez. After their relationship ended, she married Rodrigo de Quiroga and outlived Valdivia by decades.

One might ask oneself why fiction features Suárez, or why so few works look to other significant figures or events in the conquest of Chile. If historical fiction of the conquest focuses on recuperating traditionally marginalized perspectives, where are the novels of the indigenous resistance to Spanish colonization? Where is the novel of the Chilean conquest that tells the story of the attack on Santiago from Picunche leader Michimalonko's (ca. 1500–ca.1550) point of view? Why do so few stories tackle Lautaro's (d. 1557) role? As a child, he was a page for Pedro de Valdivia before he ran away and brought the knowledge he had gleaned from his time with the Spaniards, particularly of warcraft, back to his people. Lautaro then led war against the Spaniards and ultimately brought about Valdivia's death before dying in battle himself several years later. In Valdivia's surviving letters, there is no mention of Lautaro; however, the epic poem *La Araucana* (1574) characterizes him as courageous and valiant (115), which is one of two broad camps into which most historical texts fall. In contrast, Pedro de Oña's rebuttal of Ercilla's work, *Arauco domado* (1596), recognizes the robust physicality and beauty of Lautaro's corpse as the vessel of a savage and fierce heart, though in life Lautaro is miserable, wretched, unlucky, and without valor or strength (44). Oña's work is an early example of a narrative that juxtaposes two visions of the indigenous person, the living barbarian and the dead noble warrior. An 1876 text by the prolific historian and politician Benjamín Vicuña Mackenna proposes to present Lautaro "tal cual fue" (*Lautaro* x): Indian, barbaric, vicious, fierce, and heroic, as well as a natural warrior and sublime patriot. Vicuña Mackenna maintains a marker of difference, emphasizing that "no por ser libertador dejó de ser bárbaro, no por ser héroe desnudóse ni de los hábitos ni de las pasiones de su raza" (x). Lautaro may have been heroic, but he is still undeniably other in a state that displaces indigenous peoples and forces them to assimilate into hegemonic Chilean society.[3]

Historical novels tell stories from the Spanish colonizer perspective through the lens of Inés Suárez's life far more often than they tell the story of indigenous resistance through Lautaro's. His story has been represented in Fernando Alegría's *Lautaro, joven libertador de Arauco* (1943), Carlos Barella's *Lautaro guerrillero* (1971), and perhaps most famously in Isidora Aguirre's play, *Lautaro* (1982). In the post-1990 period, however, Lautaro most often appears as a secondary character in novels dealing with Inés Suárez and Pedro de Valdivia. An exception to this trend includes the deformation of the relationship between Lautaro and Valdivia portrayed in Nona Fernández's *Mapocho* (2002). This follows the general trend of historical novels of the conquest noted by Kimberle López, who observes that even though recent Latin American literature privileges marginal perspectives, "the overwhelming majority [of historical novels] have European protagonists" (10) and the narration, even when filtered through marginalized voices, rewrites the conquest from a European perspective.[4]

What does it mean, then, that the focus on narratives of the conquest stays so fixed on the love story between Valdivia and Suárez? One answer is that through the two the marginalized indigenous perspective forms the undercurrent of the romance of the conquest. It is of a piece with how fictional narratives of the conquest narrate the indigenous peoples as other while positing gender inclusion in the machinery of the conquest itself. Isabel Allende's 2006 novel *Inés del alma mía* illustrates this opening toward previously marginalized discourses of the conquest. Earlier Chilean novels of the conquest also emphasize the Spanish perspective on events, even if marginalized figures—notably, women— participate in them. This chapter will elucidate how Suárez functions in fiction through an examination of the relevant historiography of the conquest, an outline of previous fictional representations of Suárez in historical fiction, and a close reading of Allende's novel. Taken together, they demonstrate how the exceptionalism of Inés Suárez provides an avenue through which to reimagine the role of women and indigenous men in Chile's sense of historical self, while also limiting how and to whom that reimagination might be applied. Power shapes belonging; it also determines who gets to be a citizen.

The *Mujer Varonil* and Historiography

Inés Suárez's relationship to historiography may be characterized by absence. Upon examining historiographical texts from the sixteenth through the twenty-first century, the reader can note patterns of (non) representation that weave an uneven tapestry of heroism, condemnation, and gendered moralization. As "gender is a constitutive element of social relationships based on perceived differences between the sexes, and gender is a primary way of signifying relationships of power" (Scott 42), men who write of the conquest—for they are generally men[5]—do not know what to make of Suárez. This instability allows for each writer to project attitudes about women's roles onto her.

When we examine documents that survive from the sixteenth century, Inés Suárez does not appear as a central character in the conquest of Chile. She is not mentioned in any of the twelve surviving letters of Pedro de Valdivia or in Alonso Góngora de Marmolejo's chronicle (1576); however, she does appear in the chronicles of Jerónimo de Vivar (1558) and Pedro Mariño de Lobera (1598). According to both men, when the indigenous leader Michimalonko attacked the recently established colonial city of Santiago on 11 September 1541, Suárez beheaded seven caciques who were being held in the city. Both chroniclers emphasize Suárez's role in healing the injured during the attack and associate it with a maternal instinct. Vivar also notes her ability to speak to the attacking groups in their own language. While she is mentioned by name in both documents, only Mariño de Lobera writes of Suárez's finding water while traversing the Atacama Desert. The earliest text that mentions Suárez is a legal document from 1548; it details accusations against Pedro de Valdivia, one of which refers to Inés Suárez as having aroused suspicions of "carnal participación" (La Gasca 567) with him. Therefore, from sixteenth-century primary sources we have evidence of three stories: Suárez defends Santiago; Suárez finds water in the desert; and Suárez is ordered to separate from Valdivia. This raw material finds its way into later historical and fictional retellings of the conquest of Chile.

Seventeenth-century chronicles continue to straddle the divide between historiography and fiction. Commonly referred to as the first history of Chile, Alonso de Ovalle's *Histórica relación del Reyno de Chile* (1646) never refers to Suárez and omits the charges brought against Valdivia in Peru entirely. Rodrigo de Quiroga, Suárez's second husband and fourth governor of Chile, merits only one mention. In *Desengaño y reparo de la guerra del Reino de Chile* (1614), Alonso González de Nájera does not refer to Suárez, but he does describe the *criollas* of Chile as

> Ejemplos de toda honestidad, de noble y señoril trato, de varoniles ánimos y de gran gobierno: administran el de sus casas y haciendas del campo con esfuerzo y paciencia ... son muy trabajadoras y en ocupaciones de varias labores y recamos muy ejercitadas y maestras, agraciadas en el vestir ... como en todos sus ejercicios se conforman con las mujeres de España, excediendo a muchas en el valor, gobierno, arreo y compostura de sus casas. (38)

While lamenting the state of siege in which all of the settlers live, González de Nájera praises the women in Chile. His description of them shares several features with the fictional characterizations of Inés Suárez in the twentieth and twenty-first centuries.[6]

In *Historia general del reino de Chile, Flandes Indiano* (1674, publ. 1877) the seventeenth-century Jesuit Diego de Rosales adds elements to the story of the 1541 attack on Santiago that are not present in earlier or contemporary accounts of the event. Suárez appears as a prize coveted by the indigenous leader

Michimalonko in a transposition of the *malones*, raids, and kidnappings that will become common strategies on both sides as the conflict between the Europeans and Americans develops. Rosales makes nothing of Suárez's role in the decapitation of the Spaniards' indigenous hostages, an action by which she demonstrates "extraño valor y varonil esfuerzo" (Rosales 412), echoing Antonio de Herrera y Tordesillas's estimation that her actions show "atreuimiēto eſtraordinario pero crueldad, ya otras vezes viſta en mujeres" (8). Other seventeenth-century historians in Chile do not mention Suárez at all.

By the eighteenth century, historiographical writers routinely include reference to Inés Suárez in their accounts of the conquest and the early years of the colony, though her role and identification continues to evolve. However, in those texts in which she does appear, she is generally represented in one of two manners: as a wife or as a hero. Vicente Carvallo identifies Suárez as "mujer de Rodrigo de Quiroga" (25) who is buried alongside him (140) but ignores any evidence showing a relationship between Suárez and Valdivia. Carvallo follows Rosales's lead by portraying Suárez's actions in defending Santiago as sticking to the orders of the military leaders of the settlement, though he minimizes her contribution by remarking that "este hecho nada contribuyó para la victoria" (25). Three other versions privilege Suárez for her heroism: the Jesuits Miguel de Olivares (1675–1768), Juan Ignacio Molina (1740–1829), and José Antonio Pérez García (1788–1810). Olivares writes that Suárez, seeing the efforts of the prisoners to escape and fearing that their success would see the Spaniards with enemies at their backs, grabbed an axe with which she killed them all (111). Such a description highlights Suárez's tactical analysis of the situation. Olivares compares Suárez, "mujer heroica" (111), to the mythical and contradictorily characterized Clytemnestra, the wife and killer of Agamemnon, who was in turn murdered by her own son. Molina extends descriptions of Suárez even further from her gender and into the inhuman to describe her actions in 1541 (39–40). This characterization removes her even further from the everyday that Olivares's use of mythical figures stresses, though such comparisons are also common rhetorical devices. Pérez García chooses to cite earlier historians in his approach to events recounted in *Historia de Chile* (1788–1810), an understandable practice given that the colonial governor commissioned his work. He also praises Suárez's actions without explicitly dehumanizing or even de-womanizing her, though he does employ turns of phrase lifted from earlier writers such as Olivares. Suárez's role in the defense of Santiago has become canon by the end of the eighteenth century, though her sexual politics and somewhat miraculous actions in the desert have been washed away from official accounts that survive today. Her romantic and legal entanglements also vanish, in that she is simply another member of the Spanish community in Chile with no special relationship to Valdivia; furthermore, if romantically linked to anyone, she is paired with her husband.

Nineteenth-century historiography in Chile contributed to the study of the colonial past through initiatives that brought to light previously unpublished texts, as well as through public disagreement about the role of history in the civic life of the newly independent Chilean state. The first national history, written by French botanist Claudio Gay by commission of the Portalian regime,[7] was praised by Andrés Bello for its attention to factual detail; Inés Suárez's absence speaks volumes. José Victorino Lastarria's *Investigaciones sobre la influencia social de la conquista y del sistema colonial de los españoles en Chile*, presented in 1844, also avoids mention of Suárez. A trio of influential Chilean historians—Miguel Luis Amunátegui (1828–1888), Benjamín Vicuña Mackenna (1831–1886), and Diego Barros Arana (1830–1907)—"represent an important departure from previous romantic liberal historiography in that they were able to link Chile's past to its present without recourse to polemical rhetoric . . . [and they] believed that history could serve socially useful functions" (Yeager 173). The reader may observe three differing orientations toward Suárez: Amunátegui seeks to modernize and correct errors in earlier texts; one of those is to turn Suárez into an anonymous Spanish woman. Vicuña Mackenna erases sexual misconduct in her story and spotlights marriage and homemaking. With that, Suárez becomes an image of idealized domesticity, which confirms his belief that other interpretations of her place in history focused on public action are erroneous. Barros Arana continues the vein of representing Suárez as a heroic figure, all the while avoiding the moral condemnation of her relationship with Valdivia that a historian such as Vicuña Mackenna, if he were to allow Suárez to leave the domestic sphere, would highlight.

In Amunátegui's *Descubrimiento i conquista de Chile* (1862), Suárez is not named, though the role traditionally attributed to her in the execution of the caciques is instead attributed to a nameless "mujer española, sirvienta de Valdivia o esposa de uno de los conquistadores, pues los cronistas no están acordes sobre su condición" (142). Having made explicit his desire to modernize and correct the errors of earlier colonial histories, Amunátegui's text prevaricates based on the archive's vacillations. The theme of inhumanity continues: "los bárbaros retrocedieron . . . delante de un espectáculo tan inhumano" (142). However, given her anonymity, in Amunátegui's text the story becomes an aside unmoored from any individual narrative.

Vicuña Mackenna includes Suárez in his collection of the founders of Santiago, though he regrets "una calumnia necia" with regard to her honor, which one assumes refers to her documented affair with Valdivia. Vicuña Mackenna biographizes her as

> Esposa del venerable Rodrigo Quiroga, castellana esforzada, hija de Plascencia i de quien dicen los historiadores casóse despues en Málaga, aunque no esclarecen si fue Quiroga su primer marido. Fué ésta la primera mujer que formara su hogar en este suelo de dulces hogares; i aquello que han contado del degüello que hizo de siete caciques por su propia mano, no es sino uno de esos plajios de escritores pedantes que quisieron pintarla como Judith, esta caricatura divinizada de la mujer, cuando fue solo dechado de virtudes privadas i sociales. (*Historia crítica* 40)

Suárez's value for Vicuña Mackenna resides not in her heroism or martial actions but in her marriage and homemaking, two aspects of Suárez's life that, ironically, do not appear to be well-documented in sources of her time. However, Vicuña Mackenna's texts dealing with women of all eras consistently glorify the domestic sphere and condemn deviation from this norm, as is the case in his representation of a figure such as the Quintrala.[8] This text also eschews earlier historians' mythological allusions to Greece in favor of biblical reference. Judith has been utilized in various and contradictory ways as both a sexual and celibate heroine. "According to the Apocrypha, a nation surrounded by belligerent superpowers would be best advised to find itself a Judith forthwith" (Stocker 67), who would, with God's grace, save the nation from destruction. Inés Suárez's militant defense, coupled with the very action of beheading, accordingly renders her a type of Judith. However, Vicuña Mackenna rejects this reading, denying Suárez a public face and relegating her to a realm of idealized nineteenth-century domesticity.

In Barros Arana's multivolume *Historia General de Chile*, Suárez is present prior to the establishment of Santiago, though her most colorful presence lies in her defense of the city. She makes the decision to execute the prisoners and carries out the deed with her own hands (193). Barros Arana's text avoids negative moral judgments on the relationship between Suárez and Valdivia, which is present in the text, and recounts President La Gasca's decree separating the two as a way to maintain the peace in Chile and "no dar escándalo a [los] gobernados" (*Historia* 256), which allows him to avoid passing judgment on the moral turpitude of the offending parties. Although the *Proceso de Pedro de Valdivia i otros documentos inéditos concernientes a este conquistador* features reproductions of many primary documents, Barros Arana also contributed various essays on subjects related to the previously unpublished sources. Unlike earlier historians who deal with the colonial period, Barros Arana details Suárez's relationship with Valdivia and, by doing so, brings to light new documents as a basis from which to speculate as to possible motivations for the situation as the historian sees it. For the first time, "love" is used to describe the relationship between Suárez and Valdivia (*Proceso* 315); moreover, the historian characterizes Suárez in a generally positive way as a clever and intelligent woman (318) and an excellent wife (320) who possesses a noble and generous heart (319). Altogether, then, Suárez is a good woman because she is uncomplaining in the labor and hardship of conquest, as well as charitable and obliging (318). Suárez retains agency in the defense of Santiago, advises Valdivia, and ensures that her legal right to property granted by Valdivia is not abrogated by other encomenderos. In Barros Arana's conceptualization of Inés Suárez, the modern reader can see a combination of aspects that become standard in fictional representations of Suárez in the twentieth century: the love relationship, a noble heart, and a servant of nature. Other aspects, such as her preservation of self-interest and agency in actions, however, characterize only the most recent representations of Suárez.

Despite Barros Arana's measured representation of Suárez, twentieth-century historiography on the conquest does not necessarily continue his sympathetic portrayal, though there is a consensus as to the worthiness of Suárez's actions. She is absent from a number of works in colonial historiography, though this may often be explained through the chronological limitations placed on some of that work. When present, however, in twentieth-century historiography, an explicit negative evaluation of Suárez's sexual relationships often returns to the forefront.

Accused of plagiarism in his *Historia de Chile* (1949–1952), Francisco A. Encina refers to Suárez as Valdivia's concubine (183), though she retains agency in the defense of Santiago. Tomás Thayer Ojeda, in a 1950 compilation of information about the origins of the first Spaniards in Chile and the origins of Chilean nationhood, notes that despite her sexual improprieties, Suárez deserves a statue for having been the first Spanish woman to set foot in Chile (16); in his estimation, she is a "mujer de gran empuje y lealtad, discreta, sagaz y caritativa ... de general estimación entre los conquistadores" (Thayer Ojeda 55). Sister Imelda Cano Roldán, in turn, values Suárez's contributions to the colony, particularly her nursing work, while at the same time undercutting her position as the extraordinary woman accompanying the expedition; Cano Roldán, instead, highlights an enslaved woman who accompanied Almagro's previous expedition. Crescente Errázuriz writes of "guilty love" between Valdivia and Suárez, arguing that it is difficult not to find her deplorable. Despite her faults, though, and the scandal they caused, "no carecía de distinguidas cualidades de inteligencia y también de corazón" (35). Jaime Eyzaguirre excuses Suárez as Valdivia's "manceba" (*Historia* 63) due to her usefulness to the expedition. He does not attribute this relationship to love, but rather that "lo que le liga a ella apenas trasciende del campo meramente fisiológico" (*Fisonomía* 27) without discounting her worth in terms of the distribution of wealth postconquest. Her characterization depends on her embodiment as a woman, as she exhibits a "corazón de mujer" (*Ventura* 59) and "intuición de mujer" (*Ventura* 118). However, despite Eyzaguirre's general valuation of her contributions to the survival of the Spanish colony, Suárez's portrayal continues full of gendered characterizations, censoring attributes considered to be feminine, including a particularly "femenina lascivia," while celebrating aspects that are identified as masculine, "voluntad y entereza de varón" (*Ventura* 56). This follows from earlier characterizations; as ever, Suárez's socially unacceptable behavior is coded feminine.

At the return to democracy, Inés Suárez does not become more conspicuous in historiography, despite late twentieth-century turns toward social history and gender studies. The general interest works of Gonzalo Izquierdo (1989) and Alfredo Jocelyn-Holt (2000–2008) do not engage with Suárez's narrative. In Sergio Villalobos's *Historia de los chilenos*, the historiographical focus is on Valdivia, though Inés Suárez is his "compañera fiel y apoyo decidido de la empresa" (48).[9] *Compañera* may imply a romantic relationship, though the text does not make this explicit. Villalobos describes Suárez's role in the defense of Santiago visually, describing her mail coat and the lance that enabled her to exhibit male-like courage in an evocation of Manuel Ortega's 1897 oil painting *Inés de Suárez en defensa de Santiago*. Villalobos also links her to the beheading of the caciques, though through his use of the passive voice it is only her determination that inspires this action. It is notable that Valdivia's relationship with the boy Lautaro is excised from this version; Lautaro appears only as the leader of the charge that resulted in Valdivia's death in 1553. Suárez's absences, as well as Lautaro's, continue to reflect historical approximation, that is, an active practice of silence and mention "of which history is the synthesis" (Trouillot 48).

For historians, Inés Suárez has feminine weakness and masculine strength; she makes her own decisions but follows the orders of others; she is both present and absent. She is intelligent and brave, though some argue that she was a distraction from the men's work of conquest. Although Susan Stringer-O'Keefe argues that "la visión de ella que sobrevive en la conciencia nacional como personaje romántico casi santo, parece estar firmemente arraigada en la realidad" (65), the reality or factual integrity of Suárez's life cannot be known to the modern reader. Rather, one might argue that her mythification can be traced through documents going back to the sixteenth century that participate in the vision of Valdivia as the Chilean nation's founder and, by virtue of that, Suárez as intimately related to that foundation.

In the End, It Is Always a Love Story

Despite prevarications in the historiography, historical fiction about Pedro de Valdivia and Inés Suárez over the course of the twentieth century has subscribed to a general pattern of emplotment that dramatizes romantic love as the line that unites the disparate events related in different narratives.[10] The collection of texts dealing with Inés Suárez represents modes that reflect their own time period's most legible option for telling her story. The overarching plot structure often constructs the story of the conquest of Chile as nothing more than a backdrop for the at times thorny relationship between Valdivia and Suárez.[11] Therefore, in my brief examination of a number of novels dealing with Inés Suárez written by both male and female authors, Chilean or not, from 1930 through the end of the twentieth century, two common threads of analysis are useful: the characterizations of Inés Suárez in each; and the forms that are used to portray love and romance. These novels, like other romances, "*retell* a single tale whose final outcome their readers always already know ... the act of retelling that same myth functioned as the ritual reaffirmation of fundamental cultural beliefs and collective aspirations" (Radway 198). This is doubly true for the historical romance for the reader possessed of historical competence.[12]

The works I examine here exhibit variety in plot, though not always in portrayal. Differences include Suárez's first appearance in the text; the inclusion of certain events during the traversal of the Atacama Desert; the portrayal of relationships with indigenous groups; the role played in the narrative by political intrigue in Peru; and the treatment of the love triangle (where it exists) between Suárez, Valdivia, and Rodrigo de Quiroga. However, Suárez's loyalty to Valdivia, particularly in the face of rebellion, is shared among the novels. The general outlines of the historical events are shared as well, though each novelist chooses to embellish, contradict, or simplify the available historiographical information.

The embellishments in American traveler and author Stella Burke May's *The Conqueror's Lady* (1930) create drama to entertain readers regardless of historical competence and have been utilized as possible source material for biography as well.[13] May dedicates her work "to the women of Chile who by their courage, their patriotism, and their Independence of spirit and of thought, won [her] admiration and [her] affection during [her] residence in Santiago" (n.p.). In it, she avails herself of materials in the existing archive, even as she romanticizes that archive to tell a "story that has never been told" (xii) drawn from documents "powdering in the hand of the reader after lying for years in the dark archives of two continents" (xiii). The author expends creative energy and narrative space to re-create Suárez's childhood in Spain and repeatedly alludes to Suárez's heroic destiny through commentary on the infant's nose, similar in shape to that of the Çid.[14] The religious imperative of the conquest is clearly upheld in this version of Suárez's life while a child in

Spain. In those years in Plascencia, she has a fascination with an auto-da-fé. She is also deeply influenced by the woman who raises her and who "voice[s] the belief of Spain. Her face was radiant. Her bright eyes shone with holy fire. So long as souls were saved, nothing else mattered" (23). However, upon the meeting of Suárez and Pedro de Valdivia by chance after mass, the narrative shifts from the exploits of the conquest through what Suárez hears in Plascencia to her own efforts to arrive in the Americas in search of Valdivia.

The question of gender difference in May's novel surfaces through the plot itself, detailing Suárez's challenges in arriving in the Americas, though her characterization as a virtuous Christian woman comes earlier when she realizes that camp followers are prostitutes. Although Suárez participates in many aspects of life in the Americas, from fighting to home decorating, her individual mettle is something unusual, as she does not have much interaction with other women of her station until Santiago is well-established; prior to that, most of the interactions portrayed are with Valdivia, other men, and her indigenous servants. However, not all of her interactions with Spanish men are positive, giving rise to the following description: "As a tigress guards her young, Ines guarded the treasures of her womanhood, assuming a masculine hardness, showing the canine whiteness of her teeth behind the red lips of her smile, meeting with a look of contempt the overtures of the daring" (112). Even though Suárez is guilty of an adulterous relationship with the married Valdivia, her honor cannot be impugned. However, as is the case in many texts ostensibly focusing on Suárez, much ink is spilled in the service of retelling the comings and goings of Valdivia and his lieutenants between Peru and Chile. A contemporary reviewer notes that

> Mrs. Burke has an entertaining narrative style. *Valdivia*'s achievements make a stirring tale. And although the incidents recorded of her heroine are none too many, she has succeeded in creating from their significance a plausible and vivid personality and has woven them skillfully into a background which adheres with creditable fidelity to information gleaned from her well-chosen bibliography, which she appends. (Clemence 484; emphasis mine)

This comment emphasizes that, while the novel ostensibly discusses the life of

Suárez, what is of interest to the reader is Valdivia's work, and, indeed, the historiographical archive replicates this bias. In the end, however, *Conqueror's Lady* functions as a historical romance, as it indulges the senses in florid descriptions of physical affections between the heroine and Valdivia while correcting the error of Suárez's general anonymity.

Where May's novel is a straightforward historical romance, Alejandro Vicuña categorizes his 1941 work as a biography, though to the modern reader it does not differ greatly from a historical novel. Published four hundred years after the foundation of Santiago, *Inés de Suárez* features a heroine characterized throughout the novel as motherly and in love, while at the same time manly and independent: "una mujer tan hacendosa y varonil" (48); "la enamorada viuda" (44); "verdadera madre de los soldados y favorecida compañera del jefe de la expedición" (61); "mujer de ánimos e independiente en sus resoluciones" (184). These somewhat contradictory depictions reflect the difficulty that Suárez poses to simple classifications in that her actions belie the ideal role for a Spanish woman of her time while other narratives often view her as an ideal romantic heroine. However, that embedding is complicated by her martial action in the defense of Santiago, described by Vicuña as "la trágica inspiración de una mujer," as well as her socially unacceptable sexual relationship with Valdivia (118). In addition to these characterizations, Suárez and the other characters are racialized through allusions to national character. Where Valdivia "representa fielmente el Capitán extremeño a la España de la época, creyente y sensual, mentalidad racial que no ha desteñido en la serie de los siglos" (57), Suárez laments her "sangre gitana y andaluza ... y mi vanidad de mujer" (82–3). Vicuña so fashions Suárez and Valdivia's illicit relationship while idealizing it in the text. Where Vicuña's novel-biography adheres to the general pattern of events between Cuzco and Santiago, it differs from other representations, including May's, in that the action begins and remains in the Americas. This emphasizes the quasi-nationalistic function of the text by shunting Spain to the background and foregrounding the story "como un tributo para la celebración del cuarto centenario de Santiago, ciudad donde nací, donde nacieron y murieron mis antepasados y donde espero dormir con ellos el sueño perdurable" (8). As "un cuadro panorámico de los albores de nuestra existencia" (7), *Inés de Suárez* commemorates the past, much in the way that Seymour Menton argues that the explosion of historical novels around 1992 is owed in part to the quincentennial of Columbus's landing in the Caribbean, even as Vicuña characterizes Suárez contradictorily as both motherly and manly, which reflects the ambivalence toward her character that derives from stringently imposed sexual norms alongside the idolization of gendered heroism.

The curious example of María Correa Morandé's *Inés . . . y las raíces en la tierra* (1964) features ideological contradictions when one considers that novel in concert with the author's biography. Correa Morandé was a prominent conservative politician and journalist prior to her death in 2009 because she participated in leadership roles in protests against Allende's democratically elected socialist government. Due to her role in this movement, the historian Margaret Power interviewed her and examined *La guerra de las mujeres*, another of Correa Morandé's works, in the context of political activism and right-wing politics. Power alleges that Correa Morandé, along with Teresa Donoso Loero, author of *La epopeya de las ollas vacías*, "explained women's courage and resistances as a legacy passed on to them by the heroines who preceded them" (177), among whom Inés Suárez figures prominently. Indeed, the historian notes that the anti-Allende opposition

> chose to demonstrate its rejection of . . . the UP government by reaffirming the role that Chilean women have historically played in defending the nation. The women who organized the march publicly identified themselves with the national symbols of Chilean womanhood—Inés de Suárez, Javiera Carrera, and Paula Jaraquemada . . . women supposedly represented the nation: lacking foreign or political allegiances, they were purely driven by the well-being of their families—and, by extension, of Chile. (148)

In addition to this political identification, however, Correa Morandé's relationship to an image of Inés Suárez is rooted in her most popular novel. It is openly nationalistic, a narrative "empapada en amor filial por la tierra y por la gente de este pequeño pedazo de mundo tan simple y tan complejo que se llama Chile," traditional in its view of the past, as well as directed to a specifically Chilean reading public, as noted in the novel's introduction:

> La narración . . . está construida sobre un relato de la primera fase de la

conquista de 'Nueva Extremadura', estrictamente ajustado a la verdad. Todos los hechos públicos que expongo son tan exactos como pudieron lograrse de un minucioso estudio de la historia y de los documentos de la época misma. Solo que todo eso irá presentado bajo un aspecto esencialmente humano, tratando de rehacer las actitudes íntimas de esos seres extraordinarios que, como personajes de leyenda, iluminaron los albores de nuestra nacionalidad. (7)

As opposed to May's version of Suárez's life, Correa Morandé's *Inés . . . y las raíces de la tierra* begins during Suárez's voyage to the New World to participate in "[la] empresa más discutida de toda América" (81) and establishes her character as mothering, though barren herself; delicate while strong; and, above all, devoutly Christian. Typical of the descriptions of Suárez is "esa extraña mujer, tan llena de coraje y al mismo tiempo de femeninas debilidades" (42). And so even for a conservative woman of the 1960s, Suárez's extraordinary nature goes beyond her mere presence in the Americas to her ability to combine the strength needed to succeed in conquest with the stereotypical femininity expected of a sixteenth-century woman.

The negotiation of Suárez's socially accepted yet irregular relationship with Valdivia, as well as her later marriage to Rodrigo de Quiroga, complicates the romantic quest narrative in this novel much as it does in others. The romance between Suárez and Valdivia "era un amor más grande que todas las incertidumbres, más fuerte que la vida y que la muerte. En este desolado rincón del mundo todo tenía que ser auténtico o morir; nada podría escapar a ese destino inexorable" (Correa Morandé 215–16). While Suárez recognizes her morally perilous situation, the narrative clarifies the security of her position thanks to the protection of Valdivia, while at the same time appealing to societal legitimacy through the recognition of changing circumstances that conquest provides: "en este mundo recién abierto había otro patrón para medir las condiciones y las actuaciones de la gente" (166). However, given the inevitable separation of the two lovers, the figure of Rodrigo de Quiroga constantly lurks in the background; where other novels elide his presence or his later marriage to Suárez, Correa Morandé sets up the possibility for a romantic relationship between the two at the same time she depicts Valdivia and Suárez's romance as a timeless love.

> Inés sentía especial afecto por ese amigo que le inspiraba tanta confianza, cuyo natural caballeresco se ganaba siempre la amistad de todos. Ella le tenía un cariño muy especial ... Muchas veces pensaba que sus actitudes podían ser ... amor ... pero nunca una palabra reveladora salió de esos labios que sabían sonreír tan sutilmente afectivos. (95)

Correa Morandé's method of dealing with the romantic heroine with two "true loves" relies on the social mores of the time and her characterization of Quiroga; the historical circumstance of Valdivia's death conveniently makes it easy to sidestep any concerns over continued contact.

While Suárez is, in the sympathetic thoughts of Valdivia, "una mujer valerosa ... sentía una admiración profunda por su inteligencia, por su lealtad y por esa manera absoluta de entregarle su amor" (72), success in *Inés ... y las raíces de la tierra* does not depend on a romantic resolution. In a romantic quest narrative, the climactic resolution lies in the stabilization of the love relationship between hero and heroine. Correa Morandé, however, figures Suárez's climactic resolution not as one of romance but of power. It is prefigured during Valdivia's return to Santiago before making his further incursions to the south when he notes that "donde ella está, es el centro de todo. Sigue siendo la Gobernadora. Esta mujer tiene algo especial, una grandeza propia que ningún cambio podrá anular" (297). The novel closes with the news that Rodrigo de Quiroga has been named governor and that therefore his wife can claim, legitimately, the title and position that she held for years at Valdivia's side. "¡Inés Suárez había llegado a la cumbre! El sueño que alentara su vida se hacía realidad" (351). This conclusion emphasizes not only that Suárez has accumulated power and property, and thus success, but also that the ultimate moment of this success depends on another person: her husband. This ideology, while consistent with popular conceptions of the period, also reflects certain attitudes prevalent in the 1960s and is an outgrowth of how being a member of a family takes precedence over other possible identifications.

As opposed to the previous novels dealing with the figure of Inés Suárez, Jorge Guzmán's *Ay mama Inés* (1993) from the democratic transition has attracted wide attention. Winner of various literary prizes, this novel, self-identified as a testimonial chronicle, falls squarely into the category of the New Historical novel and fits alongside other novels of the conquest published about the same time. It plays with the idea of the chronicle and absolute knowledge of the past, becoming what Cristián Cisternas has termed a historical conjecture (98). Fully cognizant of the unknowable quality of absolute knowledge of the past, Guzmán's novel nevertheless offers possibilities for interpretation of the conquest of Chile. The closing of the novel features a deathbed monologue by Inés Suárez in which she articulates her vision of the results of the dream of the conquest—concluding that idealism is always trumped by the corruption of human nature—while looking for hope in the mestizo future. Despite her prominence in communicating the message of the novel, "*Ay mama Inés* no es sobre Inés, sino sobre don Pedro. Desde la situación privilegiada de su intimidad con el conquistador, Inés entrega la información que está más cercana al corazón de Valdivia" (Martínez 22). That is, the true heart of the novel is Valdivia.

Ay mama Inés differs from earlier novels in that it does not follow the formula of a historical romance. Romantic love has a place in the novel, but it is not the driving axis around which the novel revolves. Indeed, Suárez herself expresses ambivalence about romantic love, musing privately that "si eso era enamorarse, tenían razón los curas cuando predicaban contra la pestilencia amorosa, que más se sufría enamorada de lo que se gozaba, y que todo el enamoramiento consistía en tener miedo de tonterías y desear imposibles" (53). Guzmán's text falls into the group of novels featuring Inés Suárez that allow for falling out of love. And so rather than portray the dissolution of their romantic relationship as a tragic sundering at the hands of state power, Suárez resents Valdivia's singular dedicación to the conquest of Chile, to the exclusión of his personal life (239). Suárez's personal growth, accordingly, culmina in her actions in defense of Santiago and is clarified by her moribund reflections on the work she and Valdivia carried out over the course of their lives.

> Fuiste [Pedro] recto y transparente de intenciones; porque tus sueños pusieron en movimiento una realidad que no tenía nada que ver con tus sueños y que fue la que produjo este país atroz, pero bellísimo; también te respeté por agradecimiento; conmigo fuiste generoso al punto de tratarme como un camarada en armas sin pensar jamás que yo fuera diferente de los demás por ser mujer; me hiciste encomendera; me diste poder y

me diste independencia, pero lo cierto es que de ti nunca llegué a saber mucho que importara a nuestra relación. (259)

Even at its close, she is still subject to Valdivia—in some sense created by him. Her very independence, both personal and economic, depends on his magnanimity. On the one hand, Suárez takes up arms in 1541 for her own sake, though on the other, the elderly Suárez credits her power, property, and independence to Valdivia, effectively re-subjugating herself. While one might argue that in the sixteenth century, power, property, and independence could only come to a woman through a man, the narrative turn to acknowledge this at the end problematizes a simple narrative of subject liberation that one might infer, absent the final chapter. This is further complicated by the expression of an ideology of mestizaje in the final pages that, while representing the conquest in a negative light, privileges the future of the mixed-race children of the conquest, including Suárez's position as mythical mother to its offspring. Her subjectivity in Guzmán's novel reifies the idea of a national parent, though through her own racial identification as white, she complicates the general construction of Chilean mestizaje as formulated by Sonia Montecino as a familial unit consisting of indigenous single mothers and their children born out of wedlock. Guzmán's Suárez replaces the figure of the biological indigenous mother in this system as the mythical maternal figure. Despite Suárez's optimism about the future of the mestizo children she envisions as offspring of her conquering and colonizing efforts with Valdivia, to found Chile her subject position functionally erases the indigenous mother.

Within this group of novels, the reader may generalize that several privilege the romantic emplotment of the conquest of Chile. If one considers that in romance novels women's "existence is circumscribed by a narrative structure that demonstrates that despite idiosyncratic histories, all women inevitably end up associating their female identity with the social roles of lover, wife, and mother," then the question is whether Suárez's identity becomes reduced to stereotypical femininity (Radway 207). Does she participate in feminine historicity, "the desire on the part of a feminine character to enter the historic process and to become an active agent of history" (Rabine 5)? Suárez's subjectivity in these earlier novels is bound up in authorial desire for feminine historicity, made explicit through introductions arguing for the inclusion of

Suárez's actions in the general knowledge of the conquest. The stories told and retold about her actions, from our initial knowledge of events from chroniclers through late twentieth-century novels, point toward Suárez as an individual figure embodying feminine historicity, that is, becoming an active agent of history independent of authorial intention.

Nation Before There Was Nation, Citizen Before There Was a State

The nation, as Homi Bhabha observes in *The Location of Culture*, requires metaphors to construct and reconstruct itself. These reconstructions can be found, among other places, in narratives such as Isabel Allende's; however, Allende's geographical remove from her subject in *Inés del alma mía* invites reflection on the role of distance in metaphors of the nation. Two of her earlier historical novels, *Hija de la fortuna* (1999) and *Retrato en sepia* (2000), replicate versions of the author's own geographical movement between Chile and California. Allende's place in literary criticism also confuses the issue, as a considerable debate has existed for some time as to whether her writing should be considered Chilean or even worthy of analysis.[15] What does the writing of an exile or an expatriate contribute to the idea of a nation or responsible citizenship?

> Identity as a national subject depends on friction and is often tied to loss, lack, and longing. Perfect self-identity would be unconscious, self-referential, with no outside coordinates. It would not betray its having to be learned. The pedagogical aspect of identification with a nation—what we might call citizenship training—begins with a system of institutions in which the nation is already inscribed as an idea[l], institutions that educate the subject in national virtues and national traits. (Kaminsky 29)

Residence outside of Chile, particularly during radical changes to society and practice, not to mention the contentious work of commemoration, complicates a reading of *Inés* as a simple revindication of a historical figure's role in a possible moment of nation-foundation. Nevertheless, the construction of narrative authority, the use of romance (love, sex, and the morality of both), the ideology of mestizaje, and the use of foodways in the novel will all illuminate the ways in which *Inés* functions as a reflection of certain notions of collective inclusion and exclusion.

Allende's earlier historical fiction, beginning with *Casa de los espíritus* (1982), followed a somewhat different pattern from what emerges in *Inés*. Whereas in those antecedent novels Allende's narrative revolved around the actions and feelings of the fictionalized Del Valle and Trueba women, their children, and friends, *Inés* features a historically extant figure with no relation to the social world of the novels set in later centuries. *Inés* participates instead in the general trend of historical novels of the conquest, reimagining and rewriting the colonialist endeavor privileging the perspective of Inés Suárez. An extraordinary woman, Suárez shares with Eliza Sommers, Aurora Del Valle, and the Trueba women the role of heroine, exceptional and unique. The novel is motivated by the conquest itself and Suárez's role therein, defined in part by her romantic relationship with Pedro de Valdivia. Valdivia's portrayal also benefits from Suárez's perspective praising him above other conquistadors. Per Suárez, glory was his motivation, and although a coward who betrayed her, he was, nevertheless, one of the bravest and most upstanding men of those who traveled from Europe to the Americas (Allende 82). Valdivia's virtues and flaws, taken together, portray him as a more humane conquistador concerned with the foundation of a just Chile. His exception to the stereotype of the rapacious conqueror finds a parallel in Suárez's challenge to the role of other Spanish women in the Americas of her time; they wouldn't have traveled alone as she did, nor would they have taken control of their own lives, as Suárez did by making a living for herself. Suárez contrasts with "esas mujeres [que] llevaban su vida puertas adentro, solitaria y aburrida, aunque lujosa, puesto que disponían de docenas de indias para complacer sus menores caprichos. Me contaron que las damas españolas del Perú ni siquiera se limpiaban el trasero solas, las criadas se encargaban de hacerlo" (98). Suárez is defined in this case, as well as in others throughout the novel, in opposition to the practices of other women.

Narrated in Suárez's first-person voice, the novel seeks to speak to the silences of Suárez's story.[16] However much the narrative values the everyday, Suárez as narrator rails against the legitimation of one kind of fictional discourse that devalues her own, the epic poetry of Alonso de Ercilla, which has often been taken as a historiographical document itself. Just as invented a history as Allende's version of events, *La Araucana*'s use of language and the positionality of its author as male and Spaniard authorize his text in a way that Suárez's cannot be. "Las palabras sin rima, como las mías, no tienen la autoridad de la poesía, pero de todos modos debo relatar mi versión de lo acontecido para dejar memoria de los trabajos que las mujeres hemos pasado en Chile, y que suelen escapar a los cronistas, por diestros que sean" (Allende 84). In addition to relating excluded aspects of the story of the conquest, Suárez claims authority through her use of spoken language, particularly indigenous language, in opposition to the privilege and prestige of formal written-down poetry. However, unlike a number of chroniclers who firmly believe in the translatability of one culture to another through language, Suárez recognizes the incommensurate nature of the relationship between the Spaniards and Mapuche. She notes that

> Ya sabíamos que el *mapudungu* (sic) no se puede traducir, porque es un idioma poético que se va creando en la medida en que se habla; las palabras cambian, fluyen, se juntan, se deshacen, es puro movimiento, por eso tampoco se puede escribir. Si uno trata de traducirlo palabra por palabra, no se entiende nada. A lo más, el lengua podía transmitir una idea general. (204–5)

Suárez experiences this inability to communicate precisely with the other at the level of language as well as ideology after learning the indigenous language from Lautaro, arguing that she has learned to understand (the) Mapuche, but that, given so much pain and bitterness, mutual understanding is an impossibility (212). The epistemological uncertainty of communication between the experiences of groups residing in Chile during Suárez's time come out in Allende's text in a way that is not ideologically permitted in the chronicles to which Suárez compares her text.

As is the case in other fictional representations of Inés Suárez, *Inés* depends on gendered characterizations. However, in many ways they reverse typical narratives of romance between Suárez and Valdivia. In comparing herself favorably with the other Spanish women in Peru, Suárez continues a practice that she begins earlier in the novel. She is introduced as the less attractive of two sisters (20); her activities and self-sufficiency contrast with Valdivia's wife, Marina Ortiz de Gaete, who not only is unable to manage a household, but also is identified as a pious girl good only when it comes to prayer and embroidery (37). Characterizations of Suárez herself depend much more on her actions and character than on her exterior appearance; the only definite description of her physical self comes through the eyes of her lover, Valdivia. He observes her work and how she carries herself in public spaces, comparing her force of character to what he seeks in his soldiers. She is intimidating and compared to a contained storm (112). He also recalls following her through the city "nada más que para deleitarse con el movimiento de sus caderas—caminaba con firmes trancos de gitana—y el reflejo del sol en sus cabellos cobrizos" (112). Although a sexualized aspect of Suárez's body—her hips—first draws Valdivia's attention, his initial impressions of her mark her character and her conquistador-like virtues. Suárez's body is even compared to Valdivia's when Suárez speculates, predicated on her own visual appreciation of his physical presentation, about what he sees in her. His virile features and blue eyes (115) contrast with Suárez's self-deprecating description that emphasizes her regular appearance. Suárez, though, never wavers from her depiction as valorous and brave (56). When she narrates herself with feminine-coded characterizations, it is in those moments that she is clearly embodied as a "woman," usually tied to physical love and sexual expression. Suárez's femininity is rooted in her incarnation, her body, and such descriptions constitute the bulk of her self-representations, just as the descriptions of Valdivia commonly have him ambitious and strong (124). In this sense, *Inés* follows the trend of masculinizing aspects of Suárez's personality, but without resorting to the correlating affirmation of her more common "feminine weakness" in twentieth-century historical fiction. Suárez celebrates her feminine attributes, indulging her physical self and drawing strength from it regardless of societal expectations. In fact, the narrative itself comments on the value of certain characteristics as male or female; Suárez notes that fortitude is virtuous for men but defective for women, as women with mettle unbalance the order of the world because, like men, they exhibit a capacity for anger and destruction (307). That, in turn, challenges the patriarchal order.

Love and sex are present in all of Allende's fictions, and *Inés* is no exception. Like those other fictions, it follows the general pattern of emplotting Suárez's story as a romance encoded by feminine historicity, though with an ideological position quite different from the negative views of the religiously condemned sexual relationship between Valdivia and Suárez. One might notice that Suárez's love relationships do not change her character, as is the case in several novels dealing with her story, and indeed characterize the journeys made by some of Allende's heroines in other historical fictions. Suárez clearly expresses her sexual desire because she is not content with the bounds society places on sexual practice. For that reason, one can compare the representation of Suárez's sexual expression with her attitudes toward societal restrictions on that sexual expression to understand the relationship between this novel, set in the sixteenth-century, and the late twentieth and early twenty-first century ideologies of sexual liberation that Suárez anachronistically expresses.

The demonstrations of physical love in the novel are not explicit descriptions or "spicy," which is consistent with how Allende writes a sex scene. In an interview she indicates its underpinnings:

> You destroy the effect if you go into the details. The reader, unless you're writing pornography, doesn't really want to know what happened and who penetrated whom. They want the feeling of eroticism, the sensuality. They want to use their own imagination, their own experience, their own sense of what sex is about. (Rodden 386)

Throughout the novel, in fact, Suárez often triggers lust in the various men around her. Her first marriage is a result of her first lust for Juan de Málaga. While rape has less to do with lust than with power and control, Suárez's first act of killing was self-defense against an attempted assault. In terms of plot, her incitement of sexual desire in Lieutenant Núñez is the push that ultimately allows Suárez and Valdivia to meet. Yet even in this positive and mutual relationship, Suárez reflects that their initial blind passion was perhaps a bit unhealthy, tracking quantities of time and physical affection: "Me sorprende que a ninguno de los dos nos asustara esa pasión que hoy, vista desde la distancia del desamor y la ancianidad, me parece opresiva" (121). She does, however, take pleasure in her sexuality, which departs from earlier versions of her sexual character that focus her sexuality on the love object. Suárez's sexual expression centers on her own pleasure. The narrative voice recognizes the unusual nature of Suárez's experience, and indeed she intends to transmit this experience to younger generations through her stepdaughter Isabel. "Mi experiencia en capitanes españoles es limitada, pero puedo decirte que los que me tocaron fueron muy poco sabidos en materia amorosa, aunque bien dispuestos a la hora de aprender" (305). The aged Suárez not only offers to pass on her knowledge but also recognizes that this knowledge is not widely shared, to the mutual disadvantage of all involved parties.

Despite the pleasure Suárez experiences in intimate relationships, sexual permissibility does not permeate the world she inhabits. Various critics of romance who acknowledge a woman's right to feel sensuality through reading have argued that the form itself restricts women's imaginative worlds and reinforces patriarchal norms. However, Allende's use of the form differs from this tendency. Cherie Meachem contends that "she has used what some have designated a 'despised' genre of literature, one that is shaped by woman's experience and woman's desires, to change the very structure of experience and desire" (43). This structure in *Inés* is still inscribed in an imagined world of sixteenth-century sexual mores in which Suárez's relationship with Valdivia, no matter how noble or useful, was not just condemned but also punished, given the hardship that ensues. This results in a division. In Santiago, Suárez is a woman with the right to the title doña, "la Gobernadora" (281), and the symbolic mother of Chile. This contrasts the hegemonic view of her relationship with Valdivia, exemplified by the perspective of Pedro de Gasca, representative of the Spanish Crown in Peru: "manceba, barragana, concubina" (Allende 281). She recognizes this double representation and standard are, in her own words, ironically satanic since the concubine is widowed and free and the man is married to another (291). Suárez generally distrusts the purported fairness in any justice system with which she is familiar, noting how most automatically suspect women. "No me hice ilusiones: a nosotras se nos culpa de los vicios y pecados de los hombres" (72). The belief that women are responsible for men's sexual behavior, a view held by some even today, has Suárez rail against this misguided attitude—much as twentieth- and twenty-first-century feminist movements have done.

> Me he preguntado a veces si fui responsable de las acciones de Sebastián Romero, el alférez Núñez o ese muchacho, Escobar. No encuentro falta en mí, salvo ser mujer, pero eso parece ser crimen suficiente. A nosotras nos culpan de la lujuria de los hombres, pero ¿no es el pecado de quien lo comete? ¿Por qué he de pagar yo por los yerros de otro? (168)

Suárez's rhetoric clearly questions the juridical reality of women's guilt in sexual improprieties; however, the historical record that Allende follows does not allow for Suárez to traipse from this point of tension despite the recognition of the injustice of the situation. In other words, "la única que salió perdiendo fui yo" (287). However, Suárez's punishment for sexual improprieties with Valdivia does not undo the foundational work of which she is so proud. The clear positive counterexamples of Suárez's life juxtaposed with dominant discourses on expected women's behavior emphasize a pro-women's rights perspective in the novel that remains untroubled by its use of an essentializing and universalizing category, "woman," while insisting on the nobility of a military endeavor that necessarily affirms the system that oppresses her.

Although a popular reading of Chilean history has it that the nation itself is founded on war, particularly the War of Arauco (1536–1810), *Inés* only tells the beginning of that martial history. This encoding of national origin as one of war and violence exists alongside other conceptions of national origin steeped in ideologies of racial mixture. *Inés* does not privilege this construction, though pieces of it are scattered throughout in representations of warriors as well as the indigenous population. This bellicosity is traced by some to the soldiers who accompanied Diego de Almagro's earlier expedition to Chile. In various chronicles, those figures are referred to as "chilenos." Allende describes them as men that have empty stomachs, empty purses, and threadbare clothing: "por eso les llamaban los "rotos chilenos". . . Chile, según la descripción de esos hombres, era tierra maldita" (124). Throughout the twentieth century, the figure of the *roto* has been praised as authentically Chilean, which is to say, poor and of mixed race, regardless of the heritage of any one individual identified as such. Allende noted in an interview that "I am mestiza. If I am not mestiza by blood . . . I am mestiza by culture. I come from both cultures, so I can understand both, and I feel entitled to speak for both" (Block). This concept, though lacking awareness of the complicated racial history of mestizaje in Chile and Latin

America, as well as the phenomenon of speaking for others, is characteristic of much of the discourse on racial difference in Chile.

Allende follows other writers in praising the Mapuche, constructing them as worthy enemies of the Spanish colonists. The narrative voice returns various times to reflections on the relative difficulty of the conquest of Chile when considered in the context of the rest of the region. It highlights the Spaniards' general error in expecting war with the Mapuche to follow the same pattern as earlier conflicts: "al llegar a Chile nada sabíamos de los mapuche, pensábamos que sería fácil someterlos, como hicimos con pueblos mucho más civilizados, los aztecas y los incas. Nos demoramos muchos años en comprender cuán errados estábamos" (207). Suárez's narrative voice appeals to the lack of understanding between the Spaniards and the Mapuche while at the same time presenting some self-representation allying herself with the indigenous peoples, particularly indigenous women. She includes herself in a category with indigenous serving women because of men's loose tongues in front of women of all ages, races, and ethnicities (169). However, Suárez does not identify herself with the indigenous, preferring instead to try to respect their culture and belief systems as distinct from her own. This attitude contrasts with what the narrative identifies as the officially authorized discourse, as represented by figures such as Alonso de Ercilla. Suárez at one point reflects on the word Ercilla uses instead of Mapuche, *araucano*, and rejects it. "Yo pienso seguir llamándolos mapuche—la palabra no tiene plural en castellano—hasta que me muera, porque así se dicen ellos mismos. No me parece justo cambiarles el nombre para facilitar la rima: araucano, castellano, hermano, cristiano y así durante trescientas cuartillas" (Allende 83). Despite the fact that Suárez allows the Mapuche to name themselves within her narrative, she clearly believes in and acts in favor of the Spanish Conquest.

In the case of *Inés*, the ideology of a nation grounded in racial mixture exists, expressed by Valdivia himself when speculating that "un día habrá una nueva raza en esta tierra, mezcla de nosotros con indias, todos cristianos y unidos por nuestra lengua castellana y la ley. Entonces habrá paz y prosperidad" (122). Many foundational fictions written in the nineteenth century in Latin America posited a symbolic founding through the racially mixed offspring of parents of different racial groups, a practice identified and analyzed by Doris Sommer. Allende's novel differs from many foundational fictions, however, in that the symbolic parents of the nation do not produce mixed-race offspring. Although Suárez does not embody this racial mixing, she embodies feminine heterosexuality and explores the complexity of blood purity on the Iberian peninsula. She observes that despite whatever official documents may say about the family's blood purity, she suspects that it is fake since without her nun's habit, her niece Constanza looks as if she belongs in a Saracen harem (61). The inclusion of Moorish heritage in a sixteenth-century Spanish identity complicates Suárez's self-assumed racial categorization, which, even today, subscribes to varied cultural standards, such as the one-drop notion in the United States and pigmentocracy in Latin America. This suspicion finds a physical echo in Suárez's chosen weapon of self-defense: a Moorish dagger. With this blade, she maintains her bodily integrity when threatened by Sebastián Romero, "pequeña y afilada como una aguja" (66); the dagger itself allows for her to take action and maintain her bodily autonomy and independence while symbolically alluding to Spain's own mixture of race, culture, and religion. This mixture is idealized and actualized in Chile, with Spanish arrogance and indigenous indomitability resulting in an absurdly imperious people (177), which underscores the pride that characterizes many efforts to define Chilean nationhood.

Foodways also contribute to nation construction in *Inés*. Even though not an originating piece of nationalist construction, what Jeffrey Pilcher terms culinary nationalism nonetheless contributes to later group-solidifying practices: "Nationalist feeling may well have emerged from the sharing of common foods, but only when used in such an instrumental fashion; culinary nationalism may also be subsidiary to and later than other affiliations" (69). Although food in and of itself might not be a primary marker of identity, a number of social scientists argue that the aspects of food production and consumption are key players in the continual definition and redefinition of collective identity.

> Food is one of the most, if not the single most, visible badges of identity, pushed to the fore by people who believe their culture to be on the wane, their daughters drifting from their heritage, their sons gone uptown. Ordinary people may not write books about how food means, but they participate in an ongoing—in fact, daily—discourse on the subject more keenly cultural than anything in print. (Camp 29)

The study of this ongoing discourse on food has identified a mass of conventions that, taken as a whole, Massimo Montanari has established as a system—a grammar—of food, which "informs the food system not as a simple *compilation* of products and foods, assembled in a more or less casual fashion, but rather as a structure, inside of which each component defines its meaning" (99). He likens this configuration to the use of language, noting that both function as codes of communication "convey[ing] symbolic and *signifying* meaning of widely differing kinds (economic, social, political, religious, ethnic, aesthetic), both inside and outside the societies that express them" (133). Allende's novel uses food in two ways that draw the attention of the reader when considering food as a system of symbolic communication: the times of food scarcity and the role of empanadas.

Despite the availability of food and Chile's described fecundity, hunger plays a role in *Inés*. As one of the episodes that Suárez recalls with minimal detail, the hunger and suffering of the residents of Santiago after its destruction in 1541 does not contribute anything novel to her characterization; she exhibits the same qualities of giving and caretaking that distinguish her throughout the novel. In this sense, the complex survival strategies at play during famine follow the general rule: "while in a forced estrangement from usual practices, the strategies continue to adhere as closely as possible to the basic individual culture and to the familiar, already known 'language'" (Montanari 105). Hunger was at times an issue for many groups of European conquerors, but in general, the food situation in the Americas during the sixteenth-century was adequate for the needs of the population. "While much of the world fought against shortages and famines, Spanish America produced surplus quantities of grains and meats" (Super 88).

The recorded culinary history of Chile dates to the colonial period. Though meager, culinary histories accept that the bottleneck of the foods present during the colonial era resulted from the destruction of Santiago. However, "gracias al heroísmo de Inés Suárez se pudieron librar: "dos porquezuelos y un cochinillo y una polla y un pollo y hasta dos almuerzas de trigo," troncos genealógicos de la cocina chilena" (Pereira Salas 15). Even though dealing with the lack of food was a greater threat than Michimalonko's attacks (Allende 250), Suárez and her unnamed collaborators continue providing for the needs of those around them with the resources at hand: the herbs "romero, laurel, boldo, maitén" and "unos puñados de maíz o frijoles de nuestras reservas, que disminuían muy rápido, papas o tubérculos del bosque, pasto de cualquier clase, raíces, ratones, lagartijas, grillos, gusanos" (250). Filled with unlikely ingredients, the common pot[17] maintained group solidarity through shared meals. However, the narrative voice recognizes deviations from the norm of communitarian sentiment. One concerns rumors of cannibalism among desperately hungry people without any other options. Ignoring the rumors that starving Europeans also engaged in this practice, the Spanish focused on it in indigenous communities and "se sirvieron de eso para justificar la necesidad de someterlos, civilizarlos y cristianizarlos, ya que no existía mayor prueba de barbarie que el canibalismo; pero los mapuche nunca habían caído en eso antes de nuestra llegada" (252). This deviation from usual food practices, allegedly practiced by both Spaniards and Mapuche in dire straits, indicates on the one hand that Suárez's memory of the suffering of hunger elides the worst experiences yet on the other draws attention to the justifications for conquest on flimsy claims of moral superiority. The novel continues its general move toward sympathy for the indigenous peoples, even as it pulls back. In the end, the narrative privileges the perspective of the conquerors.

As is the case with her nourishment of the colony through the common pot, Suárez's activities relate to the construction of a nation through her production of food in more bountiful times as well. Meat wrapped in dough is common throughout the world's cuisines, but Suárez's descriptions of empanadas correspond to traditional Chilean meat empanadas. According to Eugenio Pereira Salas,

> La *empanada* figura en la gastronomía española desde el siglo XIII y era de uso común en Europa . . . La empanada europea de masa de hoja, se transformó en empanada criolla, horneada con grasa y rellena con el *pinu* (voz indígena) para designar el picadillo de carne, cebollas, pasas, huevo y ají. En nuestras búsquedas hemos encontrado pocos datos sobre la empanada, pero al menos podemos acreditar su relativa antigüedad con un documento grafico como es el lienzo de 'La Santa Cena', de 1652, que se conserva en la sacristía de la Catedral de Santiago. Al hacer la descripción del cuadro, el fino historiador don Luis Álvarez Urquieta apunta: 'y sobre

un plato se ve nuestra clásica empanada'. La empanada pasó en los años coloniales a la categoría de indispensable guiso nacional. (60–61)

Empanadas and the women who make them are not unique to *Inés*. Upon arriving in California, Eliza Sommers, for one, makes empanadas to survive in *Hija de la fortuna*. The name of the traditional filling stems from indigenous language, emphasizing the local nature of the product. As part of a symbolic system, food products, particularly in a narrative of discovery and conquest, bring memories of the home culture and serve as a medium for the integration of the new cultures encountered.

> The relationship between culture/language and the sensory experience of the body can be glimpsed in the way we tend to deal linguistically with food, for words for prepared food are on some profound level untranslatable. There are ways in which 'empanadas' are not and cannot be 'meat pasties.' The experience of eating can be unmediated by language, and language always follows the experience of food. (Kaminsky 62)

Empanadas, as mediated through the language Suárez uses in *Inés* represent much more than simple sustenance for biological survival.

The function of the empanada and, by extension, Suárez's acts of cooking range from signifiers of economic independence, mediums of physical defense,[18] and adaptation to difficult situations. Her physical being, in fact, relates to empanadas, as they are sustenance not only for flagging energies but also for good will from those around her. For Suárez, as for many, smell activates memory, and she reflects that her body absorbed the aroma of meat, onion, cumin, and dough to such a point that she thinks she will die smelling of empanadas. (Allende 108). This sensorial emphasis underscores the importance of corporeal experience to the character. Suárez embodies sensation throughout the text, particularly pleasurable ones. Her physically lived experience, highlighted by her enjoyment of sex and food, is used to legitimize her symbolic role. Sex can lead to creation of new life, and food, particularly food that symbolically links Suárez to Chile, sustains new life.

Suárez's introduction to the world of empanada production came as a result of her marriage to the ruffian Juan de Málaga; while working as a seamstress in Spain, Suárez made empanadas on the side, ultimately making more money through her culinary pursuits than her tailoring. The empanadas from Suárez's ovens differ from others, and perhaps share their maker's extraordinary nature, though the narrator argues that their preeminence is due to experience with trial and error (25). When she is shipboard, her fried empanadas varied day to day according to the fillings made available to her, from lentils and beans to cheese to octopus and shark (61). Suárez's labor satisfied a need among her shipmates; the collectivization of her food production here prefigures her organization of the common pot during times of hunger.

> The perpetual need of the organism for nourishment means that the platonic empanada, widely recognized as the symbol of Chile for its exiles, is endlessly made material and consumed. The empanada is produced, devoured, and reproduced with ingredients that only approximate those of home, where, in fact, not all empanadas are created equal either. (Kaminsky 62–63)

The variations in empanadas that Suárez produces throughout the novel, adapted to the foodstuffs available—such as the switch from wheat flour to corn flour while in Cuzco—emphasize the ever-mutating content of a form thought to be emblematic of the nation. In this sense, the empanadas themselves represent the making of the nation, continually adapting and being adapted to changing situations. Suárez's role as the shaper of the dough can be read as symbolically foundational; however, rather than defining one correct way to be Chilean, Suárez's culinary exploits open a space that allows for dynamic negotiation of identity.

Negotiation, Identity, Self

Inés, though different from Isabel Allende's earlier historical fiction, is as concerned with definitions and versions of Chilean history as her previous works. Allende has noted that knowledge of the past, however incomplete, is essential to the betterment of humanity. "I think that we learn from history. First of all we realize that things weren't very different before, and then we make the same mistakes over and over. I think it's particularly important to look at the past and see what people are capable of doing" (Block). Far from a simple cautionary tale, however, Inés Suárez's story, as told in her own (imagined) voice, constructs a vision of selfhood grounded in national and gender identification. The novel legitimates a woman's voice and, accordingly, questions the hegemonic value of epic poetry much in the way a modern historian questions the emplotment of the conquest in the epic mode. "Valdivia es un comienzo porque ciertas exigencias narrativas de una historiografía hagiográfica así lo han dispuesto" (Jocelyn-Holt, *Los césares*, 194). But still, Allende's novel does not go so far in devaluing the epic mode of historiography; indeed, the novel strives to place Suárez alongside Valdivia within an epic discourse. Doing that calls for valuing other kinds of discourse concerned with the past.

Inés's figuring of Inés Suárez as a symbolic marker of nationhood develops along several different avenues. As those who travel move between cultures, the negotiation between home culture and the new cultures that the traveler encounters is borne out in several aspects of daily life, such as food. Allende's novel utilizes empanadas as a symbolic marker of belonging to the Chilean nation, and as such, Suárez's role as the producer of food places her at the center of identity-creation. The novel uses symbols such as the capital city and patriotic foods that purport to include everyone, but in practice few belong due to elements they cannot control, among them their race or gender. In the context of Chile's transition to democracy, the disconnection between rhetoric and reality approximates the competing narratives of what happened, to whom, and what the consequences should be, with no single shared conclusion. Despite this lack of resolution, Suarez's embodied selfhood also functions as a base for a possible community that, while allowing women full citizenship and empathizing with the indigenous resistance, nevertheless invests unitary symbolic freight in a particular and extraordinary white woman.

CHAPTER TWO

The Viceregal Period

> La figura de La Quintrala—apelativo otorgado a doña Catalina—ha sido más un material para la imaginación, la leyenda, el chisme y las murmuraciones elevadas a verdades históricas. Es indispensable ahora revisar la historia, conocer el contexto en que se desarrolló la existencia de una señora que hemos convertido en una Lucrecia Borgia propia. Es necesario hacerlo y no por posesionarnos de una película sangrienta y misteriosa propia, sino para asumir una verdad que rompa los clisés de los prejuicios y de una moral discutible. (Mansilla 8)

In 1604—or was it 1605?—Gonzalo de los Ríos and Catalina Lisperguer welcomed to the world one of their two children, a daughter they named Catalina. As the daughter, granddaughter, and great-granddaughter of conquistadors, German settlers, and indigenous rulers, she inherited great wealth. Her mother was accused of being a witch and of killing her stepdaughter; Catalina's strong-willed reputation depends on an accumulation of crimes as much as her exercise of and relationship to power. Did she poison and kill her father? Did she lure a respectable gentleman to her bed to kill him? Did she beat, disfigure, and otherwise abuse her enslaved workers? How many deaths could be laid at her feet? Was she in league with the Devil himself?

We don't know. Her father's sister, her aunt, accused her of his murder in 1622; in 1634 a bishop requested an investigation of her holdings and practices. The Real Audiencia, a court, began an investigation in 1660. However, she was never found guilty of any of the accusations. She left her estate to the Church with the stipulation that it be used to pray for her soul. Despite the lack of evidence proving many of the more salacious accusations made, the myth of Catalina de los Ríos y Lisperguer (1604?–1665) remains strong in Chilean society. She appears repeatedly in history textbooks, novels, films, television series,[1] educational comic books, and as a term for criminal women. In spite of this, historiographical archives regarding her life and alleged crimes are scarce. As such, those who tell and retell her story depend on popular legend and a few scattered documents to reconstruct their versions. The result of this accumulation of accounts is what Olga Grau calls a "densidad simbólica" (260), with each new layer responding to earlier stories while also reflecting ideologies—especially related to gender and race—particular to its author and period of creation. The myth of Quintrala reproduces anxieties about racial mixing and gender politics that are presented alongside a gamut of truth-claiming narratives, even though Lucía Guerra emphasizes that there are no unmediated documents in existence that tell Catalina's story. "Su voz y más que nada su discurso, han quedado sepultados en el silencio y ni siquiera nos es posible conocer los trazos de su firma porque no sabía leer ni escribir" (48). As Trouillot reminds us, we can seek the story living in those archival absences and silences.

The archival challenges related to studying Catalina de los Ríos y Lisperguer reflect the challenges of studying difference in the seventeenth century. In the Chilean context, historiographical focus on the colonial era during the democratic transition has shifted toward an interest in moving beyond facile caricatures of individuals who are taken to represent the entire era in its ever-evolving complexity. A sampling of recent work includes studies of Spanish-Mapuche relations; public liturgical events and other rituals; practices in colonial urban development; and the practice of everyday life in the colonial period. Under this new regime, a figure such as Quintrala functions as an effort to thicken the tapestry of knowledge about the period in which she lived. The observation that the history surrounding Quintrala "más parece novela, que verdad histórica" (Maturana 675) dates to the first decade of the twentieth century and has made her, overwhelmingly, a figure to be novelized, rather than researched, thanks to her star billing: Catalina de los Ríos is "una de las estrellas femeninas en la historia de Chile" (Cumplido 14). Jocelyn-Holt argues that the fascination Quintrala has held for generations of Chilean creators of culture reflects ideas and practices related to power, particularly those that inhere in nineteenth- and twentieth-century state practices. He speculates that her mythical impunity can be read as an analogue to the impunity of similarly violent exercisers of power. As the "símbolo máximo del poder," (*Los césares* 259), Quintrala represents the ambivalence present between accusation and conviction, the truth-value of gossip and rumor versus the legal language of culpability.

Despite the lack of historiographical interest in this figure, Quintrala doesn't escape the narrative role that has been assigned to her. It is the content of this role that shifts, not its mythical function. To understand these shifts, it is imperative to be familiar with the Ur-narrative, that is, the version found in Vicuña Mackenna's *Los Lisperguer y la Quintrala* (1877). Many texts follow in its footsteps, including influential historical novels such as Magdalena Petit's *La Quintrala* (1934), in typifying Catalina de los Ríos as the embodiment of feminine and mixed-race evil. A counternarrative of the Quintrala exists as well, but doesn't clearly coalesce until the novels of the democratic transition—Mercedes Valdivieso's *Maldita yo entre las mujeres*, Virginia Vidal's *Oro veneno puñal*, and Gustavo Frías's *Tres nombres para Catalina: Catrala* (2001) and *La doña de Campofrío* (2003)—in which the trend shifts toward the recuperation of Quintrala's humanity and a questioning of earlier narratives' orientations with regard to difference. As Chile's autochthonous version of the femme fatale, narratives of the Quintrala posit her demythologization while nonetheless seeking to integrate Catalina de los Ríos into an ideology of national belonging.

The Ur-Narrative: Vicuña Mackenna's Quintrala

The vast collection of cultural productions dealing with the figure of Catalina de los Ríos y Lisperguer lies along a mythologizing spectrum. At one end are texts that mythologize and generally demonize her and, at the other, those that demythologize her, usually accompanied by an ideological project of reconceptualization. Despite historical fiction produced post-1990 that undermines the traditional story, Quintrala as the archetype of the bad mestiza remains the dominant narrative in contemporary Chilean society. As noted earlier, many critics, journalists, and academics refer to Quintrala as a myth. The historian Cecilia Salinas even disqualifies her from historical consideration because she finds her "un estereotipo femenino, que se ha mostrado, hasta ahora, difícil de desentrañar y fácil de manipular con escaso rigor histórico" (20). In fact, colonial chronicles never mention Catalina de los Ríos. Various Lisperguer men, most prominently her uncle, Juan Rodolfo, appear in accounts of the War of Arauco in the ostensibly historical works of Diego de Rosales, Alonso González de Nájera, Alonso de Ovalle, Vicente de Carvallo, and José Antonio Pérez García, all composed in the seventeenth and eighteenth centuries. Women in general are absent from these chronicles, including Inés Suárez. González de Nájera describes women in Chile positively in general terms, but does not refer to any one individual or group. It is not until the nineteenth century that historians, particularly Vicuña Mackenna, bring to light new documentation that allows them to elaborate the bases of the Quintrala myth.

Ronda Ward has addressed the issues with Vicuña Mackenna's selective use of privately held archives to create his image of Quintrala.[2] He lists his sources at the opening of *Los Lisperguer*, which include various familial archives, as well as unpublished correspondence of both Francisco González de Salcedo (bishop of Santiago between 1622 and 1634) and Alonso de Ribera (Royal Governor, 1601–1605 and 1612–1617). Ward notes the limitations of the documents when she writes that

> None of the 1660 documents insinuate, let alone prove, that [Catalina de los Ríos] was a cold-blooded murderer. Salcedo's 1635 denunciations, which even his contemporaries ignored, were not only rife with prejudices against women and native Chileans but also contained significant inaccuracies. Determining the innocence or guilt of a specific individual who had lived in Chile during the colonial period, however, was not the motivation.... In fact, Los Ríos was not the central character of the work, despite her prominent presence in it. Although Vicuña Mackenna's case against her was weak at best, it became the definitive version of her life story and continued to win audiences despite its flaws. The reasons for its success lie in the fact that this is not an account of Los Ríos's life, but the story of *La Quintrala*, the personification of the corrupt Spanish Empire. (94–95)

For Vicuña Mackenna, Quintrala is always a them, that is, an exteriorized other. His invention of Quintrala does not make history, but myth.[3] Accordingly, he describes aspects of the popular legend about Quintrala that his work intends to codify to impart an appearance of intellectual rigor: whippings, bloody voluptuosities, sacrilege, pride, impunity, and ultimately a soul held by a string above the fires of Hell (7). The woman who "mataba a destajo i por su propia mano a niños, a ancianos, a doncellas, a sus capataces de vacas, a sus mujeres, a sus pastores humildes" (Vicuña Mackenna 113) is also compared to historically depraved women, including Valeria Messalina, Lucretia Borgia, and Margaret of Burgundy. Later authors replicate these comparisons, and seek others.[4] In addition to historical comparisons, Vicuña Mackenna uses a number of different adjectives to describe Quintrala, including "sinister," "irresponsible," "damned," "cruel," and "unnatural."

His explanation for the actions of Quintrala centers on ideologies of mestizaje and witchcraft. Catalina de los Ríos descended from a combination of German, Spanish, and indigenous individuals. The historian-mythmaker erases any Spanish heritage, instead assigning Quintrala a "casta que no era castellana ni cristiana vieja, sino cruza de bárbaros, jentiles i de alemanes escomulgados" (36). The mixture of these barbarians, gentiles, and heretics, embodied in this woman, implies an inclination to evil that, while unnatural, should not be a surprising result for Vicuña Mackenna's contemporaries, particularly when he asks rhetorically whether or not "¿habia en esta mezcla de razas fundidas rápidamente en un solo tipo algo que predisponia al crimen i al mal?" (78) These characterizations, particularly of excommunicated Germans, resurface periodically in other texts, especially with regard to gossip that links Pedro Lisperguer, grandfather of Quintrala, to Protestant pirates harassing the Chilean coast. While a number of critics have connected mestizaje in Vicuña Mackenna's text to preoccupations of national identity linked to Europe rather than to the indigenous past, the text also ties the practice of witchcraft, *brujerías*, to Quintrala's mixed racial heritage: "es mas probable que el jénio altivo de aquella familia, su misticismo frailesco, i especialmente sus afinidades íntimas i cercanas con la raza indígena de que procedian, las arrastrase a aquellas practicas cabalísticas" (66–67). It is worth noting that Vicuña Mackenna proposes that the Lisperguer family's close relationship with indigenous people and practices is one among several possible threads linking the women of the family to the occult. His connection of religious mysticism and witchcraft mirrors Inquisitorial doubts about the veracity of women's spiritual experiences as illustrated by the processes against nuns, *beatas*, and other women claiming theological insight.[5]

In *Los Lisperguer*, Vicuña Mackenna encodes Quintrala within a heritage of women engaged in the dark arts. Referring to rumors and superstitions, he nonetheless presents the women of the greater Lisperguer family as witches complete with "encantos, brujos, duendes aposentados en su morada, i hasta pactos con el diablo" (66). In his attribution of these supernatural acts and relationships, the historian follows the general pattern of dealing with witchcraft that Ruth Behar identifies as distinctively Hispanic:

> Unlike the secular judges of northern Europe, who viewed women's power as illegitimate in the sense that it threatened the state and society through the conspiracy of the "coven," the inquisitors of Spain and Mexico viewed women's power as illegitimate in the sense that it was a delusion and therefore not really a form of power at all. By thus devaluing the discourse of women's magical power, not taking it altogether seriously, the Hispanic religious élite trivialized and denied what on the local level was viewed as a source of power for women. (184)

By attributing accusations of witchcraft made against Quintrala and her relatives to rumor and supposition, Vicuña Mackenna thus effectively delegitimizes that power at the same time he constructs what Rebecca Lee and Ronda Ward have identified as an apophatic manual for gendered behavior based on the negative example of these women. And so when Vicuña Mackenna picks selectively from legend, he renders impossible any wholesale dismissal of that kind of power. In other words, Quintrala and her female relatives, like so many tarred from association with witchcraft, have "mysterious power which do[es] not derive from the established order"; in the late nineteenth century, this served as grounds to argue for a restricted view of women's spheres of influence (Larner 273). Lucía Guerra attributes Vicuña Mackenna's reaction of horror when faced with Quintrala not to her powers or acts, but to her gender (53). This conclusion is mirrored in various later texts that take Vicuña Mackenna as their primary source.

Following in Vicuña Mackenna's Footsteps

Twentieth-century historian Jaime Eyzaguirre mimics Vicuña Mackenna's attitude toward Quintrala: "¿qué podía resultar al fin sino un engendro monstruoso e inverosímil de esta confluencia de sangres degeneradas en que volcaban su vena un noble alemán, presunto descendiente de los duques de Sajonia, una india picunche, cacica de Talagante, y una bruja gallega?" (24) In the cases in which historians have engaged with the Quintrala myth, the terms set by Vicuña Mackenna dominate their narratives. Other nineteenth-century historians, most markedly Miguel Luis Amunátegui, also attempted to use previously unpublished sources to bring certain facts and rumors to public attention. His 1882 publication *El terremoto del 13 de mayo de 1647* does not focus exclusively on Quintrala, but he does devote a chapter to her story. He echoes Vicuña Mackenna in attributing her criminality to "una inclinación hereditaria" (38); and, as ever, she is characterized as "la Lucrecia Borgia chilena" (41). Amunátegui also values access to original documents and, because of that, flaunts his superior knowledge by arguing that the colonial period was much more violent and socially loose than generally believed.

> La biografia de doña Catalina de los Rios es un testimonio fehaciente de la corrupción de las costumbres, i del desenfreno de las pasiones en la primera mitad del siglo XVII. Una joven soltera perteneciente a una familia acaudalada i principal que se exhibe en la vida haciendo matar a palos a su amante delante de sus propios ojos, es algo de monstruoso que, en la actualidad, apenas se concibe. (79–80)

Emphasizing that in his own era the alleged crimes of Quintrala are barely imaginable, Amunátegui gestures toward an incommensurability between past and present that finds a strong echo in Western postmodernism. His account of Quintrala, alongside Vicuña Mackenna's, serves as a citation for the encyclopedic work of Diego Barros Arana. Rather than engaging the lack of understanding his contemporary reader might experience when faced with the alleged crimes of the Lisperguer family, Barros Arana instead accentuates their impunity as proof of the corruption of the moral fabric of the era, including its judicial system. Even though he resists the impulse to attribute gendered simplifications about criminality and justice to the case of the Lisperguer women, Barros Arana does generalize that actions such as those taken by the family in question were not exceptional due to their wealth and social position.

A wide variety of texts take up Vicuña Mackenna's ideological lead: plays, novels, and essays depend on the Quintrala trope to make sense of women's roles and racial mixing in their own contexts. Romantic, *modernista*, and *costumbrista* works revive and perpetuate Quintrala as a myth of negative womanhood in Chilean culture, while at the same time affirming problematic moralizations of female sexuality and ethnic difference. Literary critics have been particularly interested in the figure of Quintrala in Magdalena Petit's *La Quintrala* (1934).[6] Although written by a woman, which may imply a more sympathetic view toward a female protagonist, "it does not differ greatly from the patriarchal version of a Catalina possessed by the forces of evil, the scourge of men and a terror to society" (Flores 278). Petit's version of Quintrala introduces the reader to the child, already marked by rebellion with her red hair. The culmination of the first section of the novel features this child discovering the pleasure she derives from self-flagellation as "presa de frenesí, como una exótica danzante, la Catralita se disciplina . . ." (29). Quintrala does not conform to the expectations placed on her by her age and situation.[7] She is represented repeatedly as feline and exotic, the image of a sultana relaxing in her ornate pillow-covered space. She is immanent to the characters around her. Petit's narrator explains

> Si una está en el paseo o en el templo, lo primero que oye, como un cascabeleo que la precede, es la risita diabólica de la Catalina; lo primero que ve, la llamarada, entre las cabezas negras, de su pelo colorín; lo primero que siente, el olor pasoso de ese perfume que fabrica sabe Dios con qué yerbas (mirras satánicas, seguramente), pues nadie huele así. ¿Y aquellos trajes descotados como los de una mujer crecida? Y, en fin, tantas y tantas cosas que a nadie más se las pasarían . . ." (57)

The diabolical laugh, the flaming hair, and the satanic perfume, not to mention the young woman's inappropriate flaunting of her sexual physicality, conform to the Vicuña Mackenna-esque style of Quintrala's representation. By describing sound, vision, and smell, the text emphasizes the sensuousness of her embodiment.

While these aspects of Quintrala's physical presence stand out, she is not simply a body to be observed. Petit imbues her with a unique intellect: "el de una mujer, y mujer poco común; ¡qué sutileza para argumentar, qué fuerza de carácter! ¡pero qué orgullo, qué espíritu de dominación, qué independencia dentro de la humareda supersticiosa!" (59) But as exceptional as her mind and personality may be, this individuality rests in negative physical traits, particularly when thought of as a combination of differences, a coded reference to racial mixing.

> Su fama de belleza era, en verdad, merecida: belleza extraña, casi monstruosa en sus contrastes. Algo mefistofélico en la combinación de las facciones: la barbilla en punta, las cejas oblicuas; luego la llamarada de la cabellera colorina sobre la tez cobriza y el reflejo verde de los ojos . . . Los antepasados germanos y el cacique indio habían logrado mezclar curiosamente sus dones. En cuanto a lo moral . . . (73)

The ellipsis is original, and this pregnant silence allows the reader to infer that the "curious mix" of German and indigenous reflected in Quintrala's physical being would also apply to her moral fiber even as she possesses strength of character. As such, in this case mestizaje implies a negative ideological orientation that determines Quintrala's bad womanhood from birth. This mix is reflected in the narrative voice of Quintrala herself, who expresses a sense that her personality is split, "como si dos personas existieran en mí; una que quiere el bien, otra el mal; una que sabe lo que hace, la otra que se olvida" (128). The "good" part of Quintrala desires to find God and heaven; the "bad" part takes pleasure in suffering.

The narratives that continue Vicuña Mackenna's lead—here represented by Petit's *La Quintrala*—are the influential narratives that revive and perpetuate Quintrala as a myth of negative womanhood in Chilean culture. This negativity is amplified by the ethnic and racial politics of the mestiza with social power. Nonetheless, challenges to this ideological position and to Quintrala herself exist as the lens through which to interpret seventeenth-century Chile.

Escaping the Myth?

The Chilean bicentennial celebrations in 2010 were rife with historical remembrances. Visual narratives greatly influence collective understandings of historical events and underline the current state of Quintrala in Chilean culture. Gary Edgerton not only expounds his understanding of television as a tool for historical education and means for constructing collective memory but also identifies a number of its functions.

> It organizes together various viewing constituencies into a web of understandable relations, which are defined mostly by their differing identities and positions of power; it loosely affirms the majoritarian standards, values, and beliefs; and it facilitates a society's ongoing negotiation with its useable past by portraying those parts of the collective memory that are most relevant at any given time to the producers of these programs as well as the millions of individuals who tune them in. (8)

This is in line with Niall Brennan's understanding of the function of the Brazilian miniseries as representative of national identity, in which "national cultures act as the signifier, national values act as the signified, and national identities act as the sign" (7). As a product designed for a mass audience, television programs of a historical nature, whether miniseries, telefilms, *telenovelas*, or other genres, interact with popular folk notions of the self as identified with the national community of viewers. This prosthetic memory, articulated by Alison Landsberg, allows people to take on the memory of events they did not experience: "the person does not simply apprehend a historical narrative but takes on a more personal, deeply felt memory of a past event through which he or she did not live" (2). A visual narrative not only informs this perspective but also invites the viewers to take on the story as their own, which is particularly salient when considering history. Edgerton affirms that the majority of people acquire historical competency through visual media,[8] and studies have shown that for those who "watch history movies without the support of sufficient content knowledge and nuanced understandings of history, a possible (or probable) outcome is for the filmic account to 'colonize' their thinking about the past—taking up residence in the mind as a kind of literal truth" (Metzger 68).

In July 2010, Televisión Nacional de Chile (TVN) began broadcast of a series of historical specials, "Algo Habrán Hecho por la Historia de Chile," in which the historian Manuel Vicuña and actor Francisco Melo discuss Chilean history in the present day by visiting important places and observing "the past" as it comes alive. Hardly a ratings-buster, the program was well-received by critics and continues to be promoted as an educational resource. The second episode, "El mestizaje, la Quintrala y el poder de los jesuitas," features Quintrala in several scenes. When she appears on screen, played by Begoña Basauri, Melo names her "la famosa Quintrala." In an exterior scene, the natural light is flattering, but the actor's eyes are cold as she converses with a priest; she does not smile, and the production has chosen to use lightly menacing music. Basauri wears a red dress, and a black mantilla covers her hair. Despite these traditional visual and auditory clues, Melo and Vicuña take apart key pieces of the myth. The historian notes that Quintrala "tuvo que pagar un alto precio por su poder. La persecución y la mala reputación la acompaña hasta hoy día." He tells Melo that she was accused of witchcraft because of her knowledge of African and indigenous rites; he also contends that these rites qualify as a form of social control. They conclude that she is no worse than anyone else of her era. Her "fault," Melo observes, is that men "no toleran que una mujer sea fuerte, con carácter." The section dealing with Quintrala closes with a brief consideration of the sources on which the myth is based, namely Vicuña Mackenna's work, and points out several flaws. As such, Quintrala in *Algo* visually cues the myth, but the dialogue between Melo and Vicuña dismantles the legend and contextualizes her story.

These few minutes of *Algo* represent, then, an anti-Vicuña Mackenna current and posit an important question: how can one escape that narrative? Prior to 1990, only a few texts try to elude it. Joaquín Edwards Bello (1887–1968) uses the myth to understand the conquest, shifting the emplotment of Quintrala away from bad womanhood. His essay does not recuperate the figure of Quintrala in the same way that writers during the democratic transition in Chile resemanticize her indigenous heritage. Edwards Bello, while recognizing Quintrala's indigenous roots, instead focuses on her as something quintessentially Spanish: the Conquistador (14). In opposition to his contemporaries, Edwards Bello attributes importance to Quintrala precisely because he imagines her to be the Chilean female archetype; as such, he avoids references to witchcraft, crime, and violence as components of her mythic nature. Instead, he places her on par with Pedro de Valdivia in terms of Chilean identity, a move that alters and reorients her myth without destroying it. Edwards Bello's Quintrala is, in short, the Chilean everywoman. He apostrophizes

> No eras bonita ni elegante, pero valiente, altiva, sufrida y dura como piedra fundamental de nuestra sociedad. En ti se batieron todos los gérmenes mejores de todas las mujeres chilenas; no fuiste caso aislado, sino parte inicial de la serie, o producción a la *douzaine* del stock femenino nacional. Fuiste la mujer superior entre hombres debilitados por las guerras y el mestizaje. No te merecieron, y tan física era en fin de cuentas tu belleza como la otra. (25)

Note that while seeing Quintrala herself as positive, Edwards Bello also subscribes to the racialized ideology that views mestizaje as a negative trait, in this case, one that weakens the male population. This statement does not exist in a cultural vacuum; intellectuals and politicians such as Argentine Domingo Faustino Sarmiento and Mexican José Vasconcelos argue for the gradual whitening of the general population as inherently desirable for the progress of the Latin American nation-state. These ideologies of mestizaje do not distinguish race from class or caste and can be read as a cultural underpinning for much Latin American literary production.

Several novels published during the Chilean democratic transition show patterns of structure and content that seek to answer the question of how to escape from Vicuña Mackenna's normative narrative of Catalina de los Ríos y Lisperguer. These patterns include: the use of multiple discourses and the confessional mode; a revaluation of the feminine and the indigenous in Chilean culture; a clear representation of power, its exercise and consequences; and the exercise of violence and the definition of agency. While all these elements are present among the authors who write about Catalina in the 1990s and 2000s and may function in similar ways in different texts, each novel offers a possible response to the question of escaping Quintrala's myth in Chilean society.

Along with Vicuña Mackenna's nineteenth-century text and Magdalena

Petit's 1934 novel, Mercedes Valdivieso's *Maldita* completes the trinity of critically appraised Quintrala texts. Writing in a confessional mode,[9] Valdivieso uses *Maldita* to vindicate the figure of Catalina particularly with regard to her indigenous heritage. Widely considered to be one of the more prominent Chilean New Historical novels, Valdivieso's work "creates a polyphony of voices that reveals the invalidity of a discourse that has erected itself as truth bearing, based on patriarchal monologism and arbitrary selection" (Flores 283). But even as the critical consensus has it that Valdivieso's work demythologizes the figure of Quintrala, Rebecca Lee argues that "Doña Catalina is also the territory over which the quest for identity is forged. And although Valdivieso proposes a revisionist reading, Doña Catalina's function remains symbolic. Like the mythic *Quintrala*, the protagonist stands as an emblem of a totalizing Chilean identity" (115). The Quintrala legend may have been dismantled, yet the figure of Catalina de los Ríos retains figurative meanings, offering what Lucía Guerra calls "una readecuación feminizada del ser y su relación con el mundo y lo divino" (62). The symbolic meaning of Quintrala shifts, but the mythic form does not.

The other works studied here have been largely ignored by literary critics. Virginia Vidal's *Oro* reproduces Catalina's story through various narrative perspectives that unify the questioning of Vicuña Mackenna's monolithic myth through both structure and content. Gustavo Frías's *Tres nombres* features two novels, *Catrala* and *La doña*, both in their second editions; Frías's death in 2016, however, means that his trilogy must remain incomplete. In 2008 Frías published *El inquisidor*, which he characterizes as a novel independent of *Tres nombres*, though it inhabits the same world.[10] Frías characterized his motivation within these novels as an effort to "recuperar nuestra leyenda, lejos de la hipocresía" (Molina n.p.) in terms of an autochthonous identity. By reconstructing her family history, Frías offers an alternate vision of main events in the life of this young woman in such a way as to humanize her while also exploring her relationship to symbolic aspects of identity.

Narrative Structures

Maldita and *Oro* are notable for their uses of multiple discourses and the voice of rumor. Valdivieso's novel opens with a letter penned by Alonso de Ribera that explains the situation in which he finds himself during his first appointment as governor of Chile. One of his reflections tells of the effect that the women of the Lisperguer family have on him, as well as his confession that he lacks the social tools to interact with them appropriately. He therefore categorizes them as different, "estas mujeres de las Indias, magas o doncellas tienen algo en común, otra forma de naturaleza que a mi inteligencia de hombre se escapa y, por qué no decirlo, asusta" (11–12). In presenting the hegemonic European male view, predicated on the incommensurability of subject positions and the fear it provokes in the hegemon, the novel shifts to a first-person narration centered on Catalina. Valdivieso's recuperative project[11] contrasts the voice of public rumor, the "*dicen que*," with Catalina's self-narrated lived experience. The gossip makes true that

> Indiferente al mal, la mujer ya había cometido parricidio, sacrilegio e incesto y quedado impune. Nada bueno podía esperarse de quien nació a la sombra de dos crímenes, el de María de Encío, su abuela paterna, perpetrado en el primer Gonzalo de los Ríos, y el de su madre Catalina Lisperguer, ejercido en la hija natural del segundo Ríos, el que iba a ser su marido. A palos dicen que mató a la muchacha en vísperas de su casorio. De ese linaje de tradición infausta venía la Catalina menor. (28)

While the narrative mode of earlier novels would authorize the truth-value of such rumors, in reproducing them Valdivieso's text challenges their veracity. The second Catalina negotiates the world that whispers behind her back in an effort to establish her own individuality, balanced with her connections to the women who came before her.

Valdivieso's novel features gestures toward multiple discourses through the inclusion of letters and rumors mediated through characters in the novel, while Vidal's *Oro* marks different discourses through formal separations. Twenty chapters vary their narrative point of view and use epigraphs from a series of different works to frame their perspectives. Throughout the novel, the reader can contrast the chapters reproducing the conversation of men at a gossipy tertulia with a separate third-person narration of Quintrala's experience. The typical descriptions of Quintrala resurface contextualized in rumor and hearsay in the men's conversation. A would-be lover calls her "mi selvática," (87), and at the news of her death, members of the tertulia refer to her as "esa subversiva" (220) and "bruja torturadora, criminal e impune" (221). Within the cacophony of the tertulia, one man, don Joan Canudos, consistently dials back the imaginative fancy of his companions. The opening session of the tertulia features a litany of rumors, many of which link Quintrala to witchcraft, sorcery, and deviant sexual practice. Canudos's response to this accumulation of accusations is simply "no digáis así, solo es hembra humana" (12). The death of Juana Talaverano, attributed in several earlier versions to Quintrala, is described as a beautiful murder, "ése sí que es obra de arte: morir de aspirar claveles, y la Quintrala, su artífice" (76); Quintrala is both desired and reviled. The tertulia, though somewhat obsessed with Quintrala, does cover other topics, among them the institutionalization of education and anachronistic connections drawn between Alonso de Ribera's government and Augusto Pinochet's twentieth-century dictatorship (the "autoasignado capitán general").[12] It is in this last comparison that Canudos foresees the attempted erasure of the indigenous peoples; the tertulia also discusses the progress of the Arauco War and issues of civilization and barbarism.

The tertulia participants use language to reflect the world they imagine they live in, though in many cases that reflection is reflexive. Nevertheless, the question of the importance of naming becomes a subject of conversation:

> —¿Os dais cuenta qué desastre ocurre cuando a uno de ellos se le borra el nombre?
> —Es borrarle su memoria.
> —Desgajarlo no sólo de su pasado sino también de toda su cultura.
> —Es enturbiar la piedra.
> —Es dispersar la bruma y quitarle el velo a cuanto protegía.
> —Es cortarle las garras al puma.
> —Tenéis razón, caballeros, bautismo y monogamia son tan importantes como fusiles y cañones.
> —Es labor de la conquista, labor misionera para salvarlos. (Vidal 126)

In the context of indigenous naming practices portrayed in this novel, the name of an individual not only identifies the person but also connects the subject to community and heritage. The Spanish attempt to eliminate the selfhood of the indigenous subject is part of the project of civilization and conquest. Quintrala, though not as closely tied to indigenous communities in Vidal's novel as in several others, gains knowledge of the origin of her nickname when she is speaking with one of the indigenous women who raised her, Potenciana. Catalina notes that "me decíais que mi pelo era de llamas y mi naturaleza, de trueno," and Potenciana responds that "—y como en mi lengua, quin es conocer y tralca quiere decir trueno y el trueno suena después del relámpago, al comienzo te inventaba mil apodos cariñosos: Quintralca, Catralca, Catrala y, después, Quintrala, la que conoce el trueno y es amparo del fuego. Y todos te empezaron a llamar así" (49). Though many works propose different etymologies for the word Quintrala—a deformation of Catalina, a reference to the plant *quintral*, or an explanation such as Vidal's—the act of naming, imbued with knowledge and affection, here connects Catalina, Quintrala, and the indigenous world in seventeenth-century Chile. When juxtaposed with the male tertulia's recognition of the power of naming and knowledge in the conquest of the natives, *Oro* privileges the value of naming and its relationship to systems of domination.

In addition to the chapters that reproduce discussions at the tertulia, the third-person narration shares a separate perspective on Quintrala, at times purporting to transmit her own words. Quintrala is constructed as intimately linked to literacy and the written word, despite her own inability to write. However, she recognizes the power of the written word as a vehicle for knowledge transmission: "si supiera escribir, anotaría las palabras, las murmuraciones, conservaría las intrigas, las historias y patrañas que me han contado y las que he inventado, apuntaría las fórmulas para el bien y para el mal" (24). She recognizes that the written word does not guarantee truth-value and that the writer enjoys power insofar as rumor, innuendo, and invention can all coexist. The constructed nature of text, and particularly texts produced with the intention of transmitting information through time, is thus ironically reinforced by the words of an illiterate woman. Vidal's Quintrala is also linked to the printed word through her German ancestry; she consistently has visions of Faust that she does not know how to interpret. This leads to a narrative of a possible relationship her ancestors may have had with the historical Johann Faust (ca. 1480–1540), as well as with Johannes Gutenberg (ca. 1393–1468) and the first printing press. Her ancestry, focus, and explanation for her violent acts in other versions here only receives passing mention in service of metaliterary reflection. A tertulia member speculates that her hatred of the world "—Debe ser la mezcla—aventura el caballero don Isidoro Torremocha. /—Mestiza por partida triple. /—Germana, india, española" (93). However, it is not until the death of her son that Catalina truly becomes Quintrala: "Ni con todo el oro del mundo le sería devuelto su hijo. Ni con todas sus súplicas se lo devolverían. Se convertiría en el azote de Dios. Todo dolor sería poco para apagar su dolor" (106). The reader may therefore characterize Quintrala's wickedness in *Oro* as an outgrowth of her mourning process.

The novels of *Tres nombres* characterize Catalina herself as a literate woman who produces these texts, as she narrates it, to preserve a unique perspective on when she lived and reflect her own empowerment. Time and again she refers to lost knowledge and the obliteration of the Picunche,[13] as well as an urge to transmit her knowledge. However, her work toward memory-recuperation[14] is consistently tied up in a parallel process of forgetting that reinforces that which is remembered.

> Instead of representing an event literally, exactly as it occurred, memory narratives incorporate the past *performatively* via modes of transmission that render the experience (or some aspect thereof) intelligible to a specific audience, and for a specific reason. In writing memory, subjects generally appeal to narrative modes with which they are familiar or which are available to them, and which create the conditions of possibility for telling. Narrating individual memories, in this sense, cannot be disconnected from the broader collective archive of discursive practices and symbols that facilitates their transmission, circulation and reception. (Lazzara *Chile* 30)

Varied novels reflect different intended and constructed audiences for Quintrala. Frías's Catalina writes to see and forget (*Catrala* 18, 195) and frames the novels as the work of an old woman "con la tarea espiritual de no morir antes de consignar estas memorias y tener el tiempo y la lucidez de quemarlas alguna noche de San Juan Bautista" (*La doña* 26). This conceit contrasts with the textual authority given to earlier source works by historians; Catalina writes not to set the story straight but as a spiritual exercise before death.[15] In this, Frías's novels follow the pattern of the Quintrala narratives that frame themselves as confessions. However, Catalina's vagueness about the nature of this spiritual exercise decouples her practice from the explicitly Christian sacrament of penance. Throughout the novels, Catalina observes the world around her, at times describing her memory as a series of still portraits (*Catrala* 60) and at others as a process of retrieving information from an architectural structure. However, not every experience or observation can be narrated, as Catalina perceives language as the medium of transmission for drama and action and less adequate to quiet introspective expression because "la lengua no sirve para contar las cosas divinas" (*La doña* 251). Catalina recognizes a limit to the power of human expression; her narrative does not purport to replace other texts, but instead centers her account around a thoroughly humanized Catalina de los Ríos, whose strengths and frailties are utilized to offer an alternative view of what it could mean to be Chilean. This speculative mode does not declare itself to be the only possible answer to the question of who we are. In fact, it makes the case for a nuanced view of an oft-demonized woman and, in so doing, promotes a wider reconsideration of what it means to belong.

Value of the Feminine and the Indigenous

Aspects of indigenous belief systems and practices are integrated into the fictional life Catalina describes in *Maldita*; she questions what it means to be mestiza, "ser mujer primero y también, mujer cruzada por dos destinos, lo que era ser mujer dos veces" (Valdivieso 37). In an effort to discipline her physical being, she turns to the figure of the *imbunche*,[16] a mythological physically deformed monster that traditionally guards caves used by witches and warlocks. The text also reproduces a conflict between the European view of God as opposed to the indigenous view; Catalina's Tatamai, a physical link between the woman and her indigenous roots, argues that God, "Dios-Ngenechén," reflects all of humanity, but that the Christian Spaniards have cut off the feminine half, "de ahí la igualdad que nos quitaron, y en esa diferencia andan todas las mujeres, también las blancas" (41). Catalina, though arguing on one occasion "carezco de hablar y de hacer" (65), shows this face to society at the same time she imagines an alternate order in which her gender would not limit her exercise of power.

> Entre el fuego, la Señora gritó una voz conocida: "¡te hago a imagen y semejanza mía!" Vi cómo hurgaba entre su chamal y salía su mando con una rosa negra: "¡te doy mi corazón!," exclamó como si de su propio corazón se desprendiera. Alargué el brazo y agarré la rosa negra, una sola espina tenía que relumbraba su acero y se ensangrentaba con el rojo del recinto. Miré su rostro y era el de mi madre: "¡madre Dios!" (64)

This world-construction depends on the indigenous world as well as the European; it allows for the female subject to imagine Genesis 1:27[17] on her own terms. As we have seen, Quintrala is most often shown in concert with the Devil. Valdivieso's transformation of this comparison as a desire to find oneself in the presence of a God recognized by both Christian and Mapuche rewrites this relationship as one that values subjectivity regardless of gender or ancestry. As such, *Maldita* posits an inclusive collective subjectivity coalesced around the occupation of a geographical space; Quintrala's role in constructing this subjectivity has her function as a symbolic representative of the Chilean self.

Accordingly, Catalina's gender practice within *Catrala* is quite fluid, as noted by her experience of cross-dressing, as well as its one lesbian sex scene. Throughout these experiences, however, Catalina's femininity remains prominent. While she is able to put on a man's identity for a period of time, she nearly always inhabits a female space and is constructed as part of the matrilineal power structure she inherits from other textual treatments of her and her line of female relatives. However, Frías's novel twists that toward a more positive direction so that what she inherits is not witchcraft and a genetic predisposition to evil but a worldview that encompasses European and indigenous perspectives and vast material resources. The same rumors reproduced repeatedly in earlier texts are given superficial airing in *Tres nombres*, including witchcraft and invisibility, as well as the ability to find lost treasure, fly through the air, make soups and stews cook themselves, bring rain, enchant serpents, break iron, and cause mortal accidents (*Catrala* 39). Catalina recognizes that the women in her family are "buenas matronas, mujeres sensuales, grandes, de caderas anchas y pechos generosos" (*Catrala* 138) while also at times "injustas, caprichosas, irritables, intrigantes, contradictorias, provocativas, insoportables, rebeldes o intransigentes, pero nadie podrá decir jamás que somos mezquinas" (*La doña* 340). Through Catalina's words, Frías responds to earlier caricatures of Quintrala and her female relatives by, for example, linking their sensuality to childbearing.[18] What some may see as difficult character traits are enumerated as an accumulation of attributes that are ultimately contextualized. Meanness implies a malicious intent which the Lisperguer women are reputed to lack and Catalina de los Ríos is enmeshed in the world of these women.

The construction of Catalina as a bridge between the Spanish and the Picunche

> reivindica su herencia materna mapuche, reconoce su sangre indígena y se enorgullece de su herencia múltiple, lo cual no sólo la distingue del resto de una sociedad que niega sus raíces indígenas, sino que la transforma en una mujer más libre, menos temerosa y más dispuesta a romper las reglas impuestas con sangre por los europeos. (Waldman "Chile" 109)

As we have seen, the novels represent this heritage through dress and syncretic religious belief and also in language use and alternate cultural practices that allow Catalina to maintain her independence in the face of paternal opprobrium. As a child, she nonviolently resists her father's corporal punishments through her ability to feel connected to the world beyond pain, fear, and her father's fury because of her indigenous ancestry (*Catrala* 93), a power to which she wants to return when dealing with the aftermath of a loved one's death: "quería volver a ser india" (*Catrala* 179). Despite Catalina's position as a link between the different peoples populating the same territory, the negotiation required is not always successful, which at times prompts her to reflect that it is impossible to inhabit a liminal space because one must always choose a side (*Catrala* 199). That said, most instances dealing with contact between the two worlds Catalina inhabits result in a relationship built between the two, rather than an incommensurable divide of the two.

Yet a constant undertone in *Tres nombres* is the war between Spaniards and Mapuche; Catalina's family goes to great pains to distinguish between their group, the Picunche, and the Mapuche in the south. While related, the Picunche have traditionally favored maneuvers to allow them to retain their culture while under the proverbial boot of Empire, be it Inka or Spanish. In any event, much discussion of the merits of war, peace, and the practice of conquest occurs between Águeda, Catalina's grandmother, and her husband, Pedro Lisperguer. When Pedro argues that the Europeans simply want to spread their way of life—their religion, especially—his wife responds heatedly, "¿Y para trasladar su forma de vida tienen que aplastar nuestros templos, esclavizar a nuestros hombres, engendrar en nuestras mujeres, borrar nuestro idioma . . . ?" (*La doña* 287), a view more in line with one expressed by Catalina's other grandmother, María de Encío. While sharing memories and stories with a friend, María recounts her experience as a *conquistadora* before coming to Chile, concluding that conquest always ends in disappointment, yet "nunca me ha conmovido tanto la desilusión de un europeo como el indescriptible desencanto que reflejan los ojos mudos de los indios conquistados cuando descubren nuestra voracidad, nuestra avaricia, nuestra crueldad" (*Catrala* 230–31). Catalina's uncle, Juan Rodulfo Lisperguer, also reflects this negative view toward Spanish motivations in the conquest. He compares the Spanish unfavorably to the Mapuche in arguing that "los araucanos son los últimos caballeros y negociar con ellos será perder el tiempo . . . Ellos no luchan por conquistas ni posesiones, padre, luchan por la nobleza" (*Catrala* 90). Nobility belongs to the indigenous peoples. Although the Europeans may propose a civilizing Christianizing mission, the reality as expressed by characters with experience on the ground is far from that ideal. Even Pedro Lisperguer, whose nobility comes directly from his relationship with the Holy Roman Emperor Charles V, recognizes that the relationship that the Europeans have tried to build with the indigenous peoples, and of which he has been a part as a *juez de hechicerías*, does not live up to its rhetoric. He argues, for instance, with other powerful groups that propose to ban an indigenous singing practice, which he judges a gross miscalculation that is as misguided as killing heretics and witches to ensure the safety of the community:

> herejías que eran sólo costumbres, conspiraciones que no fueron tales, brujerías que eran ritos religiosos, y el resultado, señor, es que los naturales me odian. Si me permite generalizar, señoría, nos odian y su odio son las sílabas de ese canto que usted quiere eliminar. Pero eliminar el canto jamás eliminará el odio. Al contrario, nos odiarán más aún. Y no sólo los indios, todos. Los ancianos, los mestizos, los negros, todos. (*Catrala* 159)

Lisperguer's rationalization for the perpetuation of the singing practice roots itself not in the theological, but rather in a pragmatic recognition of the situation in which the Europeans find themselves. This pragmatism opens a space for Catalina to dream of utopia: peace. She argues for the end of the war of conquest, from the foreign perspective, and of defense, from the indigenous one, so that the rupture between her peoples finds resolution in a single community (*La doña* 252). She embodies a possible route to this utopian peace, in which an "us-versus-them" ideology is rejected in favor of the idea that every individual is subsumed into a singular category of belonging. Frías constructs Catalina as a figure who extends the definition of identity to include European, indigenous, and their offspring. As such, she lives up to her title as "creadora de linaje" (*La doña* 189)[19] by offering an alternate vision of what it means to belong to a collective Chilean identity.

Power

All of these novels of the democratic transition engage with the question of power—the exercise of control or authority over others—to one extent or another. Their structure questions the power of historical narrative and proposes a new exercise in which the subject is able to name herself. Political conflicts over property and twentieth- and twenty-first-century adaptations of the baroque dichotomy between being and seeming also reflect the exercise of power. Thus, these works undermine the Ur-narrative put forth by Vicuña Mackenna.

Much of the conflict in *Tres nombres* revolves around the exercise of power and struggles for it. While a number of the exercises of power are limited to family politics—such as Águeda's orchestration of marriages within the family—the mechanics of power in the wider society also figure. Although Pedro Lisperguer argues that in America "creamos nuestra propia aristocracia" (*Catrala* 25), the narration's characterization of the local aristocracy defines it in negative terms, not because of their names or relationships with power structures in Spain, "sino por haber matado más indios en las batallas, o robado una propiedad de buen rendimiento o por dignidades eclesiásticas conseguidas en el clero secular o los conventos" (*Catrala* 24). The corruption inherent in the colonial system results in injustice. Catalina, however, does not rebel to change the system but to liberate herself from personal strictures. "La heredera del orden no puede hacer más que conservarlo" (*La doña* 167), even when that order is described as hypocritical, sanctimonious, repressive, excessively pious, and overly interested in the misfortunes of others. This world as depicted is an authoritarian state in which public opinion does not matter and obedience is accorded to the loudest and most powerful. "No podemos decir cómo son o deben ser las cosas; apenas podemos pensar cómo no son" (*Catrala* 160). The overt restriction on free thought, expression, and commerce is accompanied by the hegemony of the Inquisition, which hovers ever-present in the background of the novels. With the death of Gonzalo de los Ríos, his lover, Bettina, accuses Catalina and María de Encío of murdering him by poison. This accusation is dealt with by an interview with familiars of the Inquisition that report to the Inquisitor General. Catalina's narration recognizes that this accusation is repeated years later by Bishop Salcedo, a source used by Vicuña Mackenna. However much happiness she feels at being free of her father's influence, Catalina's narrative demonstrates her innocence.

In *La doña*, Catalina begins to exercise more formal power, but always within the context of her legal right to do so, which sets Frías's version apart from many others. Once informed by her servants of the goings-on of her guests at Toda el Agua, she feels simultaneously like a monarch at her court and a spider at the center of her web. Both images carry the implication of the manipulation of absolute power, but the spider image carries malignant overtones in Western culture. The theme of manipulation emerges again as Catalina imagines individuals as dolls or marionettes that perform the same play time and again. She also enjoys the thrill of the first time she is called "doña," "implicando lo que doña significa: el poder y la propiedad . . . fue como si me bautizaran por segunda vez" (*La doña* 63). The child Catrala becomes doña Catalina of Campofrío. This naming progression, reflected in the titles of the constituent novels, is left unfinished as is the cycle of texts. At the close of *La doña*, Bettina curses Catalina and names her Quintrala. However, Catalina remains herself, a woman exercising power between European and indigenous worldviews and offering an alternate vision of what Chile could be.

As within colonial Latin American societies appearances mattered, clothing and appearance fulfill important narrative and symbolic functions in Frías's novels. Sumptuary laws regulated how individuals could present themselves to

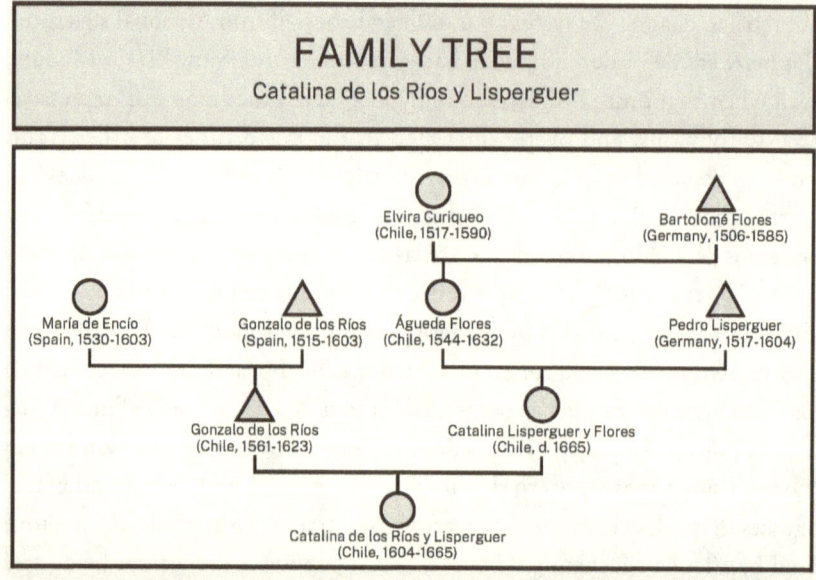

Figure 1. A visualization of Catalina de los Ríos y Lisperguer's family tree. Courtesy of Katherine Karr-Cornejo.

avoid confusion about proper places in society. Many of these laws restrict clothing choices, be it in terms of fabric, colors, or design, in a society that believes appearances should reflect the true nature of a person and their position. Catrala, the name used for the girl who grows into the woman Catalina, is described as an attractive person with "cabellos rojos . . . estatura de princesa alemana, encerrada en un delicado cuerpo sevillano" (*Catrala* 18). The trope of pairing separate heritages with physical attributes allows her to embody racial and ethnic mixing: "tienes el pelo rojo fuego de los godos, los ojos verdes del norte alemán, la piel mate y los pómulos altos de la tribu de Tala Canta, que es nuestra propia tribu, y los labios abultados, ese árabe sensual de los De los Ríos, represor como buen descendiente de españoles andaluces" (*Catrala* 112). Later characterized as "la mujer más peligrosa del reino" (*La doña* 446), Catrala consciously uses the rhetoric of dress to bridge the gap between her practice of life as a Spanish Catholic in Santiago and as the indigenous *cacica* of Toda el Agua. The first section of *La doña* details the day of Catalina's installation as the leader/owner of Toda el Agua, a shift in property ownership announced in *Catrala* by her grandmother. Catalina recognizes the importance of her dual European-indigenous heritage, expressing a desire to wear pieces of clothing that recognize her double origins (*La doña* 23).

To do so, she wears

> una camisa sevillana de muselina blanca, encima una blusa picunche de lana de alpaca negra, bordada con grecas teñidas de rojo con las flores del quintral, y una falda española del color de las castañas, apta para montar. Llevaría también un poncho corto de lana blanca de vicuña, que usaba la gente de Toda el Agua en días calurosos como este. (*La doña* 23)

Two shirts, one Spanish and one Picunche, alongside the Spanish riding skirt and Picunche poncho, visually mark Catalina as bridging two cultures, as she also bridges two systems of religious practice. During the day that celebrates the transfer of power from Águeda to Catalina, the "longest day," Catalina reflects on similarities and differences in Catholic and Picunche cosmologies. She sees similarities between the cannibalistic practice of eating an enemy's heart to consume his power and the sacrament of Communion, as well as the practice of repetition in prayer. However, the belief systems also clash, when, for example, Catalina considers that "las culebras no son malditas, dañinas ni agoreras para nosotros los indios, pero yo también era cristiana y la serpiente oculta en el paraíso me resonó como la del relato bíblico del Génesis" (*La doña* 28). Her language reflects her dual identification as she speaks in the first person to refer to both cosmologies. However, she does not offer her own identification as representative; her position is presented in both novels as a unique heritage, though her family of origin and its power are dangerous gifts (*La doña* 68). Catalina is constructed as an extraordinary individual whose position between worlds alludes to the mestizaje that becomes part of the symbolic foundation of the Chilean nation, a process that Frías has spoken of in interviews and in which he discusses the importance of legends as a way to examine Chilean identity. Sociologist Gilda Waldman argues that in negating the pejorative idea of mestizaje in Catalina, Frías "reconstruye a un ser cuya inteligencia, pensamiento y acciones provienen, precisamente, de su compleja raigambre mestiza" ("Chile" 109).

Catalina's appearance in Frías's novels also plays with concepts that commonly appear in baroque artistic production, such as the difference between being and appearance, as well as the use of mirrors and masks as foils for the identity of the subject. After the death of her lover Esteban de Britto, Catalina describes her face as a mask (*Catrala* 277) behind which her thoughts are but a nightmare.[20] She wears a different kind of disguise when she sneaks out of the house to visit the doctor Francisco de Maldonado,[21] traversing the evening streets of Santiago dressed as a man.

> The apparel is not only of *another* identity but of passing through forbidden (and therefore exotic) portals into the world of the opposite. Clothing is the clue and the passport to this because it acts as such a significant marker. To enter into the clothing of the opposite sex is as close as one can come to *being* one of that sex; to participating in activities which would otherwise be proscribed. (Suthrell 8)

Though Catalina does not routinely cross-dress in the novel,[22] she recalls childhood aspirations to imitate her father. She installs herself in front of a mirror to examine her reflection in light of her father's model. The reader is thus privy to the disconnect present between the self and the aspirational appearance. Catalina "comparaba los rasgos de mi rostro con los suyos e imitaba sus gestos, tratando de copiarlos lo más fielmente posible, con la intención de producir en los demás el mismo respeto tímido y servil que provocaba mi progenitor" (*Catrala* 207). The mirror serves as a tool in which to practice her performance of domination. Yet in revealing this practice, however, the narrative refutes any naturalization of the exercise of power. When at the close of *La doña*, Catalina again gazes in a mirror, she sees a woman exercising power, "una ñusta poderosa y terrible a quien todos podían amar y temer" (688), which contrasts with her earlier desire to imitate her father's male practice. Between these two episodes, Catalina also experiments with inhabiting a male space through dress. She recalls that

> Vestirme de hombre esa noche fue como encajarme entera dentro de una máscara, una actitud, un sentimiento. Hasta el día de hoy creo haber comprendido entonces, de una vez y para siempre, el secreto de la monja

alférez . . . Para mí, las ropas dispuestas ordenadamente sobre la cama eran solo un disfraz, pero a medida que las iba vistiendo sentí cómo me traspasaban su aplomo y seguridad, dotándome con una voluntad decidida y fuerte, de esas que al tomar una determinación no vacilan hasta que la han realizado, ni ceden aunque el miedo les haga temblar las verijas. ¡Es magnífico ser hombre!, recuerdo haber pensado. (*Catrala* 307)

Catalina's use of a man's clothing does not merely disguise her: it transforms her worldview. The importance of dress, therefore, to signify her double heritage cannot be overstated. Frías's characterization of Catalina may be read in light of Judith Butler's idea of performativity, that is, that "what we take to be an internal essence of gender is manufactured through a sustained set of acts, positioned through the gendered stylization of the body" (xv). Catalina's dressing actions respond to racialized and gendered views of what her body should represent; the power and freedom she feels while dressing as a man is not replicated in her women's dress, though over the course of two novels, she sees instead within herself, reflected in a mirror, a woman holding great power.

Violence

Key to the Quintrala myth is the exercise of violence by a mestiza woman. Vicuña Mackenna's text expects its audience to be horrified by these actions and guides readers to associate the exercise of power through violence in the person of Catalina with demonic activity. On her death bed, Vidal's Quintrala describes a dream in verse, detailing the violence she has inflicted on bodies other than her own, "cuerpos llagados, / a sus ojos aterrados / a sus labios rotos" (208), searching out those who would in some way challenge her power to discipline them or, better, to resist her willful creation and destruction of docile bodies. Although Michel Foucault examines the creation of docile bodies through disciplinary institutions in a later time period than that in which Quintrala lived, the societal framework that enforces ideal practice through vigilance and selective violence can be observed throughout the novel, both in the words of the tertulia and in the commonly portrayed practices of the Inquisition. Where Quintrala's actions deviate from a Foucauldian model comes in her excess, that is, in her use of violence for violence's sake, as opposed to restraint to maintain a disciplinary system. She wants to create fear as a strategy for the preservation of her own power and property; she confesses "los descuartizo / para armarlos de nuevo / y zurcirlos y dejarlos mansos" (208), though her true aim in the process of violence is to

> Sembrarles
> una semilla de miedo eterno
> que les heredan hasta a los chozonietos
> ninguno osará posar la vista en mis tesoros,
> ninguna hambre les hará codiciar mis bienes (208)

A perversion of her grief for her son drives her cruel practices. Without an heir, her obsession with the conservation of her wealth connects her both to her conquistador ancestors and the society in which she lives. Her value to society and power to exercise violence is rooted in her assets as interiorizing patriarchal values of worth and wealth. This situation is not simply a relationship in which Quintrala exploits her disciplinary power over her workers, wherein she hopes to instill the idea, with the resonance of a grieving mother, that "el dolor dura más que el deleite" (209). When she physically tortures their bodies to satisfy her grief, her own body is victimized.

> Se me montan encima, me envuelven, me visten,
> y mi cuerpo se baña y se empapa
> de sus babas, de su sangre, de sus lágrimas.
> Me persiguen, me acosan, me amarran.
> No me abandonan jamás.
> Sí, son mi propiedad y yo soy su dueña.
> Pero los malditos piensan.
> Los malditos sienten.
> Los malditos callan.
> Y todo el miedo
> y todo el odio
> y todos los reproches amordazados
> les brotan por los ojos (209)

In this passage Quintrala relates that her property, the damned, physically cover her with their bodily fluids even as they retain an independent collective identity that resists the punishment Quintrala tries to impose on them. They still think and feel for themselves, no matter how much violence Quintrala uses. Unlike earlier versions in which Quintrala's powerless victims are represented as righteously pleased at her death, Vidal's Quintrala is haunted by the agency her prey exercises. No matter how much suffering she inflicts, she cannot stop thought or feeling, which continues to be expressed through nonverbal cues. At death, Quintrala does not turn to the Christian God, nor does she repent her abuses; she describes, instead, her failure to dominate another human being completely. *Oro* doesn't partake in myth-writing or symbol-creation, as is done in *Maldita*. Vidal is more interested in what the role of narrative and the refraction of multiple discourses can contribute to an understanding of the constructed nature of our knowledge of the past than in facile repetition of well-worn tropes about Quintrala.

As Frías uses Catalina as a symbol for mixed-race identity in Chile, however, her figure is complicated by the violence traditionally attributed to her. Frías adapts the myth of the black widow, who lures men to her bed only to kill them, by shifting murderous intent from Catalina to a man jealous of her love for someone else. Esteban de Britto's death mixes blood and semen, as Catalina's earlier sexual experiences also mixes death and sex as she masturbates a man in a coma. Death and the violence that leads to it are naturalized in the novel cycle, with Catalina going so far as to instruct her maid that "la violencia no es mala . . . es solo la naturaleza que nos rodea . . . y yo soy señora de todo, de la gente, los ganados, las tierras, incluso de los animales salvajes que merodean por aquí" (*La doña* 27). Catalina's position of power grants her agency to commit violent acts with impunity. Despite this agency, Frías's Catalina does not abuse the power given to her and is portrayed as a benevolent mistress. This is accomplished through a series of contrasts between Catalina and her father. Although, as a child, she aspired to imitate him, Catalina constructs a complicated dance of identification and rejection with regard to Gonzalo de los Ríos. Their relationships with Gonzalo's mistress Bettina are quite different. Catalina's sexual experience demonstrates a positive regard for the female body, but Bettina's relationship with Gonzalo is steeped in violence, given that his rapacious mouth repeatedly bruises her breasts. Frías identifies Gonzalo de los Ríos with the figure of the minotaur, in Greek myth the mythical beast at the heart of the Cretan labyrinth who is ultimately defeated by Theseus. Catalina alternates between identifying with the minotaur and wanting to defeat it. She sympathizes with its in-betweenness, recognizing that she is neither a man among men nor indigenous among the indigenous: she is a woman, and she is mestiza (*Catrala* 107). By the close of *La doña*, however, the metaphorical minotaur is dead.

Circumscribing Catalina de los Ríos y Lisperguer's story are sex, power, and violence. As a woman who navigates and exercises her own sexual desires, she falls outside the expectations of a woman in her social position. As a wealthy landowner, she undermines the view of an elite that has excluded women from its ranks. As someone who uses her power and wealth to exercise violence against those over whom she has power, she both inhabits her social position and stands outside of the stereotype of her sex. Her construction as a subject worthy of fiction depends on the relationship between all three themes, even as Mercedes Valdivieso, Virginia Vidal, and Gustavo Frías shift the weight between them and seek different rationales for that balance.

Reconceptualizing Quintrala

During the period between the publication of *Maldita* and *Tres nombres* (1991–2003), Chilean responses to memories of violence construct a series of prosthetic memories. Historian Steve Stern characterizes the 1990s in Chile as an era in which "competing emblematic memories, skewed power, and [a] politicocultural impasse" (271) dominated national culture. By the later years of this period, "Chileans created a culture of unfinished memory work—inflected by a sense of shared tragedy and by struggles over practical consequences" (Stern 312). The memory struggles attendant with the figure of Catalina, dead for over 450 years, do not share the same urgency as the moves to deal with the more recent past. However, the shift in agency that the reader can observe between works written prior to the dictatorship (1973–1990) and those written during the democratic transition fundamentally alter the narrative of Quintrala, the latter reading her not as a bad example of Chilean womanhood but as a complex figure that makes possible the recuperation and integration of aspects of mestizaje and the indigenous colonial past distilled into concepts of contemporary Chilean identity. Catalina's characterization as evil and diabolical previously excluded her, as the nation's construction depends on both inclusionary structures and exclusionary practices. Despite the recuperative and inclusionary gestures made in the works I examine, the overarching myth of Quintrala continues to live on in earlier versions of her legend.

> Hace rato que se acumula evidencia que estaría apuntando a una posible *genealogía de la crueldad chilena* aún por escribir. En dicha genealogía, o si se quiere, *historia general de la infamia chilena*, no me extrañaría que la Quintrala, amén de protagonista de primera línea, fuese una pieza fundante, una clave maestra explicativa de nuestra atávica propensión por la brutalidad . . . un punto en especial habría que dilucidar al respecto: ¿Todas estas Quintralas que periódicamente "reaparecen" entre nosotros, todas estas distintas a la vez que sospechosamente similares versiones de una—suponible—misma crueldad sin límites, significan que estamos condenados, destinados fatalmente, a su repetición? (Jocelyn-Holt "La Quintrala" VII)

Perhaps those who identify with the first-person plural referred to are not condemned to a continual cycle of cruelty, as one might see emphasized in the newer versions of the life of Catalina. However, fiction has yet to imagine an escape from the mythical worldview of Quintrala even as it resists the strictures imposed by the cultural underpinnings of a nineteenth-century polemic.

Postlude: What About the Men?

Catalina is undoubtedly the main route through which fiction writers seek to represent the seventeenth century in Chile. Even though she is the highway, there are byways that authors also travel. A focus on Quintrala implies a focus on the center of the Kingdom of Chile, that is, Santiago and the central valley. However, a number of texts undermine the idea that the only stories worth telling are in the center and remind the reader that while political and theological intrigue dominated there, at the periphery battles and bloodshed continued. Works such as Jorge Guzmán's *Deus machi* (2010) and Isidora Aguirre's *Guerreros* employ seventeenth-century history on its borderlands and from the perspective of a culture that still circulates anti-indigenous racist ideologies (Merino and Mellor 224) that are articulated through lived experiences of racist stereotyping, prejudice, and discrimination. Catalina represents an assimilated mestizaje in which indigenous resistance to Spanish rule is only alluded to, even in the most recent portraits. Scattered stories from the seventeenth-century periphery of the Reino de Chile—the center of armed conflict between Mapuche and Spaniard—highlight figures that embody indigenous resistance.

The typical narrative of a Mapuche warrior has him dying young and violently, so a story that ends differently intrigues us. Lientur does not have the fame of heroes of the mid-sixteenth century like Galvarino, Lautaro, or Caupolicán. Nevertheless, historical records of his role in the War of Arauco in the first half of the seventeenth century do exist, as well as accounts of his role in the treaty of Quilín, which ostensibly governed Spanish-Mapuche relations from 1641 onward. Most chronicles[23] narrate Lientur's strategies against the Spanish, attacking estancias and retreating before the Spaniards could mount a defense. In the words of the nineteenth-century writer Claudio Gay, Lientur, "como sin duda los lectores no [lo] han olvidado, era el jefe araucano terrible que mandaba el paso de las Congrejeras, y se calificaba a si mismo de hijo primojenito de la fortuna. Siempre o casi siempre a la cabeza de las mas temerarias espediciones, al fin renuncio al mando, hallándose ya muy viejo y cansado" (*Historia física* 482). In contrast to the image of the heroic warrior who died young in glorious battle, Lientur retired.

This "terrible caudillo" (Aguirre 163) is the subject of Isidora Aguirre's final work, *Guerreros*, a novel that was completed before her death in 2011 and published posthumously the same year. For *Guerreros*, Aguirre's research included reading histories, especially "pasajes de mujeres indias que tras parir a sus hijos en los campos, los ahorcaban con sus propias manos para que no tuvieran que repetir su mismo destino de esclavitud" (García 29). The plot of the novel is set between 1600 and 1641 and follows the Jesuit priest Luis de Valdivia (no relation to Pedro) and the Mapuche child Lientur. The theme of liberty related to Mapuche existence is brought up repeatedly, and this has particular resonance within the historical context of early seventeenth-century Chile. While the New Laws in 1542 abolished indigenous slavery, exceptions were made for rebellious groups, among which were the Mapuche.[24] Therefore, the threat of enslavement was constant, and in Aguirre's novel the good Spaniards—the Jesuits—fight against it. The novel, narrated in the third person, summarizes the colony's attitudes toward the Mapuche accordingly: "Porque a aquellos que otrora ensalzara don Alonso de Ercilla en su poema *La Araucana*, habían pasado a ser para los colonos «gente degenerada, bárbara y borracha»" (25). This characterization of difference between the Europeans and the Mapuche prefigures nineteenth-century attitudes that are explored at length in chapter 4.

Lientur finds himself taken to Concepción at the age of ten and placed under the care of the Jesuit mission. He embodies the Jesuit's vision of the indigenous peoples,[25] which values the traditional characterizations of the Mapuche as brave, quick-witted, and adaptable, who are admired and valued for their "valores éticos, la dignidad, el espíritu libertario, la fuerza de los lazos familiares así como el amor al terruño. Amaban y respetaban la naturaleza, la que les parecía estar llena de vida" (27). The narrative additionally emphasizes the privileged place of the warrior within the Mapuche cosmological understanding of the world. Freedom defines group identity and remains linked to a specific geography: "Los mapuches además de odiar la esclavitud, no soportaban la idea de vivir lejos de sus bosques y sus ríos." (27). Although Lientur initially experiences the conflict from the Jesuit viewpoint, his perspective changes over time; ultimately, he attributes the conflict between groups in southern Chile to different understandings of property.[26] Quintrala's perspective on property and wealth reproduces patriarchal and colonialist norms of accumulation and ownership, which contrast with Lientur's observations of his community's fundamentally different worldview.

> Si bien eran [los Mapuches] belicosos y solían enfrentarse entre ellos en rencillas, ahora estaban siendo injustamente despojados de sus tierras y atacados por el ejército de unos extranjeros que intentaba someterlos. Sufrían los ataques de gente de la peor calaña . . . a quienes no los movía el ideal como a los de su pueblo, e defender su tierra, sino el de enriquecerse con la venta de esclavos . . . Y quienes lo seguían, acostumbrados a habitar un terreno comunitario, no entendían la avidez de los blancos por apoderarse de su terruño para ser dueños exclusivos de un campo, o de un trozo

de tierra que explotaban con fines comerciales. Al término «propiedad» no le hallaban una traducción en su lengua. ¿Quién puede afirmar, se preguntaban, que es el dueño absoluto de una pradera, de un cerro o de un bosque?" (116)

Lientur's shift toward the indigenous perspective continues to emphasize the rights for which contemporary indigenous groups fight, namely, for the recognition by the state that ownership of property does not function crossculturally, that is, that the neoliberal state's concept of ownership does not correspond to that of the Mapuche; nor should the state supersede it.

Lientur returns to his people when he is forced out of the mission by violent and greedy Spanish soldiers. It is at this point that Lientur shifts from the role of a mediator between leaders to a leader himself. As he leads a group of indigenous young men away from danger, other leaders recognize his capabilities and send their youth to train and fight with him. One of these leaders stresses Lientur's qualities when he justifies sending his people to Lientur "¡ . . . porque sé reconocer a un caudillo!" (107) The word caudillo is used to describe Lientur on various occasions; it distinguishes him from the rank-and-file warriors by connoting leadership, power, control, and knowledge. *Guerreros* affirms the just cause of the Mapuche rebellions, often emphasizing that the conflict's root is in the Spanish denial of indigenous liberty, land, and the right to live in peace. Lientur's desire for peace leads to an almost humorous contradiction in his last battle before retirement: his presence on the battlefield proves so frightening to the Spaniards that they abandon their position rather than fight. Years after this event, at the close of the novel, Lientur is chosen to represent all of the disparate Mapuche communities at a peace conference with the Spaniards, which leads to the Treaty of Quilín. Aguirre's text emphasizes Lientur's bicultural upbringing when he writes:

> Tuve suerte al formarme a la sombra, o más bien, a la luz, de personas luchadoras que se entregan por entero a las bellas causas. Eso fue lo que me inculcaron en la misión, el afán de combatir la injusticia y buscar un modo más digno de vida. No deberían los hombres resignarse a estar siempre en guerra. (161)

Aguirre's Lientur is a man of peace raised in a time of war, a warrior whose abilities were lauded by his enemies, and who chose to live a quiet domestic life rather than continue the fight in the flesh.

Isidora Aguirre's heroic indigenous warrior represents the combination of Mapuche heritage and Spanish childrearing that reflects facets of colonial power in Mapuche life, including areas such as education and property rights. The identity of the colonial power—Spain or, later, an independent Chile—is immaterial. Within this cultural structure, Lientur utilizes careful tactics and the fight for freedom as a just cause. He represents the warrior-as-peace-maker whose name has faded, more or less, as has the treaty he helped create.

So why, then, might one see Lientur as a counterpoint to Quintrala? She and Lientur represent different modes of mestizaje in seventeenth-century Chile, with Quintrala embodying racial mixing and Lientur culture and knowledge. Both figures seek a world of peace, but their visions are not aligned: the one seeks peace in the obliteration of difference, while the other seeks the justice that will lead to peace. Quintrala's understanding of property and wealth confirms her social position as a colonial elite, while Lientur's privileges community and collective solidarity. Lientur neither suffers nor benefits from the same pervasive mythology in Chilean culture to which Quintrala is subject. He is the hero of his story, unlike Quintrala, whose actions and exercise of power are always qualified by her gender and use of violence. In these two figures we observe the importance of intersectionality in our understanding of identity formation: the male indigenous figure heroically fights for the interest of his people, while the female mestiza fights only for herself—or, depending on the version, the devil. The differing power dynamics within which both figures operate reflect distinct geographical concerns and emphasize the danger of depending on a singular narrative to make sense of seventeenth-century Chile. Regardless of this difference, however, neither figure's cause triumphs—making it much like the democratic transition, which, in consolidating power, fails to usher in a just and peaceful world.

CHAPTER THREE
Independence

EVERY SEPTEMBER MUCH OF Chile stops. The reasons are varied: the protests and commemorations of the 11 September coup; the bacchanalia of food, dance, and drink of Independence Day celebrations on 18 September; and, then, Armed Forces Day on 19 September. Only Christmas surpasses them. When Chile celebrated the bicentennial of its independence from Spain in 2010, other events prepared the way. An editorial in *La Tercera* the same year reflected that

> La ciudadanía ha apoyado siempre la existencia de una autoridad impersonal y respetada, la vigencia de la ley y el amparo a las personas y sus derechos. Por eso, los momentos más difíciles que el país ha vivido son precisamente aquellos en que los conflictos internos pusieron en peligro estos elementos esenciales para la paz social y para el progreso. Esas experiencias, duras y dolorosas para el alma nacional, nos han enseñado la importancia de preservar los consensos fundamentales que permiten la sana convivencia y la integración de todos los habitantes en forma armónica y colaborativa al desarrollo del país. ("Chile celebra")

Authority, the rule of law, and refuge for others are held up as necessary values of a shared community. Consensus and coexistence were the touchstones for Chilean society entering its third century of independent existence. We are all Chile, so long as we conform to the ever-evolving target of respectability politics. This editorial leaves little space for justice or truth in its valuation of harmony and collaboration.

Two hundred years after a first attempt at limited self-governance—rejecting Napoleon Bonaparte's puppet in Spain as a legitimate authority and affirming loyalty to the deposed Fernando VII—the cover of satirical newspaper *The Clinic* featured in its bicentennial special issue the deformation of a recognizable portrait of José de San Martín, the Argentine general, into the face of the beloved Argentine coach of the Chilean National soccer team, Marcelo Bielsa. As a general, San Martín led a series of independence movements throughout southern South America. Chile's passing good fortune in soccer, in addition to her independence, has strong links to Argentines. And so the satire *The Clinic* depended on was straightforward: that jingoistic nationalism denies any virtue to those who do not belong to the group. Both the editorial in *La Tercera* and the cover of *The Clinic* participate in discursive practices that the literary critic Lauren Berlant, writing of the United States, identifies as part of a "National Symbolic." It is

> the order of discursive practices whose reign within a national space produces, and also refers to, the "law" in which the accident of birth within a geographic/political boundary transforms individuals into subjects of a collectively-held history. Its traditional icons, its metaphors, its heroes, its rituals, and its narratives provide an alphabet for a collective consciousness or national subjectivity. (20)

The bicentennial of Chilean independence is an event that serves as a locus of icons, metaphors, heroes, rituals, and narratives that are repeated, re-created, and relayed to define what it means to be Chilean in 2010 and beyond. The bicentennial, however, builds on a multitude of other moments and occasions—quotidian or extraordinary—in which this alphabet for a collective consciousness is constructed and reconstructed. In historical fiction written prior to 2010, women's historical actions and the function of space both contribute to an expansion and resemanticizing of that alphabet.

The bicentennial brand was used to market, sell, commemorate, and project into the future ideas of what Chile is and should be.[1] Historical fiction isn't immune to this brand. Historical fiction set during the independence period has been popular since the nineteenth century; however, its production during the democratic transition can be divided into those texts that constitute and transmit the National Symbolic as related to Chilean independence from Spain and those that seek to remold or undermine the National Symbolic as transmitted through television, film, and public education. It is this second category that occupies this chapter. Three novels—Jorge Edwards's *El sueño de la historia*, Virginia Vidal's *Javiera Carrera, madre de la patria*, and Juanita Gallardo's *Déjame que te cuente*—tackle iconic images related to Chile's independence struggle to expand the acceptable limits of the meanings associated with these images. Edwards's novel, set in the last decades of the eighteenth and twentieth centuries, dances in the shadows of familiar independence narratives. However, the parallelism between pre-independence decades and the seventeen years of military dictatorship implies a relationship between independence and the return of democracy in 1990. In addition, the focus on an architect famed for creations that have become iconic symbols of Chile and its government prompts the question: how does the built environment reflect ideologies of exclusion and inclusion? "Literary works serve a cartographic function by creating a figurative or allegorical representation of a social space" (Tally). An examination of the figure of the architect and his most well-known creation in *El sueño* raises important questions about the representation of difference in Chilean historical fiction and how that difference can be understood beyond subjects and their identity by inviting a mode of analysis that links narrative, space, and power. Vidal and Gallardo's novels recuperate the stories of elite women related to two major leadership camps in the independence struggle against Spain. These stories of independence link individual women's stories to larger symbolic structures that have traditionally emphasized the martial exploits of men. All three novels portray this shift in how symbolic structures—pieces of Berlant's alphabet—are constituted. As preludes to the 2010 bicentennial, these novels invite parallels between their historical referents and the democratic transition and do that by avoiding the triumphal celebration of either.

Prelude to Independence: Joaquín Toesca and La Moneda Palace

How does an Italian architect become one of the most notable figures of the colonial period?[2] Why do he and his work represent a transitional moment for

Chilean independence? Joaquín Toesca (1752–1799), born in Rome, studied architecture in a series of European academies and worked with notable figures such as Francisco Sabatini (1722–1797) before coming to Chile in 1780 at the invitation of civil and ecclesiastical authorities. During the last portion of his life, Toesca designed and oversaw the construction of iconic elements of the built environment of Santiago, such as the Cathedral, La Moneda Palace, and the Cabildo, in addition to dikes to minimize the habitual flooding of the Mapocho River. While this lasting urban footprint remains, he, or, rather, his relationship with his *criolla* wife, Manuela Fernández de Rebolledo y Pando (1765–1808), also inspires interest.[3] While seismic instability occasionally prevents the preservation of colonial-era construction, differing economic models have imposed building styles and philosophies of preservation that have resulted in juxtapositions such as those seen in the Plaza Mayor, today's Plaza de Armas. An individual facing the northwest corner of the plaza will note a mirrored office building at Catedral 1009 that reflects the images of late eighteenth- and early nineteenth-century constructions such as the Metropolitan Cathedral, its façade designed by Toesca. The buildings and public works that he designed, and his training of a generation of architects and engineers in the decades prior to the Chilean independence movement, have left a lasting mark on the city that a third of the Chilean population calls home. The staying power and the symbolic meaning imbued in the built environment of Santiago, and particularly in structures designed and overseen by Toesca, inform an understanding of the contemporary cultural perception of the space and place[4] of Chile. Therefore, a brief reading of the presence and function of urban space, architecture, and La Moneda Palace enriches an understanding of how fiction reflects ideologies of difference, while emphasizing the connections between the two transitional moments represented in Jorge Edwards's *El sueño*—the shift from Spanish colony to independent republic and the shift from military dictatorship to a limited democracy.

Toesca, Space, and Difference

Toesca was the originator of symbols that permeate memory and history, so to consider the relationship between architecture and identity becomes paramount to understanding the representation of difference in the context of the decades before independence from Spain. The work of feminist geographers and spatial feminists illuminate a way architecture functions in society. Per Leslie Weisman, architecture "is a record of the deeds done by those who have had the power to build. It is shaped by social, political, and economic forces and values embodied in the forms themselves, the processes through which they are built, and the manner in which they are used" (2). By portraying a historical figure who designed buildings representing imperial power that have shifted in time to represent the Chilean government by metonymy,[5] space and place in *El sueño* reflect this symbolic power while also undermining its representation through the narrative structure of the novel.

Not unlike the narrator of *El sueño*, Jorge Edwards went through the papers of historian Eugenio Pereira Salas and highlights "uno de nuestros personajes simbólicos" ("Mito" 10): Joaquín Toesca. In an essay from 1980 based on his reading of Pereira Salas's *Historia del arte en el Reino de Chile* (1965), Edwards links Toesca's work and philosophy to the Enlightenment and Chilean independence. In spite of this, Edwards carefully avoids any conflation of what he terms "this ghost, this Toesca" with the historically extant man, about whom few contemporaneous documents survive. In the historiography related to Toesca, two tendencies emerge. The first confirms the relationship between power and architecture: Toesca is erased as originator of his work, with credit instead going to the political leadership overseeing and paying for his work, Royal Governor of Chile Ambrosio de Benavides (1718–1787).[6] The second highlights and praises Toesca's work,[7] coalescing around a consensus that he is an artistically extraordinary man whose influence on the later development of architectural aesthetics and building practices in Chile cannot be exaggerated.

The process by which Toesca and his creations emerge in *El sueño* has been underlined in a number of studies that deal with Edwards's narrative in general terms and the novel itself.[8] In *El sueño*, the narrator—the character known as Ignacio, who does not narrate the entire novel—makes no attempt to hide his mediation of documents. Where documents are found lacking, Ignacio affirms the narrator "supone, y se imagina" (Edwards 55) or that "no sabemos" (292). Verbal tenses also distinguish borders between documentary historiography and the narrator's invention, as when one notes the differences between "was said" and the conditional "would say" (37), the latter marking Ignacio's forays into conjecture. As the novel develops, Ignacio's sympathy and identification with the architect blur the separation between the amateur historian and his subject, made explicit when the subject of an action becomes him, I, Toesca (203) and is followed by a verb conjugated in the first person. In spite of that, Ignacio retreats into a supposedly objective pose at the close of the novel. And so when pressed to give his opinion of the 1988 plebiscite on the rule of Augusto Pinochet, he protests that he is the narrator and "me corresponde estar en todas partes, en un lado y en el otro, y en ninguno" (363). By abrogating the responsibility of a perspective, this so-called neutrality harks back to the language of the editorial quoted at the beginning of this chapter. Ignacio's language when narrating the past indicates a consciousness of the constructed nature of his story, yet he actively ignores that consciousness when forced to decide about his own life. By retreating into a supposed objectivity that he has previously shown to be a ruse, Ignacio demonstrates an inconsistent attitude toward his own narrative position.

Other aspects of the narration of *El sueño* continue to emphasize the instability of an absolute understanding of narrative of the past, as when the narration shifts away from Ignacio's voice—in, for example, the chapter his son narrates from a first-person perspective. Earlier, Ignacio is characterized as "el historiado aficionado y narrador en proyecto" (29). He interrogates his role in society, both as the prodigal son and as a person who is more comfortable situating himself outside of current events rather than a protagonist in them. Returning to Chile after years in Spain, he reflects on the city's signage, written in a familiar language that is nevertheless strange, "porque el país, al fin y al cabo, no tenía nada que ver con el de su memoria, era otro, y él también" (Edwards 14).[9] By the close of the novel, Ignacio has consumed the memories constructed by others, represented by the papers he reads in his attic apartment in the Portal Fernández Concha. However, his self-positioning as a narrator, rejecting his own agency in the present day, continues as he creates an ever-expanding archive. He seeks more papers and books as he wanders through alleys and holes-in-the-wall to spend his nights "en aquella ciudad tan machacada y que había escogido, por reacción defensiva, la indiferencia, en aquel país amnésico" (376) accompanied by the archive he has assembled. Ignacio lives in an obsessive pursuit of documents, searching constantly for physical remains of the past, positioned at the heart of a city that avoids remembrance. Adrian Santini argues that the physical location of Ignacio's archive, above the heart of the colonial city,[10] "parece decirnos que otro de los principales protagonistas de la novela es la ciudad misma" (157). This positioning, as well as the importance of the built environment within the novel, emphasizes Joaquín Toesca's centrality to this proposed understanding of Chilean identity and difference during the democratic transition.

The shifting protagonism of Toesca, Ignacio, and Santiago itself shines in metanarrative moments so extraordinary that, for example, the narrator is in doubt about the very topic of his study. This instability, typical of the novel, does not extend to the depiction of Toesca at any point in the narrative. The order characteristic of neoclassical architecture is mapped onto Toesca's personality and profession, as one might consider that part of the engineer's work is to give form to the natural world. Built elements of control—such as dikes—are part of Toesca's legacy to the city and his mark on the urban landscape. As a lieutenant in the royal army, military engineer, and architect, he was "hombre de orden: al menos en apariencia. O sobre todo en apariencia . . . el hecho central es que conocía por experiencia, por educación, incluso por instinto, la fuerza del orden establecido, y tenía una tendencia a respetarla" (Edwards 231). Later characterized as respecting authority and at times himself authoritarian (126), Toesca and his creations impose and dictate; they exercise power in ways that exclude, for instance, women, even his wife.[11] However, the novel does not simply affirm a connection between authoritarianism, Toesca, his creations, and an implied link to dictatorship Chile. The ambiguities of documentation and memory are brought to the forefront when Ignacio discovers that enigmatic answers exist, but they are not entirely convincing (Edwards 126). Despite this doubt, or perhaps because of it, the narrator also asserts that we, readers and narrators alike, know more of Toesca than Toesca knew of himself (Edwards 172), a paradoxical affirmation that descends to pessimism when an anonymous narrative third-person voice emphasizes that Toesca has been forgotten by all and sundry. Ignacio's work to recover documentation that will allow Toesca to live on in memory, constantly questioned and problematized, reveals that Toesca's legacy lies in the physical artifacts he designed and built, not in archives.

Built Environment: Santiago Through Edwards's Eyes

Santiago's urban landscape features a mix of buildings of different styles and architectural philosophies. In the center of the city, few early colonial buildings survived the ravages of flooding, earthquake, and the consequences of constant war with the Mapuche.[12] Much of the older physical plant of the central city dates to the late eighteenth century; successive waves of reform have aimed to preserve some older buildings, though the criteria for preservation vary between the different municipalities that make up the metropolitan region. Despite the engineering innovations that allow for safer construction in earthquake-prone zones, the question remains: "¿para qué edificar en Santiago monumentos que un terremoto, un incendio o una inundación echarían por tierra en minutos, sin dejar señales de ellos?" (Cádiz 30). The cycle of construction, destruction, and reconstruction contributes to a description of Santiago in 1814 as a city lacking in architectural flavor (Pérez Rosales 1). Even though Kelly Donahue-Wallace affirms that "architecture was the visible manifestation of local pride" (165) during the viceregal period, Chile's seismicity and peripheral geopolitical position limit the expression of this pride. Therefore, the architect works against the vagaries of the natural world while also reflecting the social and political mores of the society in which they function. The creative products of the architect's works are cocreated with each new interaction as "the projection of meaning is inherent in both the creation of built form and the act of observing it" (Weisman 16). *El sueño*'s narrator speculates that Toesca thought of architecture as "una defensa contra el tiempo, un dique de contención o algo parecido. Una defensa precaria, en todo caso, y que al final se desmoronaba" (301). Despite Toesca's personal and artistic desire for order and its corresponding representation in urban space, change comes.

A late eighteenth-century response to challenges to remembrance is an enlightened search for better solutions—new methods, new materials, and thoughtful designs. Edwards's Toesca, like many other enlightened reformers, displays a desire to bring order to the world around him. His attempts to give meaningful form to his personal life, though, met with mixed success;[13] his professional work, on the other hand, was more successful in embodying an impulse toward stability. Order has been seen as a central tenet of the exercise of power in Chile, particularly with regard to the establishment of both formal and informal mechanisms to maintain governmental authority.[14]

Toesca, a foreign architect whose ability marks a change in the urban development of Santiago, embodies a parallelism between physical and social stability. According to architect Myriam Waisberg, the works of the late eighteenth century in Chile "conjugan la presencia de una arquitectura al día, hábilmente implantada en la trama formada por el sentido del proceso cultural en desarrollo y por los factores condicionantes propios de la organización de este país. El resultado fue una arquitectura de calidad" (14), generally judged worthy of preservation. Toesca functions as an inflection point in which the built environment reflected greater stability, as it was able to survive seismic shifts. However, this stability also excludes other practices, as it reflects the power of the colonial elite through the imposition of specific European aesthetics.

The development of cities in Spanish America followed patterns set out by the Spanish governing authorities, dating to the sixteenth century. Although the codification of these rules did not occur until after the founding of many of today's major cities, the content of the rules reflected many of the commonalities between places. King Phillip II's rules, first published in 1573 and updated in 1680, required a certain stability of construction and uniformity of style to reinforce Spain's colonizing and civilizing presence in the face of indigenous opposition. The central square's form was dictated both in terms of location and arrangement, and the rest of the city was laid out with an eye to defense. In general, then, "the city embodied Spanish culture and civility by an appeal to ancient and Renaissance authority; it likewise symbolized divine sanction of the colonial effort and operated as the physical manifestation of the new social hierarchy" (Donahue-Wallace 77). Even though bureaucratic documents concentrate on directions themselves, without explanation, they reflect a way of thinking about space and power that has influenced the development of urban life throughout the region.

> Space, like language, is socially constructed; and like the syntax of language, the spatial arrangements of our buildings and communities reflect and reinforce the nature of gender, race, and class relations in society. The uses of both language and place contribute to the power of some groups over others and the maintenance of human inequality. (Weisman 2)

Minimizing Joaquín Toesca's role in the built environment of late colonial Santiago in favor of emphasizing the men who authorized and funded his work mimics this operation. Exploring these spaces through *El sueño* implies an understanding of the way in which space reflects, embodies, and enacts power in such a way as to define difference and exclusion in a given place and time.

Within Jorge Edwards's oeuvre, *El sueño* is more spatially oriented than any of his other novels, even though all depend on a human geography that is bound by class segregation in twentieth-century Santiago. Edwards specifies his own cartographical identification: "básicamente soy ciudadano no de Santiago de Chile, que es una ciudad muy extendida, sino de un lugar muy preciso de la misma, del Cerro de Santa Lucía . . . mi fidelidad patriótica está dedicada al cerro de Santa Lucía" (Alfieri 132). This connection confirms urban historian and architect Dolores Hayden's explanation of the link between identity and memory, inclusive of both the individual and the collective. "Urban landscapes are storehouses for . . . social memories, because natural features such as hills or harbors, as well as streets, buildings, and patterns of settlement, frame the lives of many people and often outlast many lifetimes" (9). In fictional terms, urban novels "domicilia[n] los sueños de sus habitantes, radica[n] las imágenes de sus dramas, y así insinua[n] un espíritu de estos barrios" (Franz 26). On Ignacio's return to Chile around 1978, he rents an apartment above the Plaza de Armas as an escape from the conservative pro-dictatorship security-obsessed world of his father and sister in the wealthy northeastern municipalities. His ex-wife Cristina lives in the downtown area facing Santa Lucía Hill, several blocks from the Plaza de Armas, the place Edwards names as fundamental to his identity. And so Ignacio's strolling along the roads bordering the hill has resonance. As pedestrian-readers follow along, moving from one street to the next, they can trace Ignacio's route via streets named after historical personages, which allows for toponymically appropriate thoughts that connect the names given to geographical places and their changing functions throughout centuries.

As represented in *El sueño*, central Santiago of the late 1970s and 1980s is a space full of varied people and noises that, paradoxically, also reflect the tense sense of observation and control perpetuated by the disciplinary apparatus of the military dictatorship.[15] Ignacio, however, feels safest in the protected anonymity of the central city: "el ruido, la suciedad, la fealdad mezquina de todo el sector, los carteles con ampolletas quemadas, le producen un curioso efecto sedante" (66). The chaos of central Santiago effects a comfortable anonymity in which one does not feel alienated as much as private, secure, and safe in belonging to it. As well, the linear passage of time in the novel allows Ignacio, from within his comfortable nest in the central city, to accumulate more social and political freedom as a military presence recedes. That parallels Ignacio's discovery of the details of Toesca's life with Fernández de Rebolledo, including his death and her widowhood. When participating in a *cacerolazo*[16] in Cristina's apartment in the early 1980s, Ignacio looks out onto the street and sees the northern staircase of Santa Lucía Hill, which features a brick arcade decorated with a royal emblem originally designed for La Moneda "que las primeras autoridades republicanas desplazaron de su sitio de origen, pasaba una cuca de carabineros, pero la calle, la escalinata, el cerro, estaban desiertos" (267). The emptiness of public space prevents the police force from using violence to suppress dissent, "las innumerables y dispersas cacerolas, una por una, de manera que el símbolo de fuerza se transformaba en su contrario, en símbolo de impotencia" (267). This passage emphasizes the subversion of power, both in the form of an architect's plan and in the police's ability to repress dissent. Plans are adapted to respond to changing realities; in short, space is contingent. La Moneda Palace as it exists, as opposed to how it was designed, is popularly presented as an exponent of a pure neoclassical style and therefore read as such. In the plan, however, it originally possessed a number of late baroque flourishes, including the royal seal transferred to the gate at Santa Lucía. This infidelity to the architect's plan runs counter to the ideal the novel expresses that the work of an architect may stand the test of time without modification.

Although a youthful Ignacio participated in a political movement that privileged a population foreign to the geographical space in which he and his family resided, *El sueño* nevertheless avoids the so-called marginal areas,[17] their black roofs appearing out of focus and distant from the narrator (27). At the same time, the distance between the center of the city and the western coastal mountain range is compared to the liminality of twilight itself (266), which removes Santiago's slums from the world that Ignacio inhabits. Toesca, living in the 1780s and 90s, would not have considered those spaces to be part of the city, as urban sprawl over the following centuries, and particularly in the twentieth century, built up the space between the Mapocho and Maipo

Rivers. Even though Santiago was founded in 1541, Edwards's Toesca views his work as city-building, that is, he is motivated by the notion of building something fundamental and new, as well as teaching others how to do so the same (60–61). Like a child playing with blocks, Toesca has the opportunity to leave a mark on Santiago, which appeals to the notion of legacy, of leaving something behind. The connection between a figure that designed and directed the construction of a city and a man two centuries later who inhabits and identifies with that place creates an interplay between past and present that inscribes itself onto a map that, no matter how faithful to contemporary Santiago, nevertheless remains grounded in invention and imagination.

> La alusión a lugares que forman parte del mismo Santiago que habita el Narrador por medio de nombres distintos a los que él usa, sugiere un diseño de mundo en el que se representa un orden distinto no sólo a nivel topográfico, sino también social y cultural . . . designan un mundo que a pesar de las aparentes proximidades resulta intraducible al lenguaje del Narrador. (Viu 205)

The places named are not only points on a map, but allusions that imply a thick history of race, class, and usage. One might imagine Toesca's colonial Santiago buried underneath Ignacio's city, the buried wall that Carlos Franz argues undergirds the relationship between identity and narrative in Santiago's urban novels.

Worthy of Remembrance: La Moneda

The work for which Joaquín Toesca is best known—his contributions to construction methods, public works such as dikes, and the cathedral façade notwithstanding—remains La Moneda Palace. Originally a place designated for the production of coin, it was opened in 1805; in the 1840s it became the presidential palace. According to the report submitted to UNESCO by the Chilean Council of National Monuments, several presidents made changes to the building as a seat of power from 1846 to 1973. The area around the palace was also changed during the 1930s to reflect the relationship between the presidential palace and other buildings housing government ministries.

Subject to a bombing campaign the morning of 11 September 1973, as part of the coup d'état that brought Augusto Pinochet to power and the site of President Salvador Allende's suicide,[18] the palace was restored during military dictatorship and continues to serve as the seat of government.[19] When one wishes to speak metonymically of the Chilean government, one can refer to "La Moneda," in the same way that in the United States one may say "White House" to refer to the president and executive branch. Keeping in mind these intrusions from the nonfictional world, the reader may notice that the palace designed as a mint by Joaquín Toesca has been used in ways unthinkable to the man at the drawing board.

First designed to show the imperial might of Spain,[20] as were all public buildings built with royal funds during the colonial period, La Moneda Palace retains a similar purpose for Ignacio: it stands monumentalized. The juxtaposition between the original design of the building and the symbolism of this space and place in contemporary Chilean culture is a texture within the novel that obscures any facile reading of historical parallels and ideas of circular history. This complication is echoed in the contradictory nature of the narrative voice throughout the novel. Architectural historians provide insight into the relationships between place, memory, and monumentality in attempts to understand how monuments function within an urban landscape.

> Place memory encapsulates the human ability to connect with both the built and natural environments that are entwined in the cultural landscape. It is the key to the power of historic places to help citizens define their public pasts: places trigger memories for insiders, who have shared a common past, and at the same time places often can represent shared pasts to outsiders who might be interested in knowing about them in the present. (Hayden 46)

The differing and multivalent functions of historic places that Hayden identifies as specific to either cultural insiders or outsiders are at work in the contemporary symbolic role that La Moneda Palace plays in an understanding of Chile and its history. In one building, an individual may read a multiplicity of memories, shared or foreign, that allow the individual to approach a culture in the present by the way it deals with its past. This operation defines a monument.

> The historic monument has a different relationship to living memory and to the passage of time. On the one hand, it is simply constituted as an object of knowledge and integrated into a linear conception of time: in this case its cognitive value relegates it irrevocably to the past, or more precisely, to history in general or to the history of art in particular; on the other hand, as a work of art it can address itself to our artistic sensibility . . . in this case it becomes a constituent part of the lived present, but without the mediation of memory or history. (Choay 13)

Hayden and Choay present two options for memory-making via the monument: first, as a historic place that requires a level of historical consciousness from all viewers (not dissimilar to the historical competence fiction requires); and second, as a cynosure that is time-transcendent. Still, that ahistorical reading would not forget or overlook the concerns and exclusions of the time and context within which it is produced. The function of La Moneda Palace in the novel can be read in either mode.

The setting of a monument within a work of historical fiction implies a reading of La Moneda Palace in *El sueño* conditioned by the historical context within which the novel operates and is created. Monuments can also be read dynamically as value-added art—as objects imbued with a historical importance and distance and also as works whose meaning is constantly being remade on a grand scale.

> More than most works of art or architecture, not to mention ordinary objects, monuments enjoy multiple social roles. As things, they share their status with other objects: the term monumentality suggests qualities of inertness, opacity, permanence, remoteness, distance, preciosity, and grandeur. Yet monuments are prized precisely because they are not merely cold, hard, and permanent. They are also living, vital, immediate, and accessible, at least to some parts of society. Because a monument can achieve a powerful symbolic agency, to damage it, much less to obliterate it, constitutes a personal and communal violation with serious consequences. While the destruction of mere things is commonplace in our takeout and throwaway world, attacking a monument threatens a society's sense of itself and its past. (Nelson and Olin 3–4)

The destruction of a monument implies a move toward the negation of its symbolic meaning, while the act recognizes the power of its symbolism as a threat to whatever performed the destruction. However, important sectors of societies may be excluded from the symbolic agency of a monument.

La Moneda Palace, representing the power of the democratically elected government, was necessarily destroyed in a military move to assure the success of the coup. That symbolic gesture, accordingly, signified a turn away from the democratic practices of earlier decades and the socialist policies of the previous government. In a newspaper article about the bombing published 13 September 1973, in *La Tercera*, the text states that

> Según testigos presenciales del bombardeo y que se retiraron del sitio a instancia de los militares que tenían acordonado el sector de La Moneda, el Palacio de Gobierno fue destruido casi totalmente. Se informó que a la primera descarga las bombas hicieron blanco preciso en la Casa Militar del Palacio de Gobierno. Posteriormente, los blancos fueron el frontis del edificio diseñado por Toesca, y así sucesivamente hasta destruirle totalmente. ("Quince Minutos" 7)

In an accompanying photograph, a Hawker Hunter jet can be seen flying over a smoking La Moneda Palace. The angle of the image suggests the danger of the situation and the precariousness of the position of the photographer. The caption informs the reader that seventeen bombs were dropped on the site and that a dense cloud of smoke was seen at the start of the destruction of "Toesca's Palace." Images of the violence of the coup were seen the world over, both in newspapers and on television.[21] Such dissemination supports the idea that La Moneda Palace can be read as both a marker for a version of collective Chilean identity and a door through which outsiders may gain access to an understanding of said identity. An anonymous third-person narrator gives a concise history of La Moneda Palace at the end of *El sueño* that mimics the content of standard histories of the building, while remaining grammatically hypothetical. Playing with perspective in this way calls our attention to how we imagine the future.

> Aquella fachada original, por otra parte, sería bombardeada desde el aire,

con precisión electrónica, y por el lado, precisamente, que había levantado el maestro. Los cohetes, en imágenes que recorrerían las pantallas del mundo (mundo transformado en una multiplicación de pantallas . . . entrarían por las ventanas que el maestro había dibujado con tanto cuidado y cuya construcción había seguido después en forma tan atenta, y retorcerían los hierros, los barandales, los marcos y espoletas que él mismo había encargado . . . Algunos años después sería restaurada, pero nunca, desde luego, volvería a ser la misma: aquella casa donde tanto se sufría, como le gustaba decir a uno de sus ocupantes, donde la gente atravesaba por los patios con toda tranquilidad para pasar del sur de la Alameda al centro . . . confundidos con el paisaje urbano, con los letreros mal pintados, con los quiltros, con los suplementeros y las puesteras, con los racimos de gente que colgaban de micros destartalados [*sic*]. (412)

The question remains, where does power reside: with the occupant of the building or with the physical presence of the building itself? As the passage progresses, it moves from the destruction effected by the aerial bombing of the palace in 1973 to the origins of the materials used to construct the original façade of La Moneda Palace and finally settles on a juxtaposition of the political and working classes coexisting in the "Civic Neighborhood."[22] Despite the grand beginning and later bombing of the built environment, the text concludes with the minutiae of daily and banal lives in the central city whose difference is erased through their anonymity.

The original plans for La Moneda Palace have been lost, but the work was begun decades before Joaquín Toesca put his stamp on it. The building has been a symbol of power and permanence while always adapted to new uses and ideologies. Connections have been made between neoclassicism, order, and Edwards's novel. Gabriel Guarda, among others, argues that La Moneda Palace, a profane temple (198), is an architectural metaphor of power. The building everyone sees today emphasizes this:

The immense façade, which runs the length of a city block, employs a severe classical vocabulary. It is symmetrical and unornamented, with colossal paired pilasters spanning its two stories and a balustrade along the roofline. The central doorway is reminiscent of Roman triumphal arches, with paired engaged columns flanking an arched opening topped by a triangular pediment. The deep recessions between the strongly projecting pilasters and columns create a dramatic chiaroscuro. The façade's regularity is echoed in the plan, which locates offices, living quarters, and workshops around a series of orderly patios and passageways. (Donahue-Wallace 238)

Symmetry, regularity, and lack of excessive ornament imply a preference for neoclassicism; however, the chiaroscuro effects throughout the building remain characteristic of a baroque architectural vocabulary. Eduardo San José Vásquez reads the unusual mixing of architectural elements in La Moneda Palace as a stand-in for the qualities Edwards puts forward as ideal for a new political model for democracy in Chile (16). This architectural mestizaje is negated in later versions of the building, as the baroque coat-of-arms crafted by Toesca's brother-in-law[23] is shifted to Santa Lucía. "Esa mutación puede leerse como un intento por erradicar la ambigüedad de un edificio que arrastra de su origen colonial la contradicción cultural de un mundo en el que conviven la superstición y el deseo de progreso" (Viu 213). Not only does this change attempt to stamp out the colonial past but also expresses a discomfort with the ambiguity of a building displaying multiple architectural styles, unwilling to abandon or embrace a purity of style that may be symbolically grafted onto issues of identity and difference. In a scene in which Toesca speaks with Juan Joseph Goycoolea after the discovery of Fernández de Rebolledo's unfaithfulness, the Italian speaks not of his personal grudge against his wife's lover but at length of his own architectural infidelities, that is, those elements of the construction of La Moneda Palace that deviate from neoclassical ideals. The plays of light and dark that ornament the palace appear to be tame perpetuations of a baroque aesthetic when Toesca details an idea, never realized during the construction of the building, to create a visual illusion through a miniature version of the building within a building. This folly would produce "una impresión de infinito, de vértigo, de huida de las líneas hacia el sur, ¡hacia el fin del mundo!, ya que desde la puerta de la segunda Moneda uno podría imaginar una tercera, una cuarta, una quinta. Un juego de espejos . . . y una entrada en el otro lado del espejo" (154).

The image of an infinite perspective paired alongside the symbolic weight of a mirror provides an insight into the artistic, not pragmatic, practice of the architect, offering a possibility for the interpretation of the forms later made concrete in the palace's construction. This flight of architectural fancy, however, is rejected and by the twentieth century changes to the building were out of keeping with the original aesthetic vision for the building, yet no one noticed them (411). The parallelisms Toesca proposed between La Moneda and its smaller mirror-cousin are lost in practical concerns, and his artistic vision is twisted away from its original form as time runs its course, though, ironically, the monumentality of the building presents itself to the individual as eternal and unchanging.

This static view of La Moneda Palace is perpetuated in the present-day interpretations of the building. Having been put forward in 1998 as a possible UNESCO World Heritage Site, it is one of several sites in Chile that appears to champion the victory of a Westernized civilization over the barbarism of other sites. The building has been subject to various changes over the past two hundred years, but these changes do not preclude the notion of the palace as outside of history.

> La Moneda es bien patrimoniable suspendido en el tiempo, impertérrito ante los embates e intermitencias de la historia, impermeable a los cambios de gobierno—sean «democráticos» , sean producidos por la violencia militar—. . . La Moneda ha borrado u ocultado su otra cara, aquella que reflejaría las discontinuidades del poder y la fragilidad de la pujanza económica, y que pronosticaría tanto el agotamiento de los valores morales ancestrales de Chile como de sus recursos no renovables. (Ramos Collado)

That the building designed as a royal mint houses the government of Chile has not escaped commentary: "en ningún otro lugar, seguramente, el gobierno se ejerce desde un edificio cuyo nombre, "La Moneda", evoca la obsesiva preocupación de sus ciudadanos, el bolsillo, la bolsa" (Franz 61). Chile's GINI coefficient, which represents wealth distribution within an economy, ranks as near the highest inequality of OECD countries (OECD). Power symbolically rests in money, and Chile's economic disparities underscore the lie that La Moneda Palace can include everyone. Neoliberal rhetoric deceives its audience into thinking that a system predicated on inequality will allow anyone to succeed. However, over forty years of a neoliberal system in Chile has shown that power and resources concentrate in fewer and fewer hands while everyone else struggles to get by. Therefore, that La Moneda Palace depends on its function for its symbolic significance distinguishes it from the geographical features commonly associated with the city and underlines the contradictions of the body politic within a profoundly unequal economic system, symbolized by a government inhabiting a money-making building.

The physical structure that inspired various copies and stylistic renovation broke new aesthetic ground in this provincial city. As Antonia Viu reads in Edwards's novel, "La Moneda tendría mucho que decir: último bastión del orden imperial en el Chile colonial, más tarde pasa a ser palacio de gobierno del país independiente para constituir, en sus transformaciones recientes, un memorial de la violencia del golpe del 73" (210). The mixture of architectural styles and the continual monumentalization of the building designed by Toesca emphasize the fundamental ambiguity with which *El sueño* represents history and narration, and through this conditionality, a critique of the facile use of space and place in the National Symbolic to represent difference.

Contingent Conclusions

El sueño centers on two men, which implies a connection between their stories in the structure that mirrors the physical plan of the two courtyards of La Moneda Palace[24]—and in a work of historical fiction that engages explicitly with the experience of Chile directly prior to the democratic transition. The highlighting of historically extant people of the eighteenth century provides a dramatic and intimate tale that resides alongside and interwoven with the absences in historiographical discourse. As individuals whose social and political position relegates their stories to footnotes in the grand narrative of the decades leading up to the movement for independence in Chile, Edwards's focus on their story displays a tendency in the historical fiction of the democratic transition to rewrite key moments in Chilean history with an eye toward recuperating human-interest angles.[25] That said, the fundamental ambiguity of the narration impedes any grand pronouncements as to the vindication of this history. In a spatial reading of *El sueño*, the novel writes the action onto a familiar version of an urban map. With that, an accumulation of meaning written onto urban spaces takes form and is rooted in the relationship between the city to which Toesca arrived in 1780 and the city to which Ignacio returns in the late 1970s. La Moneda Palace, Toesca's masterpiece, marks the relationship between the two historical referents and reminds the reader of the thickness of symbolic meaning surrounding the building. However, even this elaboration of meaning is destabilized by the fundamental ambiguity toward narrative truth-value displayed throughout the novel. Edwards's narrative playfulness centers on a place "donde cosas importantes se deciden, aunque no siempre se tenga del todo claro qué" (Jocelyn-Holt "Amos" 221), which accounts for why *El sueño* emphasizes the theoretical instability of a collective sense of identity and difference through national monuments. For that reason, these monuments continue to be used and reused within the narrative and contemporary Chilean culture in the resemanticization of the alphabet of Chile's National Symbolic.

Independence: Recuperating Elite Women

The practice of naming public spaces and municipal buildings in honor of illustrious citizens is a fact that no individual who walks the streets of Santiago can escape. The preponderance of these streets, plazas, and buildings are named for the men considered the founding fathers of Chile—which should surprise no one. Where the main street through the city from east to west is named for Bernardo O'Higgins, a major thoroughfare to the southwest is named for José Miguel Carrera, though both are commonly called something else, either the Alameda or the Gran Avenida. The great men of Chilean history litter the commemorative toponyms of the city to the point that in honor of International Women's Day in 2019, the feminist organizing collective Coordinadora Feminista 8M renamed metro stations in honor of significant women of more recent Chilean history (@Coordinadora8m). None of the women associated with O'Higgins or Carrera was featured, however, and these monumentalized men continue to reappear all around Chile.

Chile's bicentennial celebrations coincided with the close of the period in which the works appearing in this study were published. Many commemorations often have a specific reason or occasion, much like birthdays; however, stories about the struggle for independence are popular irrespective of day, date, or occasion. Bárbara Silva notes that "'Bicentenario' parece una marca del 'signo de los tiempos', mostrando un tranco coherente con el ritmo del mundo actual, globalizado, moderno y posmoderno, frenético y acontecido" (151). While the government funded and completed a number of construction projects, as well as public commemorations and cultural keepsakes,[26] the bicentennial celebrations around 2010 were not limited to government acts. Various television stations took it upon themselves, often with the help of government funding, to produce a variety of programs to celebrate the bicentennial. These popularly consumed versions of Chilean history offer both the reification of the heroes of independence and a clearer metahistoriographical orientation toward the way that these stories have been told. Historical novels of the transition also extend the possible foci of the text toward the recuperation of the figures of elite women who participated in the Chilean independence movement and were linked through affective ties to the *padres de la patria*. These novels are part of the collection of cultural artifacts that form part of the contemporary Chilean National Symbolic. The discursive practices studied here relate to the figures of Javiera Carrera[27] and Rosario Puga. Both are participants in a larger cultural project to make legible a shared national identity—a set of current and historically cherished codes and practices—that also depend on the (re)created subjectivity of historical figures and an erasure of difference.[28] The tension between ideal democratic practice within the National Symbolic and historical fiction of the democratic transition can be productively understood through readings of two novels: *Déjame* by Juanita Gallardo and *Javiera Carrera* by Virginia Vidal. These novels and their representations of an alternate conception of the trope of the founding fathers expand and give needed room to feminine elements. That inclusiveness, denied by the hegemonic masculine ideal, enlarges the symbolic possibilities of the Chilean state for inclusion and exclusion.

Patria Vieja, Patria Nueva

Scholars of the Chilean independence movements have disputed the relative merits of the men commonly regarded as Chile's founding fathers: José Miguel Carrera (1785–1821), Bernardo O'Higgins (1778–1842), and, to a lesser extent, Manuel Rodríguez (1785–1818).[29] Carrera, the central figure of the *Patria Vieja*,[30] which lasted from 1810 with the first Junta to the military disaster at Rancagua in 1814, has been hailed for his progressive rhetoric. Carrera had studied the philosophical underpinnings of the American and French revolutions and dedicated himself to the cause of independence, but his inability to accept responsibility for political and military failures and eagerness to consolidate power in the hands of his family members darken his portrait, as did his execution in Mendoza by Argentine authorities in 1821. O'Higgins, the central figure of the consolidation of Chile's independence from Spain between 1817 and 1823, the *Patria Nueva*, was the voice of definitive freedom from Spanish rule. At the same time, he has been described as a dictator whose skills in government were inferior to his skills on the battlefield. Both men have had vocal detractors throughout history and historiography. For those who would like to construct one as the ultimate and singular hero of independence, the other must be pulled down from his pedestal and trampled. The tension between differing interpretations and collective memory with regard to both men thus weaves an intricate tapestry of overlapping interests, testimonies, documents, and judgments over the course of the past two hundred years.

The historiography of Chilean independence is, to be sure, a vast field of intellectual inquiry that covers not only the narration of the events between 1808 and 1823 but also the ancillary investigations into the role of Enlightenment thought, the American and French Revolutions, and pan-Americanism. Documents from the era have been preserved in national archives; individuals present during the times of upheaval, many of whom were British travelers, wrote memoirs that served as primary sources for later historians. A number of nineteenth-century historians were able to speak with participants in the independence movement and to use their interviews and privileged access to personal archives to advantage. These nineteenth-century documents later informed twentieth-century historians, a number of whom wrote to rectify what was seen as bias in earlier historiography. Conflict over the roles assigned to the governments of Carrera and O'Higgins, as well as characterizations of the two men and their followers, distinguishes much historiography. Major events are not, however, in question; indeed, their emplotment changes depending on the sympathies of the author. Authors such as Vicente Pérez

Rosales (1807–1886) and British travelers such as the well-studied Maria Graham (1785–1842)[31] write from their own experiences; the Rosales family had ties to the Carreras; and Maria Graham met O'Higgins during her visit to Santiago.

Broad strokes that characterize both Carrera and O'Higgins form the basis on which many literary accounts of the lives of these individuals take form; the descriptions of the women in the lives of the founding fathers of Chile respond to societal gender expectations at the time of their writing. Stories and history link Carrera to her brothers and Puga to her lover. Carrera is more commonly portrayed, particularly given her political and symbolic role in the *Patria Vieja* while she was in exile and after her brothers' executions. Puga, on the other hand, is mostly absent from historiographical accounts of independence and, when present, relegated to the archetype of the hero's lover, not unlike the traditional representations of Manuela Sáenz vis-à-vis Simón Bolívar.[32]

Although the other Carrera brothers were also well-known, a number of nineteenth-century historians, and most particularly Vicuña Mackenna, make interesting mention of Carrera, sister to the three brothers and "venerable matrona chilena" (Vicuña Mackenna *Doña* 5). Despite the greater attention she gives O'Higgins, María Graham describes "the sister, Donna Xaviera, a lady of great beauty and address, [who] both by her first and second marriage was connected with some of the principal families of Chile" (202). Graham's characterization of Carrera emphasizes her role in connecting her family to the rest of society, above and beyond the more active role that documentary evidence indicates she had during the *Patria Vieja*, particularly in terms of crafting the symbolic language of the new nation. She is repeatedly characterized as intrepid and independent (Vicuña Mackenna *Ostracismo de los Carrera* 19), as well as resolved, full of talent, and pleasant (Gay *Historia de la Independencia* 225). Miguel Luis Amunátegui recognizes her as a "fiel i cariñosa hermana" (*La dictadura* 202) and notes that she shares negative personality traits with José Miguel, even though she was "señora de salón, que daba el tono en la sociedad de Santiago. Hermana de don José Miguel, no solo por la sangre, sino también por el jenio, aunaba a las gracias de la mujer una arrogancia i una decisión verdaderamente varoniles" (66–67). This masculinization as a positive quality can be seen in several other women in this study, such as Inés Suárez. Carrera's agency and action in support of the political gains of her brothers do not earn general esteem.

> En todo esto tuvo, a no dudarlo, su parte de culpa i de responsabilidad la señora Carrera, bien que a nosotros nos cuesta más todavía absolverla de su innecesaria participación en los negocios públicos de su patria, por meritoria que aquella fuese. Pero la señora Carrera había heredado la imperiosa voluntad de su madre i el espíritu turbulento i osado que era peculiar a su raza. (Vicuña Mackenna *Doña* 19)

The actions supporting independence are laudable, but even these cannot overcome Carrera's gender and certain stereotypes about the "raza chilena." Vicuña Mackenna's ideology with regard to the role of women in society continues to reflect, as it did with Inés Suárez and Catalina de los Ríos, an idealization of women's domesticity that does not conform to Carrera's actions between 1810 and 1824.[33] His narrative apologizes for her perceived usurpation of a man's role by emphasizing instead her womanly abnegation to care for her family members (*Doña* 20). Thus, in nineteenth century historiographical narrative, the Carreras, as both individuals and a family, are presented as worthy of limited praise for their work toward Chilean independence.

Carrera is recognized as an individual capable of wielding power within what was at one time the most powerful family in Chile as "a woman as intelligent and as restless as her brother, but also more fanatical and vindictive" (Clissold 123). Antonio Ondarza describes her as "de tez blanquísima, de cabellos rubios como las espigas de trigo maduro, de grandes ojos azules, soñadores y de muy bien delineadas facciones" (18), mirroring the colors of the flag representing the *Patria Vieja*, reportedly designed and sewn by her: blue, white, and yellow. In this sense Carrera embodies the symbols of the new nation, which, according to Bárbara Silva, symbolize the power and personalism of the Carrera regime rather than the society it purported to serve (65). Exceptionally well educated for a woman of her era, she was, as some historians assess her actions and legacy, an exception among women of the colonial period:

> Era mucha hembra y su figura de heroína ha afincado en la leyenda a

mejor título que la Quintrala colonial, pues se mostraba desprendida de liviandades, y si odió como pocas, aun siendo virtuosa y recatada, tuvo la excusa de una pasión fraternal, de una nobilísima pasión que la coloca en el rango de las grandes mujeres de Chile. (Orrego Vicuña 113)

Named heroic, Carrera occupies an unstable position in the pantheon of independence heroes, due to the ultimate failure of policy of the Carrera family as well as her gender, which generally excludes her from the kind of memory created around and about men such as O'Higgins and her brother.

The women of O'Higgins's life, though mentioned periodically in earlier texts, are of interest due to the lack of conformity in their representation in twentieth-century texts. Some refer to Isabel Riquelme, O'Higgins's mother, and at times one of O'Higgins's half-sisters, Rosa Rodríguez, as background characters. Puga, mother of O'Higgins's son, also appears. Rosa, or "Doña Rosita," shares many attributes with her brother (Clissold 200), in contrast with her "perennially youthful" mother. Isabel Riquelme, though described as exhibiting behaviors that would be considered inappropriate, was engaged in a "mission . . . to lavish on [her son] the care and affection which no other woman could give" (200). O'Higgins's sexual relationship with Puga invariably is judged negatively as an "ill-starred affair," (Clissold 200), the result of "una triste debilidad" (Eyzaguirre 181) that recalls O'Higgins's own illegitimate birth. Puga herself is subject to a number of derogatory descriptions; she is referred to her by a vulgar nickname as well as "a flighty red-haired young woman of twenty-one who had left her husband to lead the life of a courtesan" (Clissold 154). By implication, Puga's intentions are driven by a lust for power that dirties the noble efforts directed at independence.[34]

Alternative Mothers: Women and the Construction of Chilean Independence

Historical narrative fiction functions as one of the forms through which "national subjects . . . share not just a history, or a political allegiance, but a set of forms and the affect that makes these forms meaningful" (Berlant 4). The shapes of these stories and the feelings—"sensations that have found a match in words" (Brennan *Transmission* 19)—they evoke contour the boundaries of the national community even as those boundaries are stretched and changed. Not as abundant as are the novels and biographies about men such as Thomas Jefferson, Simón Bolívar, or José de San Martín, fiction set during the Chilean fight for independence from Spain, whether as historical novel or novelized biography, have been fairly common. Despite that, these two novels undermine the common tropes of early nineteenth-century women and armed conflict. These novels expand the historical imagination to feature historically extant women related to O'Higgins and Carrera. The preponderance of historiography of Chilean independence focuses on "great men" and battles. In contrast, these novels focus on "great women." This realigned frame represents difference in a limited sense, but in no way equals the full spectrum of humanity in early nineteenth-century Chile.

Though Carrera figures prominently in most accounts of her brother's life, Vidal's position in *Javiera Carrera* can be distinguished productively from earlier texts by the gender politics in play as well as the narrative resources used.[35] The novel contributes to the pattern of a lionized Javiera, a representation consistent with a number of other works. Vidal's work contrasts with Gallardo's *Déjame*, a novel that represents the relatively absent Puga, Bernardo O'Higgins's lover and mother to his son, as a sympathetic protagonist in Gallardo's pantheon of historically recoverable women.[36] Both novels emphasize in their own ways that "heroes' stories resemble women's stories in that the hero is simultaneously adored and marginalized, being more often an object of veneration than a holder of power" (Hughes-Hallett 8), most obviously through the failures represented by political downfalls. Apropos of the Carrera family tomb, Vidal's narration asks "si los tres hermanos son los padres de la república, puede reflexionar el visitante, entonces ella, doña Javiera Carrera, es la madre. ¿Qué méritos tiene esta mujer, la única considerada madre de la patria?" (13). The documented roles that women played in independence, though traditionally marginalized, were varied and useful, including espionage and the organization of the war economy.[37] However, these actions and participation are rarely portrayed in historical fiction set in this period.

Both Vidal and Gallardo have written a number of historical novels since 1990, and both have told the stories of a number of the same figures and eras, such as Catalina de los Ríos y Lisperguer and José Manuel Balmaceda. Vidal's *Javiera Carrera*, published in 2000, appears to be constructed through a variety of different narrative forms—monologues, letters, and third-person narration—voiced from different perspectives. The narrative invades the interiority of the characters, jumping from one intimacy to the next, and interspersing these with the reproduction and invention of correspondence between the characters; these variations are reflected visually on the page through changes in the typeface.[38] Though other perspectives add color and context to the narrative attributed to Carrera, she emerges from the totality of the novel as the creator of the text and, through it, the creator of a history. Carrera directs the story in Vidal's novel, and as the conduit through which knowledge passes, gains power. Unlike the military power exercised by her brothers, Carrera's power derives from her control of language and expression to further her political goals. Possessed of the power of knowledge diffusion, Carrera communicates official orders. As the student of textual transmission is aware, a copyist can influence a text in myriad ways, making the text the copyist's own. Therefore, *Javiera Carrera* functions differently from traditional novels in its textual embodiment of an ideology that values Carrera's contributions as an active individual and not as a passive repository. Vidal's version of Carrera seizes on the power inherent in knowledge transmission. This Carrera is presented as an agent of history beyond the stereotypical markers of nationality.

Carrera's excellent communication skills—her command of spoken and written language—are equally commendable and set her apart: "qué bien se expresa. Nunca había conocido a una mujer tan elocuente no sólo en el decir, sino también en el escribir" (Vidal 43). Among other things, it marks a departure from the life she once led in a convent. The duty of women did not include the accumulation of power through speech acts. The enclosed space of the convent does not hermetically seal, however, as Carrera's vague knowledge of the scandalous conflict between spouses Joaquín Toesca and Manuela Fernández de Rebolledo emphasizes.[39] Despite the convent's gendered disciplinary mechanisms failing spectacularly in that case, Carrera observes the values instilled in the women educated in the convent. "Las mujeres debemos callar y aceptar. Y acallar" (28). However, she, too, struggles against the imposition of silence: "Le cuesta callar, pregunta, inquiere. Y opina" (31). Thus the idealized feminine space of the convent, with its rules and disciplines, fails to tame Carrera. Her continued use of language and the power inherent within it belies an idealized view of a late eighteenth-century woman obeying without thought the commands and decisions of the men of her family. Vidal's emphasis on Carrera's resistance to the societal silencing of women does not base itself in any trait unique to Carrera; rather it reflects a personality inclined to fluency and intellectual inquiry, as so happens, embodied in a woman. The novel constructs Carrera as a literate subject capable of speaking and highlights the subversive nature of that agency in its time.

Vidal's version of Carrera, empowered by her fluency and knowledge, nevertheless, participates in the symbolic construction of Javiera Carrera as the titular Mother of the Nation.[40] In practice, she cogoverns with her brother, and documents allude to that practice. Carrera's connections to authorities are associated with her symbolic functions within her brother's regime: "Javiera ejerce en muchos actos oficiales la función de primera dama" (110). Her name is used as a rallying cry for the supporters of the *carrerina* cause, which references secret meetings at which Carrera served as a hostess. This novel depends on Javiera Carrera's lived experience to allude to the construction of a feminine power in contrast to earlier works' maternal metaphors for nation foundation. That said, her role during the secret meetings contributes to an image of Carrera not only invested with power through her communicational roles both within the text and as the text itself, but also to Carrera as a nurturing figure. *Javiera Carrera* engages in a recuperation of the figure of Carrera from both historical oblivion and the earlier writers who utilized her as a model for idealized femininity despite her unflattering political involvement. The criticism of societal norms on gender performance, particularly tied to the power of speech and knowledge transmission, reflects late twentieth-century gender politics that value the contributions of women and other marginalized groups in history who carried on even when faced with powerful systems of oppression.

Whereas Vidal's novel reinterprets a well-known figure, Gallardo's novel re-creates a lesser known woman involved in Chilean independence: Rosario Puga. Her family was prominent in Concepción, and she was separated from her husband. She is best known as the mother of Bernardo O'Higgins's only acknowledged child. In earlier texts, Puga appears as a momentary distraction from O'Higgins's other pursuits. Gallardo, "la autora que se ha escondido tras

Demetrio y Candelaria" (243) (the two characters through which the narrative is filtered), details a part of her research process while writing *Déjame* and concludes that the "founding family," or at least one of them, is missing a number of people. *Déjame* extends the idea of the familial unit of Bernardo O'Higgins to include his mother Isabel Riquelme and half-sister Rosa Rodríguez, as well as his lover Puga, his son Demetrio O'Higgins, and his other half-sister Nieves Puga. This recuperation of a domestic side of the life of the Liberator finds echo within the information and orientations deemed worthy of remembrance.

> La novela presenta en una mirada íntima, familiar e incluso doméstica de la Historia de Chile, las casas, las calles, el campo, los escenarios bélicos, las fiestas, la provincia y la capital como lugares significativos de decisiones políticas, de convivencia y de un sinfín de prácticas culturales que realizan sus habitantes, alentados por el devenir republicano. (Larrea)

Domesticity matters as authors reconsider the nation-as-home metaphor inherent in constructions of mothers and fathers of the nation; this interest in fiction writing mirrors the rise of social history.

The practice of everyday life reconstructed and fictionalized within the novel relates to what María Isabel Larrea identifies as the heteroglossia of Gallardo's discourse by presenting tensions through a wider and more complex presentation of early nineteenth century society. In the novel, the servant Candelaria tells Demetrio O'Higgins Puga stories that draw from various discourses to piece together a mosaic of the era sympathetic to the figure of Puga. However, *Déjame* does not present itself as some monolithic history designed to replace all that has been written before. Instead, it offers a conscious alternative among many possible interpretations. Demetrio emphasizes that "a esas alturas de su vida sabía que la Historia de Chile, así como la historia de su padre, la suya y la de cualquier individuo siempre serían susceptibles de interpretaciones diversas, dependiendo de la época y lugar en que el interpretador respirara, sintiese y pensara" (Gallardo 235). Self-conscious awareness of history, modeled by this fictional character, offers an option for the implementation of historical competence within the novel as well as a strategy for readers of historical fiction. As one voice among many who write of the Independence era, Gallardo presents a unique focus on the era of the *Patria Nueva*, highlighting contributions by figures who are lesser known and reflecting an intimate relationship that, while passionate and loving, refuses to obey any idealized concept of Bernardo O'Higgins's consort as extraordinarily unique and therefore necessitating a retroactive process of symbolization.

O'Higgins, though a man like many others in Gallardo's narrative, "era un hombre sin familia en un país donde esa era la única filiación posible" (72), which sets up an ironic juxtaposition between his origins and his eventual symbolic role as father of independent Chile. His illegitimacy defines him, serving as another marker of otherness, despite the relatively common practice of the birth of children outside of marriage, as well as other social practices that fell beyond the pale of a church-sanctified marriage.[41] Although the legal impediment to the formalization of Bernardo and Rosario's relationship appears to be Rosario's marriage to another man, the narrative configures Bernardo as similarly unavailable, as he is married to the independence movement "y el poco tiempo que le sobra se lo dedica a mamá" (Gallardo 56). This move, along with the representation of Rosario's husband as an unfaithful lecher, equalizes the moral footing on which the relationship is based. Neither participant is entirely free to pursue the course of action each desires; as such, neither participant is at fault. As the novel develops, though, fault lines emerge, and not all of them can be traced back to tensions between Rosario and the women officially part of Bernardo's life. Gallardo's novel points toward tensions between national political identifications, as Rosario asks Bernardo whether he feels more Irish or Chilean, to which he responds, "Yo soy americano, Rosario; igual que tú;" Rosario disagrees—"Yo soy chilena; del sur de Chile" (171). This friction between hemispheric and localized identification mirrors conflict between O'Higgins, dedicated to the liberation of Peru from Spanish control, and other provincial interests that viewed Chilean independence as a separate matter. In this way, O'Higgins's relationship with Puga replicates his larger governmental challenges. It also undermines the idea of a unified and singular Chilean identity; not all Chileans claim or are recognized as such. In O'Higgins's world, Chile is not a "we."

In that vein, the narrator consciously manipulates stereotypical markers of Chilean identity to help the reader place the narrative within a system of symbolic signs. She calls them lies,

> Con la intención de que muchos las reconocieran como tales y así supieran en qué terreno se movían: Jaime Eyzaguirre, como coetáneo de O'Higgins, expresando su asombro por el enamoramiento del Director Supremo; el origen de la palabra "onces", de la paila marina, el mariscal y las animitas; el tono agudo que usamos los chilenos para hablar; partes del poema de Neruda acerca de Manuel Rodríguez. (Gallardo 246)[42]

The use of anachronisms emphasizes that *Déjame* is a fiction and, for that reason, does not assert absolute truth value in its claims. As a product of the author's imagination, symbolic language places Puga firmly within the web of the National Symbolic as it exists in 2000. As Isabel Allende uses the production of food as a marker of gendered symbolic foundation and sustenance related to Inés Suárez, so too does Gallardo when fictionalizing the origins of the *paila marina* and *mariscal*, both inventions attributed to Puga's mother, Isabel Vidaurre. While these aspects of the text wink at the reader with appropriate cultural competence to recognize them, their presence reflects a modern ideology of *chilenidad* that encompasses food, historical-political discourse, iconic poets, and the very act of speech itself. The case of speech is complicated by its ostensibly foreign origin, attributed to Lady Catherine Cochrane, wife of the man hired to lead O'Higgins's naval squadron. Women imitated Lady Catherine, and "el resultado fue un sonido agudo, distinto, en todo caso, a la gravedad del habla de las españolas. Las santiaguinas lo consideraron un tono patriótico que las distinguía de las realistas y entusiasmadas con el hallazgo, se lo enseñaron a sus hijas y nietas" (157). The contemporary reader recognizes this description of feminine timbre in certain social classes. The patriotic attribution of this custom, however, introduces a novel ideological orientation for this practice. That said, its symbolic function is indicative of only certain class-limited belonging.

Given the play and critique with the alphabet of national difference within the symbolic structure of *Déjame*, can Puga be considered a foundational figure for the nation? Can one read Puga within the tradition of foundational heroes such as O'Higgins and the Carrera family? The novel opens with a speculation voiced by Candelaria "si no se hubiese casado tan joven, Rosario habría sido la Madre de la Patria" (9). From the start, the narrative plants a nagging concern in the minds of readers, prompting us to consider what could have been. In doing so, however, the text answers its own question: Rosario is not the Mother of the Nation. Nevertheless, she could have been, and the novel's course highlights this unfulfilled promise. Puga's commitment to the cause of independence is unwavering, and affirmed within her family environment: "muy de familia insurgente sería, pero que así y todo, era una dama" (34). Puga, whose dedication to independence is accented by her own independent spirit, benefits from her elevated social class, despite warnings that her gender and age put her at risk. The young girl who prefers the idea of going to war with her father to staying home becomes the woman whom soldiers refer to as "Generala" during the march from Concepción to Santiago. Her physical being, however, denies any accusations of masculinization; in the same breath she is given a martial title, readers are told that "con su embarazo era más mujer que nunca" (84). In this way, Puga maintains her femininity, despite her challenges to female behavior. Her corporeal embodiment of reproduction contrasts sharply with the practices of *santiaguinas*, who "gustaban de comer poco, verse pálidas, sufrir jaquecas y desmayos y, sobre todo, cultivar la fragilidad y el recato" (100). The overdetermined nature of *santiaguina* femininity, emphasized by the obvious preference for fragility, contrasts with Puga's ostensibly natural feminine subjectivity that values strength and independence. Even as the narrative highlights the integration of Puga into an idea of the shared story of independence, it does so at the cost of women viewed as insufficiently meritorious.

In Santiago, Puga's position is less assured than in her home territory. Her relationship with the women of the city, as already noted, is constricted by conflicting values of femininity, between Puga's outspoken agency and the reticent and delicate flowers of the capital. These physical and temperamental contrasts are mapped onto regional differences that reflect the situational nature of identity. Despite these disparities, *Déjame* represents Puga as constantly in community with other women, whether family, neighbors, or friends. As opposed to O'Higgins, who is often portrayed as solitary, Puga is never alone. In Concepción, she functions as "el sostén de los ánimos de su madre y de su abuela; la encargada de rebuscárselas para conseguir dinero y mantener los trueques necesarios para la sobrevivencia . . . indispensables para mantener a la familia viva" (44). Even when in conflict with Isabel Riquelme and Rosa Rodríguez, Puga still participates in events celebrating the women contributing to the independence effort. This all-woman space—outside the disciplinary all-woman space of the convent—contrasts with the typical expectation for a commemoratory event, in which one person, usually a man, speaks while a rapt audience listens.

> No hubo discursos, sino que hablaban todas a la vez, incluso a la hora de los brindis y no llegaron a ningún acuerdo, pero tampoco lo pretendían. Quedaron felices al sentirse hermanadas después que todas contaron, ahora entre risas, las desgracias que habían afrontado. "Somos sobrevivientes," afirmaba doña Gertrudis Serrano y doña Cornelia asentía. "Un brindis por la Patria," pidió doña Isabel Riquelme en más de una oportunidad. (154)

The celebration within the text constructs women's solidarity within the groups supporting independence and reflects a more informal speech pattern than generally expected for an official event. Puga's participation in such events emphasizes her humanity through her sense of community and, accordingly, contributes to an image of her as an everyday woman whose convictions lead her toward certain behaviors and sympathies. Despite her association with certain moves toward symbolic meaning, such as the birth of the child of the Liberator, Puga maintains her humanity in the face of mythification.

Where Vidal's Carrera represents a feminine subject-construction grounded in the value of literacy, Gallardo's Puga stars in a text that resists her mythification by maintaining a local sense of identity embedded in a community of women. Both novels, in centering women during the early nineteenth century, participate in one of the trends in historical fiction in Chile: the recuperation of the role of (elite) women in history. At the same time, this focus adds depth to the body of fiction of the era in that historically extant women are attributed textual power while also maintaining their humanity. When one considers both texts in the light of the construction of national foundation and questions of inclusion and exclusion, one is confronted with two separate options, though both novels imagine the possibility of a founding mother in concert with the institutional founding fathers. Whereas Puga could have been a founding mother, Carrera is represented as a viable founding figure whose utilization of the power of communication places her on the same level of importance as men, among them her brothers and Bernardo O'Higgins. Puga, while very much an individual, works within a community of women where Carrera is set apart as extraordinary. Playful moves toward symbolic construction like those made explicit by Gallardo unpack the tendency to lionize figures such as O'Higgins; Vidal's text does not question the process of mythification. In post-1990 historical fiction of independence as represented by these two novels, the structures of identity and belonging are opened to new inhabitants, but the structures themselves are not transformed by them, which complements the democratic transition itself.

Conclusions: Independence and Instability

The narrative forms of the three novels studied here all contribute to different ways of thinking about the independence movements in Chile and the symbols and monuments that have come to be associated with them. In *El sueño* the relationships between spaces and symbols are explored through a narrative that resists certitude in its portrayal of parallel stories of umbral moments. The place of La Moneda in the Chilean national imaginary is both reified and questioned, leading to the possibility of a breakdown in symbolic systems that exude power and exclude difference. *Javiera Carrera* concentrates on the ability to speak about a reformation of the national foundation myth centered on Carrera above and beyond the men involved in military exploits, encoding the importance of and power attributed to speech acts in the metanarrative of the novel itself. Puga, on the other hand, does not function as an extraordinary foundational figure in *Déjame*, a novel that enacts and undermines pieces of the material culture and symbols of everyday life that make up large swathes of Chile's National Symbolic. Whereas Edwards's novel features one symbolic building/monument, and Vidal's version of Carrera, with its emphasis on extraordinariness, another, Gallardo's Puga lives and functions in a community of women who all contribute to the movement toward independence.

All three novels invite an analysis of the parallelism between the times they represent and the democratic transition. Edwards's novel offers the most clearcut comparison with its dual historical referents; their narrative connection posits a link between independence from Spain and the return to democracy. This optimism—the return to democracy as a new independence for the nation—is nevertheless tempered by the permanence of physical edifices that only allow for a limited resemanticizing within existing structures. The connection between independence and the democratic transition is less explicit in Vidal, as the novel shifts the meaning of existing symbols of foundation and power related to independence to the person of Carrera. Gallardo's self-conscious awareness of symbolism and anachronisms, common throughout her historical fiction, pokes fun at the symbolic structures while focusing on the human elements of historical figures. A major critique of the democratic transition is the lack of structural change in the transition from dictatorship to democracy. As *La Tercera*'s editorial quoted in the introduction to this chapter notes, respect for authority has been and remains an important piece of the narratives about Chilean political and social life. Authoritarian structures leave little space for difference; these novels carve out limited spaces for the exploration of the differences confronting Chilean identity post-1990, though they remain bound up in symbolic structures implicated in the power of homogeneity.

CHAPTER FOUR
The Occupation of Araucanía

WHAT KINDS OF STORIES can be told to make sense of an unjust conflict? What purpose do these stories serve? Stories about the Occupation or Pacification of Araucanía (1860–1883) coalesce around a particular figure: Orélie-Antoine de Tounens, King of Araucanía and Patagonia (1825–1878). In the film *La película del rey* (*A King and his Movie*, 1986), Argentine director Carlos Sorín tells a story in which impossibility triumphs. The protagonist, David Vass, tries to make a movie about Tounens, enduring a series of comic mishaps until the entire project fails. Nevertheless, in the moment of failure—having been dragged out of the desert by military helicopters, leaving behind his few remaining actors and an army of mannequins—Vass starts talking about another dream, trying to tell yet another impossible story.

While novels do exist that deal with other stories that could be told about the Occupation,[1] the majority of twentieth-century fictional texts feature the strange story of the king of Araucanía, though post-1990 only one text follows this pattern. In this chapter I will show how representing Tounens makes the Occupation legible to those who identify or empathize with majority Chilean culture. This legibility emphasizes the ways in which specifically indigenous others are still not legible within contemporary Chilean society and so betray a failure of narrative imagination: "the ability to think what it might be like to be in the shoes of a person different from oneself, to be an intelligent reader of that person's story, and to understand the emotions, wishes, and desires that someone so placed might have" (Nussbaum 270). The focus on Tounens reflects this failure, which also serves to emphasize how democratic Chile's artistic production reflects the failure of the democratic transition. The first constitutional proposal in the 2020s suggested Chile is a plurinational state.[2] As with the complex processes at work in both historical and contemporary public discourses around difference and multiculturalism, this expansive view of belonging challenges the traditional story of "una nación monocultural y homogénea que niega su morenidad y sus raíces. El colonialismo triunfante construyó un relato de una nación compuesta por un solo pueblo" (#Constitucionalista) and that a single Chile continues to shape identity formations and belonging.

The Occupation of Araucanía and Historiography

The processes known today as the Occupation of Araucanía take place over two decades and coincide with another key military venture of the relatively young Chilean state: the War of the Pacific. Unlike the heroic tales of the War of the Pacific, the stories of the Occupation aren't fodder for didactic films, nor are they particularly popular in general remembrances of the nineteenth century. The historiographical discourse surrounding this era follows some general patterns, though narrative differences distinguish orientations. One example of this is the distinction between talking about the birth of *la Frontera*, the border[3] or the Pacification or the Occupation of Araucanía.[4] In terms of that border, the land in question is emplotted in a manner at one with the Chilean perspective that views land ownership and value as definable, divisible, and developable; in terms of Araucanía, valuing the epistemology of native peoples remains an untaken opportunity.[5]

How to make sense of this conflicted geographical area has had historians produce a variety of readings and emphases. On one hand, a number of them study the Occupation as military history, detailing the role of particular leaders and the development of military strategy. This means writing about the establishment of forts, battles, lines of defense, and reproducing correspondence between individuals such as Cornelio Saavedra (1821–1891), the intellectual architect of the state's campaign and the minister of defense.[6] On the other hand, important work has been done in the past few decades privileging a Mapuche perspective and social history as it pertains to the Occupation.[7] Still, over a century passed before "marginalized histories began to be incorporated into mainstream narratives of the past" (Crow 26).

After independence was won from Spain, Mapuche groups were ostensibly separate from the Chilean state south of the Bío-Bío River and north of the island Chiloé. Nevertheless, agrarian activities of Chilean and European immigrants encroached on this territory over time in what historian José Bengoa has described evocatively as "ant-like colonization" (153). As the Mapuche did not reliably support the Chilean state's military endeavors,[8] Chilean military and political leaders began making plans to definitively integrate that territory into the state. Actual military action was preceded by legal maneuvering involving both commerce and property rights. By 1859, Chilean *colonos* were moving south of the Bío-Bío River and German immigrants were establishing themselves farther south. In the uprising of 1859, nearly all nonindigenous settlements south of the Bío-Bío were destroyed, prompting action on the part of the Chilean state. In 1861, Cornelio Saavedra presented a plan to Congress in which the border would be moved south to the Malleco River, lands between the Bío-Bío and Malleco Rivers would have their titles transferred, and colonization would be better planned and controlled.

As is the case with most conflicts over an extended period of time, the Occupation ebbed and flowed between 1861 and 1881. While skirmishes were ongoing prior to the end of the decade, by 1869 the battles grew larger and more violent, in what Bengoa repeatedly refers to as a war of extermination. Though the border was shifted south through this period of intensified conflict, between 1871 and 1881 the tenor of the Occupation shifted again to a holding pattern prior to what is viewed as the final defeat of the Mapuche at Villarrica in 1881, at which point surviving Mapuche were corralled onto reservations.[9]

Historian Jorge Pinto Rodríguez argues that the causes of the conflict were a lack of land available for sale, the necessity of land for immigrants and migrants from other parts of Chile, and an ideological belief that pitted native barbarity, so imagined, against Chilean civilization (149). While the contrast between civilization and barbarism has often been seen as a product of its time, the idea of the barbarian on the other side of the river preventing the integration of a contiguous territory as a state proved unacceptable to the Chilean center. Even in the 1980s, Ricardo Ferrando wrote that "el mapuche fue vencido por el único sistema que podía producir este efecto, por incorporación a un sistema superior de vida" (653). This sentiment remains palpable in Chilean society today, as Patricia Richards shows when she describes the attitudes of Chileans and the descendants of *colonos* in Araucanía in the 2000s and observes that one individual "opposed discrimination against people like himself but implied that discrimination against the Mapuche was their own fault" (*Race* 6).

The anti-indigenous position also recurred in public discourse during the Occupation. The narratives of this conflict began to appear with the conflict itself in newspapers, letters, and public debates. The notable historians of the day not only made public statements in favor of the machinations of the Chilean state but also excluded indigenous perspectives and contributions in their own writing of history. Journalistic rhetoric in the late 1850s prefigured the nasty characterizations that political figures would make during parliamentary debates; thus, the Mapuche were portrayed as inherently uncivilized, wild, and animalistic (Pinto 154). Figures such as Vicuña Mackenna wrote and spoke virulently against the indigenous peoples,[10] and the negative force of his rhetoric became stronger as the conflict wore on (Bottinelli 109, 113). While some figures, such as José Manuel Balmaceda, a fictional and historical protagonist in chapter 5, resisted this rhetoric, it dominated public discourse and understandings of the indigenous people in Chile during the 1850s, 60s, and beyond.

Making Resistance Legible

In telling stories about this conflict, one eccentric figure surfaces repeatedly, both in fiction and in historiography. Described repeatedly as picturesque, unbelievable, and fairytale-esque, Orélie-Antoine de Tounens inspires the imagination. Having declared himself king of Araucanía and Patagonia, the appeal of his story to writers of fiction is easily understood. The French law clerk arrived in Chile in 1858 with knowledge of neither Spanish nor Mapudungun and proclaimed himself head of an independent monarchic state south of the Bío-Bío River. Shortly after securing support from various Mapuche groups and composing fundamental legal documents for the new kingdom, he was arrested and nearly committed to an insane asylum before being expelled from Chile. His dream of an independent Araucanía was firmly stamped out, as his two subsequent attempts to return to Chile to rally indigenous rebellion illustrate.[11] Beyond Tounens's quixotic character, his presence at the beginning of the concentrated military campaign to fortify Chilean state sovereignty and pacify Mapuche space and bodies offers narrative margins for reflecting on that campaign and its lasting consequences. As the vast majority of authors of Chilean historical fiction identify with majority culture, the representation of Tounens allows for the exploration of ideas of how the center works by including and excluding groups from both the physical and metaphorical space of the nation.

Texts available to illuminate the historical reality of this French would-be king range from his own autobiography to the texts of a few historians of the late nineteenth and twentieth centuries, as well as the emergence of recent historiographical work related to social history and indigenous history. No one appears to disagree with some basic facts: Tounens goes to Chile to establish a kingdom of the Mapuche with himself as leader; his mission also participated in the nineteenth-century project of Western civilization processes in colonial contexts. He has various run-ins with the Chilean state and is roundly mocked for his plans. However, the Chilean state eventually equates Tounens's projects with a possible competing colonial endeavor from Napoleon III's France, prompting his arrest, trial, and expulsion. Returned to France, he continues to rally support for the cause of the kingdom of Araucanía and Patagonia but faces considerable financial ups-and-downs as well as several failed expeditions to return to Mapuche lands. To this day, however, the line of succession maintains its royalist practices and represent certain Mapuche interests in international arenas.[12]

Tounens's autobiographical version of his dream fails to provide a skeleton for his understanding of the history of the Mapuche people and involvement with them prior to his expulsion from Chile. Much of the text is dedicated to vindicating his legal position vis-à-vis the Chilean state, particularly in terms of his claims as the leader of a sovereign state and the abuses that he suffered at the hands of Chilean agents. Originally published in French in Paris in 1863, *Orllie-Antoine I Rey de Araucanía y de Patagonia. Su asunción al trono y su cautiverio en Chile. Relato escrito por él mismo* also served as a mechanism for raising funds to support his work in establishing the kingdom of Araucanía via the sale of copies of the text for F3.80. The self-portrait this text depicts assumes legitimacy and points out apparent contradictions in Chilean attitudes toward his project. For example, after proclaiming the establishment of the kingdom, Tounens interprets his nonarrest in Valparaíso as evidence that the Chilean state did not effectively govern Araucanía. For Tounens, the Chilean state's nonaction is an abrogation of responsibility that effectively leaves the path clear for his project and informs the outrage with which he treats his later arrest, interrogation, and trial. Indeed, he claims that "Chile jamás ha tenido ningún derecho sobre estas dos regiones, ni por conquista, ni por sumisión voluntaria; sus leyes siempre han sido ignoradas allí; por lo tanto, yo no podía violarlas ni directa ni indirectamente" (92). He supports this claim through the reproduction of documents of the kingdom and letters concerning his legal woes, though he does not produce any documentation beyond his assertions of Chile's illegitimate claim on Araucanía and Patagonia.

Many of the quoted documents in Tounens's version of events deal with the Chilean state's efforts to curtail his activities, efforts that Tounens characterizes in conspiratorial terms. He argues that those individuals sent to arrest him "tenía orden, me resistiera o no, de cortarme la cabeza y llevarla al gobierno, como prueba irrecusable de mi muerte" and that the presence of merchants on the road were all that prevented this "salvaje ejecución" (42). No other text verifies this claim. In his narrative the representation of the Chilean state and its agents varies between incompetence and malevolence. The state has laws that are not obeyed and this lack of compliance is used to delegitimize the state's claims to Araucanía. At the same time, the state that cannot enforce its laws in a particular territory nevertheless sends a goon squad to eliminate the threat Tounens poses to Chilean sovereignty. The narrative also constructs two poles of power: the kingdom as represented by Tounens and the Chilean state. The absence of the Mapuche leaders from the pole of the kingdom speaks volumes as to the power relations Tounens recognizes in his interactions once expelled from Chile and living in France, where he wrote his autobiography.

Tounens's self-identification remains French throughout the text even as he argues for the legitimacy of his royalist independence project in Araucanía and Patagonia. He consistently refers to France as "mi país," even though he recognizes that the French press sees his projects as "una lluvia de malos chistes" (37). He turns to France for support, writing letters "con objeto de obtener que reconociera el reino que yo acababa de fundar, y que quisiera ayudarme a fortificar mi poder, aclamado por los Araucanos, y a proteger a mis súbditos contra toda eventualidad" (Tounens 37), and expresses disappointment that none of his compatriots is willing to journey to southern Chile. Having arrived in 1860 with no knowledge of Spanish or Mapudungun, Tounens learned some of each yet still refers to French as "nuestra lengua" (66). One should recall that this text was published in France and directed toward a French audience seeking support for colonial enterprise. In this context, the consistent affirmation of Tounens's Frenchness emphasizes connection with his audience and reaffirms the kingdom as part of a Western project of civilization. Indeed, when interrogated under arrest, Tounens explains the objective of his election as king of Araucanía as "puramente filantrópico, . . . a civilizar esa región, introduciendo en ella la religión, la educación elemental, la agricultura y las artes" (75), betraying his ignorance of the people of Araucanía and Patagonia in his assumption that they completely lack religion, education, agriculture, and art. Whereas Tounens represents his work as philanthropic—promoting the welfare of others, embodying generosity and benevolence—he devalues the people he purports to serve. Thus, he subscribes to the paternalistic and patronizing view that indigenous peoples are barbaric and inferior to the enlightened West.

Tounens's first-person narrative focuses above all on a defense of himself and the righteousness of his own actions. Despite that, many of the notable nineteenth-century historians remained relatively silent on the occupation of Araucanía and the role of Tounens. Among the exceptions are Horacio Lara (1860–1897) and Tomás Guevara (1865–1935), who offer interpretations of both in *Crónica de la Araucanía* (1889) and *Historia de la Civilización de la Araucanía* (1898), respectively. As a text that refers to the arcs of Mapuche history as "mas bien un drama, una epopeya" (Lara 15), *Crónica* represents what other major nineteenth-century historians ignored while participating in the epic literary tradition in which the representation of indigenous figures, especially heroic ones, follows models that are predominantly European (Sutton 418). Moreover, Alonso de Ercilla's *La Araucana* permeates nineteenth-century Chilean culture's understanding of the indigenous figure, and it can be argued that in defeat the Mapuche "son despojados definitivamente de todas sus antiguas cualidades míticas, de las que toman posisión, junto con el territorio, los oficiales criollos triunfadores y sus soldados mestizos" (Castillo Sandoval 233).

With the triumph of the Chilean state in the Occupation, the delinking of living and breathing indigenous populations and the mythical heroism portrayed in Ercilla's poem is completed.

Both historians feature Tounens's story as part of the narrative they create about the Occupation. Lara interprets Tounens as an agent of the French empire taking advantage of Araucanía's "absoluta independencia" prior to 1860 to make common cause "con las aspiraciones de su primitiva poblacion" (278). Lara repeatedly describes him as an adventurer who consorts with liquor merchants, calling into question his moral fiber. Some adjectives such as famous, celebrated, clever, daring, and audacious do, however, modify his figure. Where the earnestness of his self-narration presents the French king as an injured and misunderstood party, Lara's description of the public perception of him minimizes his importance. His articles published in the press were ignored "por creer que el autor de esos artículos ocultaba su nombre con el disfraz de esa firma elijiéndola por seudónimo" (280). His physical appearance was mocked: "una figura rara i extravagante que lucia una gran melena, como la que acostumbraban vulgarmente los indios . . . lo que causó naturalmente iralidad general" (281). Where Tounens portrays the disparagement of his figure as misunderstanding, Lara's narrative links this attitude to a natural reaction to his public persona, which attempts incongruously to concatenate the European adventurer and performed indigeneity through dress, which underscore the grotesqueness of his person. Cultural mixing, therefore, is an object for ridicule, as it betrays an ideology of difference in which the European must inhabit a circumscribed space of civilization that allows for no legitimate contamination by others. In Chilean society "the idea of the "Chilean race" built on . . . elided indigenousness" (Richards *Race* 43) seeks unity in identification but that, in practice, pacifies racialized class conflicts. Therefore, in this context, cultural mixing does not celebrate a future of a whiter "cosmic race" but points, instead, to something that fundamentally resides outside of hegemonic Chilean discourse. Lara's text represents a society—dominant Chilean society post-Occupation—that uses humor and derision to delegitimize the pro-other discourses (not without issues) of a figure that, in elevating himself in the eyes of the excluded members of society, threatens the structures that support his identity—white, male, French, Christian—as the top of the hierarchy.

The manufacture of Tounens's public image is emphasized by the way in which Lara describes his arrest and defense: "Comprendiendo éste [Orelie] la gravedad de su delito, trató de aparecer como loco, i al efecto empezó a dirijir circulares a los representantes de todas las naciones, sin dejar de empeñarse i de suplicar a las personas que lo visitaban en su prision para que influyesen por el perdon de su vida" (288). Lara's Tounens is not a true-believer: he is a treasure hunter out to save his own skin. The (il)legitimacy of indigenous claims to independence are never addressed, obfuscated by the figure of Tounens whose calculating actions and confusing societal positioning allegedly speak for these indigenous claims. Tounens becomes a talisman of sorts for indigenous uprisings, portrayed as taking advantage of the rebellious spirit of the indigenous peoples (Lara 279) and instigating later rebellions in 1869 (353). Lara eventually links Quilapán (d. c. 1876)[13] with Tounens. Quilapán supplies the military might behind Tounens's ideas and, in turn becomes "el formidable adversaro" (Lara 340). Lara tells stories of the Occupation that other historians of his era did not, but he does so within his own time and culture; the legitimacy of indigenous claims are never seriously considered, just as the legitimacy of the claims of the Chilean state are never doubted.

Tomás Guevara's *Historia de la Civilización de la Araucanía* also underlines the legitimacy of the claims of the state in Araucanía. When introducing Tounens, Guevara describes the events as "un hecho que, con tomar un sesgo cómico al fin, vino a poner de manifiesto la necesidad de cerrar la Araucanía a la peligrosa presencia en ella de los aventureros" (7). Tounens is the model figure of the adventurer, writing articles that no one took seriously, deceiving Quilapán into supporting his project with lies, and costuming himself in the indigenous manner to deceive his marks. Indeed, "Esta circunstancia y las maneras corteses del aventurero, impresionaron favorablemente a algunos de sus oyentes, contra la opinión acertada de otros de mejor juicio, que sospechaban en todo esto simples embustes" (8). Appealing to the authority of letters and witnesses, Guevara weaves a tale in which some indigenous people suspect Tounens while others take up arms against the state in his name.

Tounens and France have a strong connection in Guevara's text. France is "su patria" (93), and it is through the influence of the French presence in Chile that Tounens is able to leave the country following the guilty verdict for disturbing public order, rather than be confined to an insane asylum. His foreignness comes to the forefront repeatedly, especially in the extensive quotation of documents authored by Cornelio Saavedra. "Aquel malvado extranjero" (qtd. in Guevara 84) bears the brunt of blame for later waves of violence in the Occupation, particularly in 1870. The "malévolos consejos del aventurero francés" (Guevara 86) to the insurgent indigenous groups force the hand of the state to respond with violence, and all responsibility for bloodshed is shifted to Tounens as a sacrificial lamb. The various indigenous leaders act only according to his advice, though with his removal from South America once again the indigenous forces are described as bending the knee to the Chilean state, with the notable exception of Quilapán (93). Territory and physical presence are important themes in Guevara's narrative. It is not Tounens's ideas that are dangerous but rather his physical presence and its effects on Mapuche communities. Guevara tied the agency of indigenous leaders who rebel against the forces of the Chilean state to the presence of Tounens. The Frenchman is a talisman, enabling conflict that ebbs with his first expulsion and again when he leaves of his own accord.

Guevara's version of the Occupation and of Tounens's role in the conflict depends on this singular figure: uniquely culpable for the deaths in the conflict and uniquely able to unite and inspire rebellion in indigenous leaders. What does this say about difference? As in the case of Lara's text, indigenous demands are never considered and the agency of indigenous leaders is silenced. This king is a talisman and representative in both texts; in removing him from the space of conflict, the agents of the state win the day. These late nineteenth-century historians make the occupation legible through the figure of Tounens precisely because his indices of difference are minimal—and when he adopts Mapuche markers, it is risible. Difference threatens the hegemonic Chilean narrative.

Considering state formation in Chile vis-à-vis indigeneity and difference, historian Jorge Pinto Rodríguez concludes that Chile is sad and fearful, the fruit of "una larga historia de exclusión, ocultamiento, avasallamiento, imitación y renuncia de lo propio, que nos ha impedido reconocer al conglomerado de identidades y subculturas que se reúnen en nuestro país" (283). Horacio Lara and Tomás Guevara's works highlight pro-state perspectives at the expense of empathy with indigenous causes. While one current of later historiography continues to neglect Mapuche perspectives and the violence enacted by agents of the Chilean state, an eddy in the main current of social and cultural history considers the Occupation from other perspectives, privileging the stories of communities most directly affected by it.[14] Some historiographical narratives elide the history of the king of Araucanía and Patagonia, or focus on conflict between men of European descent. Those that exhibit more sympathy toward the Mapuche perspective must also address the wacky king in the room.

Historian and anthropologist José Bengoa's references to Tounens and his role in Mapuche rebellions reflect not only on the events as they might be understood today but also on the way they have been constructed over more than a century. "Sin duda hoy día se valoran más los elementos surrealistas . . . que su posible valor histórico y . . . el valor etnohistórico que posee" (Bengoa 189). The surreal elements of the story attract attention like the shiny object drawing a magpie. One might argue that these dramatic touches "explican la acogida permanente de Orélie en los anchos salones de la literatura: el rey es un personaje muchas veces escrito" (Álvarez 113). Bengoa includes in his archive a series of fictional texts[15] to make historical sense of "un francés con trazas de aventurero, iluminado y loco, que se proclamó Aurelie Antoine I, Rey de la Araucanía y la Patagonia" (Bengoa 188). Bengoa affirms that the unresolved historical issue remains the relationship between Tounens's project and possible French imperial ambitions, utilizing the evidence of the role Alberto Blest Gana played in tamping down Tounens's projects in Paris. This also calls into question the view of his "adventures" as nothing but the ravings of a man with mental illness; however, as both Bengoa and Ignacio Álvarez attest, we neither can know nor does it truly matter what role madness may have played in Tounens's life. Álvarez notes that the unstable diagnosis given to Tounens—monomania[16]—depends on an understanding of Tounens's use of reason, and therefore declaring him deficient in its use also serves the political purpose of undermining his arguments in favor of the kingdom of Araucanía and Patagonia (112). While there may have been "una extraña conjunción de intereses y una total identificación imaginaria entre el rey y sus súbditos" (Álvarez 110), this connection and its relationship to possible mental illness depends on the ways in which the nineteenth-century state used medicine as a tool to exercise its power of inclusion and exclusion. In accentuating the mental illness of the man that Chilean leaders identified as a leader and threat—French, white, male—the Chilean state undermines the legitimacy of any claims made by the Mapuche or on their behalf.

Tounens can be a disturbing symbol. He can be made to make sense as a white man of questionable sanity who took the side of the indigenous peoples not for their own benefit but for the benefit of the West, whether represented by French imperial ambitions or the notion of civilizing the uncivilized. The agency of the Mapuche themselves is subsumed beneath a figure that is legible in power systems that privilege the recognition of legitimate exercise of power by those who look and act like those already near the top of the hierarchy. However, anthropologists and historians associated with the history of indigenous peoples shift this emplotment of the Occupation of Araucanía. While Bengoa recognizes the role that Tounens played, it is couched in the political and cultural realities of the Mapuche in the late nineteenth century.[17] Where earlier texts saw the connection between Tounens and French imperialism as a dangerous threat to the legitimate claims of the Chilean state, Bengoa ascribes political agency to the Mapuche, arguing that a possible French alliance was in their favor, even though "lamentablemente para los mapuches, el apoyo no se hizo efectivo" (190). The importance of Tounens is not his embodiment of a legible political threat but in his representation of a failed alliance that might have enabled Mapuche independence from the Chilean state. Centering representation on Tounens shows a failure of empathy in that hegemonic narrative imaginings are limited to the power exercised both in familiar ways and by a certain kind of person. This results in the exclusion, inadvertent or not, of the Mapuche from the exercise of possible political and social power.

The Quixotic Dream of an Independent Araucanía

Just as Tounens's story makes its way into historiographical texts examining the Occupation so does it captivate the imagination of fiction writers. To understand the shift in representation of the Occupation vis-à-vis the return to democracy in 1990—a shift that maintains the Occupation's general underrepresentation in historical fiction while also diversifying the specific stories told about it—we must take account of its antecedent representations, including a series of fictional texts written in Spanish and French about Tounens and the kingdom. For the purposes of this study, I focus on a selection of representations created and consumed in Chile and Argentina: Armando Braun Menéndez's *El reino de Araucanía y Patagonia* (1936) and Víctor Domingo Silva's *El rey de Araucanía* (1936) in Chile, as well as Berta Tabbush's *El intruso* (1967) in Argentina. While these texts exclude others,[18] my selection centers the story orientations of texts that may speak to changes in the representation of the Occupation of Araucanía in *La corona*, the only novel addressing Tounens published in Chile after 1990.

The 1930s witnessed a small boom in Chilean historical fiction, though, as Antonia Viu notes, the production of historical fiction is fairly constant in the twentieth century and particularly so in its first half (127–28). Authors such as Sady Zañartu and Magdalena Petit published texts on other topics studied here; however, relatively few authors turned to the Occupation of Araucanía, the majority mining history to tell stories set during independence, the colonial period, and the War of the Pacific. Víctor Domingo Silva published a series of texts about the mestizo Alejo[19] set during the seventeenth century; he also published one on Tounens. *El Rey de la Araucanía: andanzas y malandanzas de S.M. Orelie Antoine I* presents a pro-Chilean view of Araucanía and endorses the interpretation of Tounens as a colonizing agent of France. Domingo Silva contrasts Tounens with the pirates, freebooters, and evil[20] mestizos of previous centuries (24). Instead, he is an eccentric and boastful adventurer; a dreamer who is good with words but has a questionable and indefinable character; a man possessed of a "teatral actitud de héroe de oleografía" (Domingo Silva 92): this version of Tounens fits with the fictional characters with whom he is compared: Don Quixote and Tartarin of Tarascon. While the early parts of the novel portray Tounens as a fairly harmless smooth talker, as the novel's plot develops these characteristics take a negative turn. Arrested by Chilean soldiers, he is "taciturno y sombrío" (110), gullible while also an impostor and usurper (112). Through the intercession of a Chilean interrogator, Domingo Silva also compares Tounens to a real-life figure whose luck in Latin America was fatal: Emperor Maximilian I, executed in Mexico in 1867. Putting these words in the mouth of an agent of the Chilean state makes them particularly threatening: "Francia está demasiado lejos . . . a vos os espera esa misma suerte . . . o quizás otra peor" (137). The question of Tounens's mental health proves ambiguous, though, as the narrative voice diagnoses megalomania (155) yet also admits that not all of Tounens's words and deeds are "impostura, alucinación o quimera" (145). And so Domingo Silva's Tounens is as much a character as the versions put forth by early historians. What grabs the attention is that the connection with France is made through the comparisons to Tartarin and Napoleon III through his proxy Maximilian rather than, as a number of historiographical texts consider, in contrast to Mapuche cultural and racial markers.

While the racial politics of *El Rey* do not depend on ridicule of racial and cultural mixing, the representation of the Mapuche as a people and culture conforms to expectations for a text written in the 1930s. Mapudungun is referred to as "el idioma de los bárbaros" (88), which labels both a people and their language.[21] Language is one index of culture; food, as seen in the first chapter, is another. French cuisine enjoyed an exalted reputation at the time Domingo Silva composed the novel. Tounens, with an assumedly sophisticated palate, reacts to the food he is served in Araucanía in a way that emphasizes its strangeness and rudimentary nature: "con más fuerza que gusto hubo de decidirse a ingerir los platos de la grosera y primitiva cocina mapuche" (67). The barbarians practice, in the terms of the text, vulgar and primitive foodways. Nevertheless, as with the language, Tounens throws himself into local customs.

Fictional invention in *El Rey* shines in the love triangle Domingo Silva creates between Tounens, his secretary Pietro Angelo Tappa, and a Mapuche woman named Piuke-Milla, which the original helpfully translates as "heart of gold." Tounens observes and admires this woman described as "suave, sonriente y humilde como todas las hembras de la raza aborigen" (69). She is sweet and caring and defined by her relationship to her father, Pinolevi. While Piuke-Milla is an invention, Huinka Pinolevi (ca. 1836–1868) was a Mapuche leader who remained loyal to agreements with the Chilean state, which brought a raid to his position in Purén that resulted in his death in 1868 (Bengoa 203–5). Tounens never speaks of his feelings for the young woman, and his secretary Tappa asks other young men about Mapuche marriage practices. After Tounens's arrest, he expresses horror on observing the Mapuche cavalry at a distance and discovering that Tappa and Piuke-Milla are presented as a couple. Where in historiographical versions Tounens performs an in-between cultural identity in his dress, in *El Rey* it is Tappa who lives in-between, a man "vestido arbitrariamente, medio a la europea, medio a la mapuche, y asimismo, con una rozagante hembra a las ancas del caballo" (110). Tounens is Caesar after Brutus's betrayal (111), only at this realization of his romantic failure entertaining the notion of a parallel suffering for his political aims. Nevertheless, when in Chile for the second and final time, Tounens meets Tappa and Piuke-Milla, at which point Tappa criticizes him for continuing his imperial projects in Araucanía.

> Aquí no se puede vivir sino como amigo del que, por tradición, tiene que conquistar esto, poseerlo, colonizarlo y entregarlo, como creación propia, a la civilización . . . Si insistís en quedaros, si esto realmente os gusta, haced lo que yo: poneos frente a frente de la selva, desmontadla, desbravadla, fecundadla, ayudad a los indios a salir de la barbarie, y moriréis tranquilo. (Domingo Silva 137)

Tappa emphasizes the inevitability of conquest and the inexorable march of progress from barbarism to civilization. Piuke-Milla, while present, does not participate in or reflect on the threats to her world, even as two men of European descent discuss the appropriate way to civilize an entire culture. Romance spices up the narrative in a familiar way: patterned after Doris Sommer, the indigenous woman and the white man together consolidate a possible symbolic foundation of the nation. Where Víctor Domingo Silva's novel deviates from the expected is in the identity of that white man, who is not the ostensible king fulfilling romantic and foundational duties. This narrative and its historical counterpart reflect the ultimate failure of both the establishment of the kingdom of Araucanía and Patagonia and Mapuche independence from the Chilean state.

Braun's *El reino* presents itself as a meticulously researched biography, complete with sources. Its narrator does not want the reader to believe that he has "abandonado el campo de la historia para adentrarme en el reino de la fantasía" (Braun 163). Nevertheless, the style with which the text is written shows greater affinity for fantastical accounts than historiography. By profession a historian, Braun is a scion of the most powerful family in Patagonia and also one of its first academic historians. Despite the author's disciplinary affiliation, however, biography here functions much like novels or the many "fictionalized autobiographies" published in the 1930s. As a member of a number of national Academies of History, Braun wrote a series of Spanish-language histories of Patagonia, Magallanes, and Tierra del Fuego. This role is complicated by his own pedigree: his family was intimately involved in the genocidal extermination of the Selk'nam nation.[22] The last few decades of the nineteenth century saw the introduction of sheep herding in Tierra del Fuego by landowners of European descent, most notably José Menéndez, Braun's grandfather. The herds of guanacos previously present in the area were wiped out and the Selk'nam, who were nomadic hunters, turned to the sheep for sustenance. As a result, the landowners pursued an extermination campaign, hunting the Selk'nam and offering bounties for others to do so as well. While the sins of the grandfather are not visited on the grandson, Braun Menéndez vituperatively defended the actions of his family. As the "official historian of the Braun, Menéndez, and Behety families" (Nicoletti 169), Braun disputed other histories written and mounted his case by using archival materials, including period newspaper accounts, as well as documents from the Salesian-run missions and indigenous reductions. Braun

> sostuvo, junto a los historiadores de la Academia de la Historia y con algunos salesianos (Entraigas y Massa), un intercambio epistolar con el que buscaba «limpiar» el buen nombre de sus antepasados y la «honra de los meritorios pioneers», justificando la extinción de los selk'nam por una «absoluta inadaptación física a la vida civilizada». Por otro lado, argumentaba que en realidad los selk'nam «ya era[n] muy escaso[s] a la llegada de los colonos» y en todo caso «si [estos] tuvieron que defender sus haciendas a balazos, jamás organizaron matanzas sistemáticas». (Nicoletti 169)

Braun's reiterated victim blaming—the Selk'nam were made extinct due to their inability to adapt to proper civilization in the form of church-run missions and reductions—undoubtedly influenced the way in which he portrays the story of Tounens in *El reino*.

Several elements in Braun's text repeat characterizations and connections made in earlier narratives. The dream of an independent Mapuche nation is described as a chimera (11) that leads to a variety of "escenario[s] de novela" (30). Tounens's physical appearance corresponds to the fortunes of his projects, most notably in the form of his hair. He possesses a prophet's beard (14) at the start of his quest, only to lose his stately mane to dysentery while jailed. More than simply hair, this was "el principal de los atributos físicos que cimentaban su personalidad" (63). Braun's narrative voice describes him as a criminal (87) obsessed with building a house of cards (103) to support his monarchical fiction (108). Tounens has Masonic connections (18) and is ultimately pitiable: "quejumbroso, acobardado y plebeyo" (63). The Chilean judge's determination of Tounens's madness is taken at face value, as are all assertions connected to the version privileging the Chilean state's perspective. Braun's narrative posits that the project of the kingdom of Araucanía and Patagonia is fundamentally national, patriotic, and, more than anything, French (76–77); emphasizing that upon his return to France, Tounens requested a state pension based on his colonizing enterprise in South America. He also highlights the work of Alberto Blest Gana who puts a stop to Tounens's machinations in Paris, again underlining that the true conflict was between competing colonial powers—Chile and France—though only France is described as such in the text.

The preoccupation of the text, as alluded in the title, is the kingdom itself. By kingdom, Braun does not mean people but rather territory. As was the case with Guevara, it is the land that is the subject of conflict; those already living on the land are an impediment to the domination of the land. The reader may note this distinction in the way Braun describes Mapuche territory as an interruption of territorial control for both Chile and Argentina (7). The border—not Araucanía—indicates "una verdadera línea de demarcación entre dos bandos irreconciliables: la civilización y esas tribus heroicas que defendían su suelo con ahínco feroz e indomable" (7).[23] The heroic image of the (defeated and dead) Mapuche warrior is again evoked in opposition to Western civilization, implicitly blocking the possibility for progress for either state. This is forcefully shown in the form of the map Braun describes of Araucanía and Patagonia: "señaladas ambas en los mapas de la época por colores diferenciados y con espacios vergonzantes en su desnudez toponímica" (9). The state doesn't recognize existing toponyms; instead, it creates a new reality by filling the map with its own invented information. In that way, it makes legible a space occupied by different people and cultures, obscured by the emptiness of the map itself.

El reino does not enter into much detail about Mapuche cultural practices; that largely blank slate makes a reference to a legend or vision from a machi particularly noteworthy. The text alludes to an apocryphal messianic legend foretelling salvation for the Mapuche in the form of a white man (33) who exoticizes them even as he ridicules their faith traditions. Tounens may be read as that particular white man, though the text underscores that he is but a false prophet and that true salvation comes through assimilation or annihilation at the hands of the civilizing Chilean state. The indigenous peoples in *El reino* are, then, objects to be civilized, a project that requires "el valor resistente de los conquistadores, o si no, el ánimo tenaz de los exploradores británicos; aunque tal vez bate la inconsciencia sublime y dominante de los iluminados" (79). Civilization is the ultimate goal, though Tounens's efforts fail and the righteousness of the Chilean state's actions is lauded. The failure of Tounens's civilizing project, in turn, contributes to the accuracy of Braun's narrative comparisons. Other texts repeatedly characterize Tounens as quixotic; Braun instead emplots his tale as one among many travel-adventure narratives. Nevertheless, Tounens's "afición inmoderada por los libros que traían el relato maravilloso de los viajes de La Pérouse, Cook, Dumont d'Urvill, Orbigny y otros navegantes" (10) compels the reader to recall the chapters of *Don Quixote* in which Quixote's reading habits are interrogated and critiqued. The supposed objectivity of the observer taking the clear position of the state as a civilizing agent reflects the mores of the author's own era and his positions vis-à-vis Araucanía.

Berta Tabbush's novel *El intruso* (1967) does not inhabit a generically indeterminate position: the novel presents a sympathetic view of Tounens while also showing the madness of his colonial enterprise. Tabbush describes Tounens in familiar terms: a "romántico caballero andante" (78) with an "aire de altiva dignidad" (49). *El intruso* itself focuses on Tounens's youth and continually reminds the reader of his affinity for stories and dreams. Early in the novel, his hair is styled like that of a poet (49); he is half-child, half-Quixote (130). Like the king in an operetta (132), he is dazzling and chimerical. As the novel develops, the narrator shows Tounens's growing belief in his own story while emphasizing to the reader that this story is fantasy—and, like the character himself, fanciful. While still in France, the young Tounens dreams of a crown and scepter in Calderonian rhythms: "imagina enormes montañas nevadas, bosques impenetrables, indígenas que se prosternan ante él, ¿y por qué no?, un harén de indias que lo rodean y veneran . . . olvida un solo detalle: que los sueños, sueños son . . ." (61). Tabbush's text orientalizes the Mapuche through Tounens's dream of a harem, which plays into readerly expectations that a European man who dreams of the Americas, as Tounens does, will find its deep structure in colonialist and imperialist desires. Tabbush's version of Tounens fashions a narrative arc in which the young dreamer optimistically pursues his dream only to face the destruction of his fantasy.

Unlike other texts, *El intruso* devotes nearly half of the novel to Tounens's life after his expulsion from Chile, both in France and in his attempted returns to South America. Tounens tells incredible anecdotes that even he ends up believing (193). His persistence in the project is described as his defining quality. Nevertheless, this self-deception leads to constant failure. In the second half of the novel, he keeps dreaming but nothing comes of it. He is wretched (221) and unfortunate (235, 303), and his tireless projects end up falling like a house of cards (219). Still, Tabbush's iteration of Tounens maintains his "incansable fantasía" (313) through optimistic imagination, despite all evidence to the contrary. The power of imagination also manifests in Tounens's gradual adaptation of visual markers of Mapuche identity. As a young man in France, he reflects that he must learn the crude (64) language of "esa gente (iba a decir "mis futuros súbditos". . .)" (63). His presumption about the unknown emphasizes the chimerical nature of his dream of commanding an independent monarchy. However, after his arrival in Chile, his hair no longer mimics that of a poet; it turns, instead, into a mane accompanied by an ever-longer beard. He maintains his elegant French clothing, though, and as time continues, one of his presumed allies makes fun of him for tying a red cloth around his head and wearing a poncho year-round. Despite this notable change in appearance, described as "el sello de localismo indígena" (134), polite society continues to ignore him.

El intruso eventually looks less intensely on Tounens's French origins as an explanatory force than do many earlier texts. Nevertheless, Tabbush's novel makes clear links between Tounens and a series of travel writers (51) whose work sought to document and categorize the unknown to European science. When speaking to a group of Chileans in Araucanía, he self-identifies as the disseminator of civilization among the Mapuche (144). The informed reader sees the source of that belief in the dichotomy of civilization and barbarism and as a major goal of imperial projects. After all, "the symbolic opposition ... between "savages" and "civilization," was constructed as part of the discourse of European hegemony, projecting cultural inferiority as an ideological ground for political subordination" (Ellingson xiii). If the land was savage and in need of domination, Tounens's self-identification with Arauco's landscape complicates his association with European travel writers:

> En este instante se siente identificado con el árbol rey del bosque araucano. Y su imaginación elabora fantásticos sueños que borran por completo todo su pasado, que hacen desaparecer toda la realidad. Se cree auténticamente señor del Arauco; su alma vibra al unísono con el paisaje mojado, con las tinieblas que lo envuelven. (152)

The trope of the dream frames this reflection, echoing the references to Calderón de la Barca's *La vida es sueño* earlier in the novel. Whereas late-nineteenth-century historiography used Tounens as a talisman representing indigenous uprisings, in *El intruso* he is lost in a dream that can never be. Rather than pathologizing his fantasies, the novel presents a sympathetic portrayal in which Tounens, as history documents, ultimately fails, but the voices of ridicule remain relatively quiet. He is neither lionized nor openly mocked, though one might consider his isolation a form of mockery.

This relatively sympathetic perspective extends to several indigenous representations in the novel. Mañil, a Mapuche leader key to uprisings in the 1850s, is described in exacting detail. Tabbush depicts him as noble, strong, and forceful; his dark eyes are intense and intelligent (21). His son, Quilapán, is also viewed as noble and strong but tempered with kindness (120). While these characterizations call to mind the image of the noble savage,[24] both men are portrayed as possessing greater agency than in other versions in which most indigenous people are an undistinguished mass and their leaders are hoodwinked by the French aggressor. Nevertheless, the fact that *El intruso* reproduces Mapuche speech as broken Spanish contributes to the representation of the Mapuche in the novel. On the one hand, the dreamer Tounens hopes to civilize them. On the other hand, they conform to noble savage stereotypes and their linguistic expression implies cultural inferiority. The agency of Mapuche leaders is further limited by a belief in the return of the king (38);[25] Tounens's presence is again presented as predestined, though ultimately a failure. As Tounens fails in making his dream of an independent Araucanía a reality, so also does he fail in acting on any of his romantic love notions: "las expansiones eróticas no son para este Amiel araucano . . ." (261). Tabbush's novel dedicates equal time to the construction of the dream of a kingdom in Chile, Tounens's exile in France, his 1869 return to Patagonia and ultimate failure there, and, lastly, to France once again. Like Domingo Silva and Braun, Tabbush focuses on literary comparisons, firmly placing Tounens in the world of dream and fantasy.

Where earlier historians utilize Tounens as a way to make legible indigenous rebellion against European civilization, in fictional reproductions the tendency is to emphasize the impossibility of Tounens's project. These texts accentuate its failure and privilege state narratives that view the threat of an independent Araucanía as quaint. These stories are encoded in Western myths, references, and frames of references, which reveal a limited narrative imagination that can only make sense of the Occupation through the cultural eyes of the conquerors.

The Crown of Araucanía

With the return to democracy in 1990, Chilean cultural and ethnic diversity entered the public conversation in ways that were not possible under dictatorship. In terms of official government policy and practice, CONADI (National Corporation of Indigenous Development) came into being with the Indigenous Law in 1993. As of 2018, the Ministry of Culture, Arts, and Heritage follows principles such as cultural diversity, interculturality, mutual respect among communities, and the recognition of, respect for, and promotion of indigenous cultures. Indigenous concerns have also been the subject of the work of the Commission of Historical Truth and a New Agreement with Indigenous Peoples (2001–2003). However, it can also be shown that the Law of State Security (Ley 12.927) and the Antiterrorist Law (Ley 18.314) have been used disproportionately against Mapuche individuals in their claims of rights and identity independent from the state; and that the popular press often conflates indigenous political activity with crime and terrorism, which erases the ethnic dimension of conflict in Southern Chile.[26] It is in this context that Pedro Staiger published one of the relatively few historical novels set during the Occupation written post-1990, as well as the only one published in Chile that focuses on Tounens: *La corona*.[27] Impossibility permeates the novel, reflecting the problematic nature of speaking for and identifying with discriminated groups when the voice of the dominant group is louder. One might read the novel's full title as a gesture toward this impossibility, as it centers on the crown rather than the person as an impossible dialogue. It is the image of power rather than the one who exercises it that the title names. This shifts attention away from the individual and extraordinary person common in both narrative and history.

Staiger's novel follows the literary trend that combines an interest in retelling historical events from differing perspectives while utilizing postmodern narrative tools that question epistemologies surrounding narrative and history. In the prologue of the novel, he argues that this episode has been misrepresented in fiction and deserves a new treatment, with the intention of "la simple invitación a imaginar un acontecimiento singular y pintoresco, como genuinamente humano de nuestro acontecer. Es reivindicar una figura que en los textos sacrosantos de nuestra historia sólo ha merecido el desprecio y la burla" (11). Tounens has at times been represented as a bit of a buffoon, and Staiger's prologue emphasizes that this text does not intend to follow that path. In addition, the author notes a balance between history and fiction in his proposed retelling of the story of the Occupation through the story of Tounens.

> La mayor parte de las huellas que dejó este singular monarca se han borrado y son hoy irrecuperables. Será imposible reflotar sus verdaderas y últimas intenciones, el grado de compromiso que pueda haber existido en la corte de Francia, la real adhesión que haya recibido de los araucanos . . . pero es, sobre todo, una novela. Una obra de ficción. (9)

As he continues, he argues that he has done his best to be accurate in his representations, consulting as vast a bibliography as he could access, but that nothing portrayed in the novel should be viewed as authoritative. The narrative frame of the novel affirms this orientation since Tounens tells his story to his niece Marie as he is in a delirium from fever. His health highlights that he cannot distinguish the truth from invention. This conceit also functions to the same effect in earlier comparisons to Quixote and allusions to madness. This narrative emphasizes the deathbed confessional structure of the novel and follows a chronological pattern of events, though always filtered through the frame of fever.

Unlike other texts in which madness implies doubts not only about Tounens as a narrator or witness but also about his imperial project as a whole, the narrative frame underscores a physical illness that also calls into question memory and knowledge. The narrative voice, sharing the perspective of Tounens's niece, describes the family's general reaction to him, which happens to mirror the point of view expressed in historiography and various fictional pieces:

> Desde que tiene memoria, la mención de su tío ha provocado una cierta irritación en la familia. Cejas erguidas en súbitos rigores, sonrisas que se congelan, risas estancadas, conversaciones que se interrumpen. . . . Recuerda vagamente que el abuelo Jean solía defender a su hermano y también, que ello atraía las observaciones irónicas de los demás. "Tu hermano rey y sus locuras." (15–16)

Tounens embarrasses the family. How different is the mad king from the king and his madness? This formula distances Tounens ever so slightly from the conflation of his projects and his mental state, using one to discredit the other. This follows the pattern of the narrative Tounens weaves throughout telling his story to Marie: he challenges the madness that explains his actions in other texts. After months of incarceration and in weak physical health, the narrator postulates that yes, his vague and weak responses might imply that "no las tiene todas consigo" (109). However, he also observes that what some identify as monomania has lead him to live an extraordinary life. Madness is an unacceptable explanation for this story, despite the night he spends in Santiago's insane asylum.

The mental consequences of Tounens's physical sufferings are brushed aside for much of the novel. Any connection with mental instability is challenged or at the least modified when he writes, for example, of "su postulada locura" (109), which plants a seed of doubt about any diagnosis. The protagonist's experience in the Casa de Orates complicates this picture; those interned in the madhouse with him accept him as one of their own (111). Tounens segregates himself mentally from the other residents, secure in the knowledge that the French diplomatic corps will remove him from this place in the morning. Despite this, the environment of the asylum doubly undermines the reorientation of Tounens's story away from the illustrative power of madness. "Aquí, en el manicomio, todos son reyes o emperadores. Todos poseen su propio mundo y ejercen en él su soberanía. Aquí, él es apenas un rey más" (111). In the asylum, Tounens loses individuality and through that loss inhabits the expected space: the mad French king.

Tounens's Frenchness remains important in the novel; while visiting Santiago and Valparaíso in search of support for his independent kingdom, he has a short interview with the French ambassador, who silently compares Tounens's project to Maximilian's adventure in Mexico. Staiger's ambassador, Cazotte, chooses not to support Tounens not because of any particular piece of his project but out of political self-interest as he does not want to be left on the hook should things go badly. This is of particular importance to Cazotte as he is early in his diplomatic career and finds himself in the uncomfortable position of losing much and gaining little (86). His reports to Paris function "bajo el prisma de una fundamentada duda sobre la sanidad mental de su visita y quedarán, obviamente, sin respuesta" (87). Even though this young and ambitious ambassador doubts Tounens's sanity, when Tounens is back in France, he secures an audience with French Emperor Napoleon III himself. However, the narrative sows doubt and suspicion in the reader over this otherwise private and secret meeting, which allows for plausible deniability of its having occurred. Tounens's unambiguous connections with France in *La corona* function primarily as political possibilities in contrast to earlier texts that overlap these political links with cultural practices.

Tounens tries to bring these political links to bear in the armed conflict between the Chilean state and the Mapuche to no avail. Staiger's text repeatedly emphasizes the injustice of the treatment of the Mapuche. Early in the novel Arauco "bleeds:"

A juicio de todo el mundo, sus súbditos no son libres ni son sus súbditos.

Los toman por un tropel de bárbaros salvajes y borrachos que han perdido su país sin saberlo. Ciudadanos de segunda clase en su propio territorio, despreciados, empleados como peones y braceros en quienes no se puede confiar por su embriaguez irresponsable. Los quieren arrastrar a que, cuando el ocaso de sus vidas se aproxime, no tengan ya dioses propios que adorar y rueguen a dioses extraños que no les oyen. Que sean huéspedes malvenidos a la tierra que los vio nacer y que llorará sus muertes en silencio. (19)

The armed conflict is described as "la más franca y brutal guerra de exterminio" (137), and it is the "civilized" Chilean state that carries out its worst abuses. Part of that war of extermination also entails the destruction of food sources and attacks on civilian populations. Eventually Tounens shares the Mapuche leadership's conviction that diplomacy is impossible. Although his Frenchness seizes on anchoring political advantage, as do other texts, Tounens himself evolves. That is evident in his relationship with Araucanía as a political entity and with his greater understanding of the Mapuche, particularly by the transformation his shared experiences with the Mapuche wrought on his life.

Still, Tounens's choice of Araucanía, never having set foot outside of France previously, remains a coincidence that invites speculation. In Staiger's novel Tounens offers several vacillating explanations, which are notable for the multiplicity of options they imply as well as their lack of consideration of the Mapuche as individuals with a culture totally foreign to his own. The public response—"que no había más reinos disponibles en este mundo, en espera de que alguien los conquistara. No era cierto, además" (27)—wasn't true by his own admission. His inspiration came from the word Araucanía itself, which was a name imposed on the Mapuche by the Spaniards that was based in Quechua, the language of the Inka colonizers. Nevertheless, Tounens imagines the word "hecha de greda y agua, de madera y música. La ha oído por primera vez y ha comprendido de inmediato que ese sería su reino. Que no era otro, que no buscaría más" (28). The people themselves only appear as less-than-ideal royal subjects, described as hostile y indispuesto toward recognizing a governor (27). This continues the mythical and stereotypical image of the Mapuche put forward since the sixteenth century. Although Tounens aspires to be leader of the Mapuche, at this point in the narrative he identifies most thoroughly with Western colonizing power:

> Él, en cambio, persona audaz e inteligente, vanguardia de un Imperio culto, mensajero de la civilización y la ciencia, podría establecer una monarquía, única forma de gobierno susceptible de grandes realizaciones. Las repúblicas vecinas de Chile y Argentina protestarían, seguramente, pero terminarían por aceptar una solución que, en el fondo, les era conveniente: que alguien sometiera a los indios y estableciese las bases de una nación civilizada. (31)

Again, civilization and barbarism reflect an epistemological perspective that seeks civilization over and against autochthonous forms of knowledge. That view is of course alien to the Tounens who desires to be Mapuche later in the novel, but this later incarnation forms a stark contrast with earlier texts in which his adoption is political and cosmetic.

When Chilean forces are pushing back again Mapuche resistance, Tounens shares the experiences of detention and exile with many Mapuche. However, he can never become one of them despite his desire to adapt to their way of life. During his time among the Mapuche, Tounens experiences a transformation:

> Se reconoce de menos en menos como huinca y comparte, en cambio, con sus súbditos combatientes el galope salvaje por la tierra, no esquiva su presencia en alguna maloca vengadora. La vincha roja que cruza su frente, el poncho que cubre sus hombros son cada vez menos un adorno exótico y curioso como en los primeros días, es el atuendo genuino que ha escogido por un rey plenamente identificado con su pueblo. (141)

Note that this sense of identification does not convert Tounens into something he is not, but it does signal a desire of becoming like yet not the same. He is not embraced as such by those he identifies with. The center of knowledge and meaning remains Tounens. He apes the actions and dress of the people he seeks to serve through his leadership as King but is ultimately asked to leave by Quilapán, who explains the strategic disadvantage of his presence. This detail of Staiger's plotting contrasts with the normative narrative in which Tounens is expelled by the state. Unlike previous narratives, Mapuche leaders have agency and use it. Despite this shift, the continued centering of the European reflects the general tendency of the Chilean state and hegemonic culture to privilege whiteness over and against nonwhiteness, even more, Mapucheness, a force still legible through Tounens.

Although Tounens is a less than perfect ally to the Mapuche in his actions, Staiger's novel contrasts his well-meaning but ineffective desire to support the rebellion against the state with the narratives of urban Chilean society. Tounens rejects the version of indigenous life found in the mainstream press, which he describes as a feverish concert of anti-Indian diatribes (42–43). He seeks to lead, but in an ethical way. He wants to learn not only Spanish but also Mapudungun; the difficulty of learning the language without direct contact with the people who speak it reflects contemporary language-use concerns (43).[28] Tounens aches to lead an Indian raid to exact vengeance for the violence of the *huincas* and the *colonos* against the Mapuche. However, at the close of the novel, he rationalizes his failure—one of many—to do so as his benevolent submission to the wishes of "his subjects" (143). In *La corona*, then, Staiger tells the story of a historically extant individual who thought he could "speak for"—congruent with a model of servant leadership—the native people of Araucanía and Patagonia. The author, however, destabilizes a view of Tounens as savior or interpreter through postmodern narrative moves that call into question the veracity of this account, particularly by his questioning the mental state of the protagonist. In that way, the novel undermines Tounens and through him his colonizing project.

Conclusion

Historical fiction about the Occupation of Araucanía disproportionately tells the story of Orélie-Antoine de Tounens, King of Araucanía and Patagonia, and the experiences of both Chilean soldiers and Mapuche residents of the lands south of the Bío-Bío River. All novels figure the relationship between Tounens and the Mapuche differently: a false prophet (Braun); a pathetic in-between figure (Domingo Silva); a conduit for parallels to indigenous leadership (Tabbush); and an individual unable to breach the chasm of his own perceptions and Mapuche reactions (Staiger). No matter the development of this relationship, the narrative focus on Tounens makes indigenous resistance to the state legible not only to Chile but also to international audiences.

Fiction has yet to come to terms with a different way to tell this story that doesn't fall into the trap of using Tounens to make sense of the resistance of a marginalized group. The closest fiction has come to breaking free of this mold are in Sorín's ironic metanarrative *A King and his Movie* and Staiger's *La corona*. Might a possible solution to this challenge involve removing Tounens from the story altogether? What might a text look like with Quilapán as a hero?[29] The civilized nature of the texts about Tounens and the Occupation belie the undergirding violence of war. While a text such as *El lento silbido de los sables* uses extreme and grotesque violence to portray the Occupation, it does so from the perspective of Chilean soldiers, which again obscures the perspective of the Mapuche. Either way, the stories of the Occupation don't make sense of a genocidal and unjust conflict: they depend on a narrative imagination unwilling to engage with victim perspectives.

Postlude: The Other War

As the military conflict in the south between Chilean government and Mapuche groups continued its cycles of violence, the government also had its eye on the northern border. In 1879, the conflict in the south simmered but would not boil again until 1881; it was in the final years of the Occupation that explicit and sustained military conflict existed in both north and south. In the north, the War of the Pacific featured the Chilean military sweeping north, ultimately occupying Lima in 1881 and defeating the Bolivian-Peruvian alliance, with treaties signed with Peru in 1883 and Bolivia in 1884. In the 1870s Chile suffered a number of problems, among them a weak economy and climatic elements that contributed to it. An agreement between Chile and Bolivia in which Bolivia promised not to raise export taxes for Chile was signed in 1874. Later, the approval and implementation of tax increases on saltpeter exports, along with the large number of Chilean workers residing in Bolivian territory, prompted the Chilean government to action. Between February 1879 and October 1883, in the case of Peru, or April 1884 in the case of Bolivia, all three nations were swept up in armed conflict.[30] At the end of the day, Chile won.[31]

As one might imagine, the stories of the War of the Pacific are plentiful. Every 21 May the current Chilean President gives a State of the Union-esque speech on a holiday marked on calendars as the "Naval Battle of Iquique." Chilean forces blockaded the port of Iquique, waiting for Peruvian ships to come south to challenge the cordon. On 21 May 1879, the Peruvian ironclad *Huáscar* arrived and engaged the Chilean corvette *Esmeralda*. Even though that battle ended with the sinking of the *Esmeralda* and the death of three-quarters of her officers and crew, their sacrifice in the name of their country is held up as exemplary to this day. What was a Peruvian victory militarily rallied Chilean citizens to fight and changed the Chilean understanding of the conflict. In contrast to the Occupation, the War of the Pacific celebrates Chilean patriotism and builds up heroes like Arturo Prat, commander of the *Esmeralda*, and the archetype of the *roto chileno*, the valiant mixed-race Everyman. These were both bloody conflicts and occurred during the same time period, though the War of the Pacific depended much more on the importance of naval power than the land-based conflict in the south. Both expand Chilean territory and end in Chilean victory. However, the northern conflict lends itself to triumphal and patriotic stories, while the southern conflict illustrates the contradictions inherent in Chilean society's origin stories.

In the period of the democratic transition, the War of the Pacific has been seen as a subject that lends itself to audiovisual historical fiction; writers practicing the innovations of the postmodern historical novel choose different time periods to tell their stories. Even in the context of the 2010 bicentennial celebrations, notable historical fiction on the War of the Pacific shows stories on the screen rather than the page.[32] The 2007 series of made-for-TV movies *Héroes* (Canal 13) features a film dedicated to Arturo Prat. Historical film drama *Esmeralda 1879* was released in theaters in 2010 after producers spent a record amount of money in its filming. As was also the case with the series *Héroes*, schoolchildren were incentivized to see the film, with two movie theaters in Santiago offering free showings and other theaters offering discounted tickets ("Cines abrirán"). Dedicating an entire film to Peru's Pyrrhic victory emphasizes the role it plays in the Chilean imagination, though the film itself was described in one review as "una notable recreación visual de textos escolares que sin duda supera con creces el esfuerzo televisivo de Prat" (Alaluf). The eight-episode television series *Algo Habrán Hecho por la Historia de Chile* (Televisión Nacional, 2010) covers the War of the Pacific in a bit more than thirty minutes spread over two episodes; in contrast, the Occupation of

Araucanía merits three minutes as a point of transition between the War of the Pacific and the government of José Manuel Balmaceda (the subject of chapter 5).[33]

To put this into perspective, the series covers Chilean history from 1540 to 1910 in about six hours, and over eight percent of that time is dedicated to this one conflict. About one-eighth of one percent of that time is dedicated to the Occupation of Araucanía. Those three minutes present a view of the Occupation that emphasizes not just its violence but also its uncivilized nature: that it was a conflict not of armies but a struggle of the Chilean army against a people, combatants and noncombatants, that resulted in the loss to the Mapuche of what they value most in "their" culture, "their" land. As if to limit that sympathy, though, the script emphasizes in its choice of pronouns that the expected audience for this program in 2010, the "we," are Chileans; the Mapuche, to be sure, are a group apart and not real Chileans.

Episode 6 of *Algo Habrán Hecho* (1840–1879) closes with the two hosts, actor Francisco Melo and historian Manuel Vicuña, going out to a buoy that marks the place where the *Esmeralda* was sunk. The camera lingers on that buoy, flying a Chilean flag in the northern sun.[34] That image represents Chile: tenacity in the face of defeat.[35] However, popular culture celebrates the northern war and overlooks or looks away from the conflict in the south. The character and use of Orélie-Antoine de Tounens, singular representative of the Occupation, differs dramatically from that of Arturo Prat, hero of the Naval Battle of Iquique.[36] The War of the Pacific resulted in territorial gains for Chile, as did the Occupation; however, where the first war fits within a framework of nation-states at war, the second does not as the normative story forgoes recognizing the sovereignty of indigenous nations. The Occupation challenges the narrative of Chilean righteousness by refusing to allow "feel-good" stories of sacrifice for the nation to paper over the underlying consolidation of national territory and belonging through violence.

CHAPTER FIVE
Civil War

IMAGINE THAT YOU ARE elected to congress when you are only twenty-four years old. Imagine that you are lauded for your public speaking and named government minister. Imagine that you are elected President at forty-six and that you preside over a country that only a few years earlier had triumphed over its regional competitors. Imagine your drive to modernize and connect your country through massive public works projects and educational reform. Imagine your role in a strongly centralized Presidential political system. Now: imagine Congress refuses to approve your annual budget. Imagine that you move ahead using the budget of the previous year, and in response Congress and the Navy declare war on you and your supporters. Imagine that after eight months of armed conflict, your forces are defeated. Imagine that you take refuge in the Argentine embassy and send your family and friends elsewhere to try to keep them safe. Imagine what you would do the day you stopped being president.

José Manuel Balmaceda (1840–1891) chose to take his own life, perhaps the most notorious casualty of the Chilean Civil War of 1891. Civil war is never pleasant. Civil wars change how communities tell stories about themselves. With a civil war, a community faces the reality of brokenness and that sundering of relationships and civil society requires a reckoning. A common tale of Chilean political history perpetuates the idea that Chile was a model democracy prior to the 1973 military coup. However, in addition to the 1891 Civil War, said model democracy featured de facto dictatorships and genocidal campaigns against indigenous persons. The conclusion of both the Occupation of Araucanía and the War of the Pacific in 1883 and the opportunities and challenges Chile's territorial expansion offered as the turn of the century approached shape the context in which political conflict and violence broke out into a formal war between the president, the Congress, and their respective supporters.

The figure of José Manuel Balmaceda focuses work on this historical process, both in history and fiction. Despite all this attention, this individual was not the only actor in the conflict. And so to understand the significance of this conflict in Chilean narratives and culture, it is helpful to gauge the shape of the conflict. Having gained significant sources for increased prosperity from two armed conflicts of territorial expansion ending in the first half of the 1880s, Chile's wealth grew, and it was this growth, along with other factors, that led to political conflict. As the fourth consecutive president from the Liberal party, Balmaceda was wildly popular when elected in 1886. However, his popularity plummeted as the opposition and members of his own party resisted the implementation of his political platform involving massive public works projects and educational reform. Resistance to this agenda, as well as dissatisfaction with the presidential system, based on the Constitution of 1833, led to his political opponents declaring war against him at the start of 1891. The Navy sided with Congress, the Army with the president. From January to August 1891, Congress consolidated power in the northern city of Iquique and several battles occurred throughout the year, though the most important battles were joined in August. The congressionalist forces triumphed, and Balmaceda sought refuge in the Argentine Embassy before committing suicide the morning of 19 September 1891. The day before, on 18 September, he had concluded his constitutionally mandated presidential period. The war itself was the bloodiest in Chilean history, with between 15,000 and 20,000 Chileans killed.

Historical fiction dealing with the Civil War of 1891 written and published after 1990 invites two questions related to difference and inclusion that coalesce around political position and social markers of class. What does it mean to tell the story of violence within the body politic? And what does the historical breakdown of developing democratic structures signify? Historical fiction enjoys a rare place to answer these questions because in it history, memory, and the archive work dynamically to re-create the past—here the 1891 Civil War—by re-fictionalizing and reimagining it beyond its historicity.

Two novels about the Civil War anchor this chapter: Darío Oses's *El viaducto* and Isidora Aguirre's *Balmaceda*. As is the case for nearly all narratives regarding 1891, lament and regret color both. Their representations of difference deepen reader understanding of how violence and social privilege, historically depicted, discover their fictional parallels in dictatorship narratives.

Historiography and Difference

Social class marks individuals in Chilean society. At the end of the nineteenth century and beginning of the twentieth, "no other identity marker proved more compelling among Chileans and more pervasive in their political culture than the idea of class" (Barr-Melej 4–5). In the twenty-first century "Chileans are more likely to elide race altogether, preferring to emphasize class as a social marker" (Richards 8), though it is important to note that elision is not erasure or absence. Constructions and perceptions of race influence social interactions without being named or recognized as such. The term social class describes a system of hierarchy within a society, and is always "contingent, experiential, and actively constructed" (Milanich 13). Patricia Hill Collins describes social class, along with other identity categories such as race, religion, age, or gender, as a major system of oppression (219). Social class also shapes inclusion and exclusion as one reads about the Civil War of 1891. Historiography often seeks to interpret the impact of the conflict on the elite—seeing an important turning point of the war in the Lo Cañas massacre, for example, in which many scions of upper-class families were killed. Fiction also emphasizes the class-based experiences of the war.

Racialized social class in Chile has developed between 1891 and the present day. Immediately after independence, Chile was a society "todavía muy jerarquizada y rígida y sin formación política" dominated politically, economically, socially, and culturally by a small and homogenous group of landowners whose economic interests began to expand into mining and trade (Sagredo *Vapor* 35). As the nineteenth century progressed, this elite, at times referred to as the aristocracy or upper class, fought among itself for political power and allowed limited access to newcomers, for example European immigrant mercantilists. That group has continued in power to the present day, identified by "hectáreas de tierra, apellidos y un fuerte sentido de pertenencia a un grupo vinculado por el parentesco" (Contardo 46–47). This "elite endogámica más blanca que las clases inferiores" (Contardo 35) illustrates the privilege of whiteness within Latin America's pigmentocracy. However, "whiteness is not self-evident; rather, it seems to be largely shaped by the nation and its history, racial ideologies, racial composition, and norms of behavior" (Telles and Flores 442). Chile, as with several other countries in the region, is a place "whose elites have imagined their nations as white in contrast to other countries of the region, [which has] also led to a more common identification as white, adjusting for actual color differences" (442). Contrary to the rhetoric of mestizo nationalism in much of the rest of the region, Chilean rhetoric has affirmed binaries between "Chilean," variably defined, and others both within and outside national borders.

The historiography of the Civil War of 1891 does not explicitly deal with notions of racialized social class. While a general understanding exists that "la estratificación social, aun aquella de carácter capitalista, siempre ha ido acompañada de un elemento racial: en Chile, de manera general, mientras más oscura la piel, más baja la clase social" (Larraín *Identidad* 232), the grand sweep of historiographical narratives of 1891 do not apply historical thinking to that stratification. "Balmaceda is often regarded as a great national hero who was brought down by a nefarious combination of selfish and unpatriotic Chilean economic interests and acquisitive foreign capitalists, particularly British, both of whom felt threatened by [him]" (Blakemore 400). James Blakemore surveys the historiography of the Civil War from the vantage point of the mid-1960s. He identifies two historical strands: those thinkers who seek to determine who had the constitution on their side and those who examine economic motivations for the conflict, especially as they relate to the nitrate industry and foreign capital. While Blakemore suggests related areas for further study, they remain occupied by the motivations, experiences, and consequences for the aristocracy. This is not unexpected, given that social history as a mode of inquiry was only just beginning to find its feet at the time Blakemore was writing. However, as social history blossomed in the 1970s and later, the study of the Civil War remained fairly old-fashioned in its preference for constitutional and economic explanations.

In the late 1970s and in the midst of the dictatorship, Marcos García de la Huerta identified three streams of historiographical interpretation of the conflict: political causes, economic motivators, and a combination of political and socioeconomic explanations (Sagredo *Vapor* 541). This small step in expanding historiographical inquiry continued after the fall of the dictatorship. Historians took advantage of the 1991 centennial of the conflict to refocus their attention on the Civil War, arguing that it is "en sí misma uno de los acontecimientos más importantes de la historia nacional" (Bravo Díaz 121) as a hinge point between political eras (that same year was also a transition point as Chile's political class tried to relearn democratic practices). Pablo Bravo Díaz surveys the historiography in the century since the Civil War to identify a series of categories within which the work can be identified. While constitutional and economic studies remain part of the body of study, topics have expanded to include the role of the church, memorials, as well as theater, novels, and music. The most common categories remain political causes of the conflict and Balmaceda.[1]

As the transition period continued, historiographical interest in the Civil War waned. Two examples that illustrate how the historiography has become more expansive in its understanding of the conflict, though still focused primarily on the aristocracy, can be found in Rafael Sagredo's study on Balmaceda's use of political theater and Bernardo Subercaseaux's work on the history of ideas and culture at the end of the nineteenth century. Subercaseaux studies the 1891 Civil War as a pivot point in Chilean cultural history and its role related to the fin-de-siècle culture locally and regionally. When he surveys the patterns in historiography of the conflict, he identifies four trends: the political constitutional argument; socioeconomic explanations; an interclass conflict; and personalist readings. Historiography at the end of the twentieth century tends to be eclectic, "a rectificar o matizar lecturas previas y a interrelacionar—o a situar en su justa dimensión—los distintos factores que incidieron en el conflicto" (*Historia* 32). Subercaseaux's project, however, emphasizes how this conflict set the stage for Chile's cultural modernization. He concludes that "no es casual, entonces, que el año 1891 haya sido concebido como una especie de metáfora del país moderno; como una fecha clave en las periodizaciones históricas; como un hito en que ya se perfilan con nitidez los principales actores sociales, culturales y políticos del nuevo siglo" (*Historia* 36). The many cultural functions of 1891 influence not only political and economic development in Chile but also cultural production and later narratives understanding Chilean identity.

Sagredo's work surveys how government travel between 1883 and 1891 represented presidential power and expanded participation in political life throughout the country. The political theater of these systematic and spectacular visits sought to build support for Balmaceda's vision for Chilean society. He

> transformó el territorio nacional en un escenario copado por su figura y por la institución que personificaba . . . se sirvió de los símbolos nacionales y de la historia patria para hacer partícipes de sus representaciones a la población nacional, pretendiendo que la sugestión que su presencia despertaba se abonara a lo que él representaba en cuanto actor político cabeza de una administración progresista y emprendedora, en un país cuyo adelanto parecía no tener límites. (*Vapor* 20–21)

Notions of progress and modernity characterize Balmaceda's policies and accomplishments, such as reinvesting the profits generated from the nitrate industry into major capital projects, including railroads and schools. Sagredo interprets Balmaceda's death as a precondition of his function as a political symbol. By committing suicide, Balmaceda "se transformó en imagen, en modelo de inspiración para las generaciones que le siguieron. En cuanto político, y con su gesto final, Balmaceda pasó a nutrir él mismo la mitología que le concediera fuerza, sentido y eficacia simbólica a su figura" (Sagredo *Vapor* 451). Both Sagredo and Subercaseaux share this perception of the importance of Balmaceda as an inspirational image, and it is this aspect of the historiography that most often surfaces in Chilean historical narratives of the conflict. Nevertheless,

> Desde el punto de vista histórico e historiográfico, la Revolución iniciada en enero de 1891 y que habría de derivar en Guerra Civil, constituye un verdadero desafío para los investigadores. No solo por el significado que la misma tuvo en la trayectoria nacional sino, además, porque hoy, a cien años de ella, y pese a la gran cantidad de títulos que la abordan, aun no se tiene una explicación lo suficientemente convincente de las causas que la motivaron. (Sagredo "Prólogo" 9)

While there may be multiple approaches in the historiography of Balmaceda and the Civil War, what dominates the historical imagination is the figure of Balmaceda and the tragedy of the war itself.

The First Hundred Years of Fiction

The historiography shows the importance of the stories of the Civil War to the development and understanding of Chilean national symbolism. Per historian Cecilia Méndez, "mental constructions really do matter because they lead humans to carry out precisely the kinds of things that we, in turn, group under the label of 'making history'" (29). That process of making history began as soon as the war concluded, as various writers put forth their interpretation of events, trying to establish their perspectives of the conflict. This meaning-making crosses genres and sides of the conflict, with prose, poetry, and theater telling and retelling events and repeating frames. Those studying these texts, primarily written and published between 1891 and 1915, have consigned to them propaganda with little literary merit. Indeed, "el legado (literario) más importante del 91, en calidad y cantidad, se encuentra no en los géneros tradicionales sino en los recuerdos, testimonios, impresiones y memorias" (Subercaseaux "El 91" 125). The literary quality of the works, however, does not change that they were the beginning of the "mitificación póstuma de Balmaceda" (Subercaseaux "El 91" 124). This process continued on and off throughout the twentieth century. One need only note the epigraph of Luis Enrique Délano's 1944 text *JM Balmaceda* to get a sense of the way the winds blew: "A la insurrección de 1891 (que derribó al presidente Balmaceda) no le dimos nunca el nombre de Revolución, porque nunca vimos que el pueblo se pusiera de parte de los rebeldes. La consideramos obra de una oligarquía temerosa de perder su imperio" (5). While this epigraph encompasses Délano's political leanings as a member of the Communist Party, its class-based assumptions foreshadow later social history.

The Civil War of 1891 motivated literary production from its own time and has continued to do so. While there were flurries of texts written and published in the fifty years or so after the war, after *JM Balmaceda* little finds its way to publication until 1991. That year not only corresponds to the centennial of the war but also marks an early year in the transition from dictatorship to democracy. Beyond the general expansion of Chilean historical fiction in democracy, the centennial provides a natural motive for reexamining the Civil War and Balmaceda. The nineteenth century was a popular subject regionally, functioning as "un artefacto para pensar algunos problemas de cultura, construido con discursos y prácticas de todo tipo" (Ludmer qtd. in Montaldo 15). Chilean critic Antonia Viu notes that commemorative dates often correspond to the publication of historical fiction that "se usa como muestra de vinculación o simpatía, y también como la marca mediante la cual se intenta consignar el mérito de una acción, en este caso de una acción no valorada justamente en su momento" (156). The majority of novels written during the transitional period on the Civil War reflect this orientation toward the past: passing judgment on past events and valuing certain figures or events differently than in their own time.

In early transitional fiction, novels participated in the overall rehabilitation of the figure of President Balmaceda, who is never portrayed as a villain and often appears as a tragically misunderstood figure. These novels reflect that his public works projects were the right path for Chile to have taken. Texts frame the war as inevitable yet unnecessary, and narratives follow a sequential progression of events, though the specifics of the events vary. All tell the story in a more or less chronological manner. Two historical novels published at the centennial follow romantic plots centered on fictional characters, with the war itself as the canvas on which the story is painted. These novels portray Balmaceda and his supporters as righteous and correct. For would-be lovers during the Civil War, things rarely end well, especially for Balmaceda's supporters. These traditionally straightforward historical novels—featuring fictional characters who are affected by but not protagonists of the main historical events—present a *costumbrista*-style portrait of Chile in 1891.

Juan Gabriel Araya's *1891 entre el fulgor y la agonía* (1990) tells the tragic love story of soldier Amadeo Caire and Dolores Balmaceda, daughter of the president.[2] Amadeo's loyalty to the president costs him dearly, as both he and Dolores are killed in their attempt to flee to Argentina at the end of the novel. Because he is the tragic hero, Amadeo diverges both in love and politics from the rest of the novel's characters. Most characters are archetypal and unindividualized. In contrast, Amadeo's upstanding character severely critiques the parliamentary position nestled within a vividly drawn environment. One of the *costumbrista*-like elements of the novel takes shape around the three Juan characters. Their stories told initially as vignettes about common people and their situations always connect to an element of Amadeo's story at a later point. The local color is not superfluous to the plot and highlights the traditional style of historical fiction the novel draws from. The Juans, distinguished by varying religious appellations,[3] both link everyday life to the grand sweep of the romance and provide the reader with the level of detail in worldbuilding that many seek in historical fiction. Juan de Dios escapes military conscription in the south to herd cattle on the border with Argentina. Juan del Carmen is a miner in the north sympathetic to Balmaceda. Juan Evangelista works as a gardener who has issues with the laicization of the state when his wife dies and he seeks to bury her in the Catholic cemetery. These men function in the narrative to show possible influences of the conflict on everyday experience and as important plot points for Amadeo's journey and purpose. And so *1891* presents the reader with an entertainingly drawn narrative of the era that uses the historical context as a backdrop for the tragic romance of Amadeo and Balmaceda's fictional daughter, while emphasizing a pro-Balmaceda ideological position.

José Agustín Linares's *El último clarín* (1991) also structures its narrative around a romance plot that ends tragically for Balmaceda supporters. This novel, which flattens the differences between a family and a nation, highlights the perception that this is an intrafamily conflict. As in *1891*, *El último* follows traditional patterns of the historical novel. It has a linear fictional plot, local color, and representative emotion; its backdrop is rich with picturesque details; and its character types represent different perspectives as a function of their type. Balmaceda remains a distant character who comes across as a bit of a patsy and is clueless about what is being done in his name. Domingo Godoy, Balmaceda's Foreign Minister and acting Interior Minister, takes on the role of a villain who, through his unjust directives and corrupt insinuations, causes Balmaceda's government to lose popular support. *El último* portrays shifting allegiances, but, in the end, only duty and honor keep people loyal to Balmaceda. Brothers Jorge and Jaime Guerrero take different sides in the war, literalizing the notion that this is a war between brothers. At the conclusion, one of the victors reflects that "toda guerra civil al final es una guerra de comadres" (319). While chronological, Linares's novel plays with an intertext to simulate verisimilitude. It ostensibly flows from a narrative voice reading the diary of Carmen Balbontín, who expresses romantic interest in the *balmacedista* Guerrero brother. Chance drives the discovery of the text, as the narrative voice thought it a recipe book only to discover that it is an eclectic collection of entries and other texts: "una cantidad de poemas, dibujos, párrafos de autores conocidos que Carmen había encontrado interesantes o hermosos, recortes de prensa y hasta hojas y flores secas, nostalgia de quién sabe qué momentos" (13). This nostalgia infuses the text by richly portraying a world in which civil strife surprises no one and by counting the regret of its survivors in broken relationships and losses.

Araya and Linares write historical novels without the stylistic innovations and historiographical reflections that emerged in the 1970s and 1980s in some Latin American historical fiction. Other authors publishing around 1991 reflect more of the characteristics associated with what Antonia Viu terms "recent historical novels" or "historical fiction narratives" (20). In that vein are Juanita Gallardo and Virginia Vidal, both prolific authors of historical fiction who occasionally have shared subjects, such as Catalina de los Ríos y Lisperguer and her female relatives, the women associated with Chilean independence, and, as well, José Manuel Balmaceda. Their novels—Vidal's *Balmaceda, varón de una sola agua* (1991) and Gallardo's work with the historian and Trotskyist Luis Vitale, *Balmaceda: sus últimos días* (1991)—re-create the cultural milieu of 1891 to tell Balmaceda's story at the centennial. The narrative function of these re-creations, with their metahistoriographical orientation, differs from the *costumbrista* elements of earlier texts.

In Gallardo's novel, Balmaceda narrates his experience of living in the Argentine embassy for the last three weeks of his life. It reproduces text from letters and articles of the era and connects Balmaceda's reflections to literary and artistic movements of the time, especially *modernismo*. The authors remark that "no pretendemos que esta sea la verdad de lo ocurrido cien años atrás en Chile. Pero, es nuestra versión" (5). Through Balmaceda's narrative voice, the novel draws the reader toward concerns about the past and future. This emphasizes the multiple narratives that could reflect truth of the conflict: how will people remember? How will people interpret remembering? On 15

September, Balmaceda asks himself: "¿Qué dirán de él en el futuro? . . . quería asegurarse que los hombres del futuro lo juzgaran de modo diferente a como lo hacían sus contemporáneos. Ya conocía el veredicto de su época: dictador, loco y estrafalario. Lo atormentaba el anhelo de cambiar ese juicio" (164). Balmaceda's concerns and desires for the future mirror the tenor of his memory in late twentieth- and early twenty-first century Chile as a divisive figure in his own time who has generally been rehabilitated, a man who "es un intérprete de la época en que vivió" (Sagredo *Vapor* 138). Contrasted with the narrative intimacy with Balmaceda in Gallardo and Vitale's work, Vidal's novel distances the reader from Balmaceda himself. The narrator, a man fascinated by books, who, by chance, has some proximity to the Balmaceda family, re-creates the era through documents and observations of social and cultural life. Rubén Darío, Sarah Bernhardt, and *Martín Rivas* dance their way across the page while the political dénouement develops it. The novels published in 1991, commemorating the centennial of the Civil War, show the costs of the war through their characters and participate in the general vindication of Balmaceda's figure and policies.

After the centennial, interest in the war waned. However, two novels published after the centennial, Darío Oses's *El viaducto* and Isidora Aguirre's *Balmaceda*, imagine Balmaceda and 1891 as keys to unlock a sense of the aftermath of late twentieth-century Chilean history and experience. Both of these novels engage in the process of making history. They also share other points of contact, such as framing the war as a family disagreement among the elite and critiquing social structures related to gender and class in ways that highlight not only the stratified nature of Chilean society at the close of the nineteenth century but also call into question commitments to social integration in Chilean society today. In contrast with other authors writing about 1891, both Aguirre and Oses have produced an ample bibliography that has caught the attention of critics and the reading public alike.

Isidora Aguirre's novel *Balmaceda* was published in 2008, but it is based on an early play. In an interview with the Chilean daily *La Tercera*, Aguirre explains that "El Ictus montó mi obra teatral *Diálogos de fin de siglo* en 1988, como creación colectiva. Pero no me gustó ese formato, así que decidí convertir esa historia en novela" (Miranda). The events of the novel are not the Civil War, and Balmaceda doesn't appear in person in the text. Instead, *Balmaceda* tells the story of the day Balmaceda committed suicide, with a thematic focus on violence and political power. This novel features ten separate first-person narrators. Several of them narrate only one chapter, while others narrate up to six chapters. These voices introduce partisans of all sides and generations, though the privilege to narrate the text remains with voices of the aristocracy. Despite this narrative perspective, the text provocatively explores the question of who suffers and benefits from the war, especially as it relates to social class and gender. In addition to Balmaceda's suicide, the narrative highlights the Lo Cañas massacre, the most notorious of the war actions in the area of the capital. During 18–19 August, scions of elite conservative families met at the Lo Cañas property in the foothills of the Andes to blow up bridges to prevent Balmaceda's forces from reaching the capital. However, the Army learned of their plan and attacked and killed the majority of those present, even after the young men had turned themselves in. This event is understood as a turning point in popular opinion supporting the government. In addition to the importance of the Lo Cañas massacre, as is the case in many other novels, a romance plot between two young people culminates in a tragic end.

Darío Oses's *El viaducto* is structurally unique among novels on the Civil War; it has also attracted the most academic and journalistic attention of the fiction of 1891. Set in the 1970s, it tells the story of a soap opera produced during Salvador Allende's Popular Unity government on the topic of Balmaceda called *En Medio de la Muerte*. The narrative trails Maucho, the leftist black sheep of an elite family, who writes the script for the program and plays the part of Balmaceda. Chapters reproduce scenes from the soap opera's version of the nineteenth century, as well as Maucho's travails in the final weeks of the socialist government in 1973.[4] The text also intersperses realia such as song lyrics, protest slogans, and political speeches. The notion of the image and the construction of a narrative run throughout the novel, as the actors playing the characters in the soap opera only exist as their characters in the narration. It is an uncomfortable text (Garibotto 78) that nevertheless amuses the reader with its carnivalesque atmosphere. The absurdity of reenacting historical events, such as the stories about Chilean presidents who commit suicide in office, unsubtly critiques parallel events even as the plot depends on those parallels.

While the novels are distinct in style, both make use of narrative practices and thematic patterns that underscore the lament that recalling the Civil War occasions while also offering tempered hope for avoiding such conflict in the future. Elements of the novels reflect on the practice of interpretation of the past, while others highlight metahistoriographical concerns. Violence and its uses intimate a systemic link to the notion of the community who matters in the Civil War. Gendered expectations of behavior influence the exercise of violence and power and its portrayal within elite family structures. In addition to the obvious forms of violence in these novels, another, less obvious form also permeates it through class warfare, particularly its effect on those with the least to gain from civil strife, yet from these lamentable circumstances the promise of hope is alive in these novelistic constructions of the Civil War, a hope, earned through remembrance, that history not repeat itself.

Interpreting the Past

Aguirre and Oses's novels portray diverse perspectives on events and personages through their narrative structures, reflecting metahistoriographical positions that interrogate various emplotments for the war, coupled with intertexts of the dictatorship and transition. These positions are also developed through how these novels use archival texts to differing ends. Representing Balmaceda provides opportunities for considering interpretation's role in these stories, while memory's function does the same, expressing a range of emotional responses to the event from lament to regret and expecting the reader to empathize with them. Each novel illustrates different coping mechanisms for tragedy figured as the Civil War. In Aguirre's novel, tragedy bookends the novel, beginning with one death—Balmaceda's suicide—and concluding with the meaningless death of a young man in love, Felipe. The tragedy in Oses's novel is implied in the parallel between Balmaceda's story and the final months of the Chilean path to socialism in 1973. It poses this question: how can fiction speak about hope after the pursuit of greater inclusion, the source of that hope, has been violently toppled? Looking at the ways that history, historiography, and memory are portrayed in these fictional constructions of the Civil War suggests a possible answer.

Fernando Moreno observes that as contemporary historical novels propose a "polifonía discursiva, los textos literarios contemporáneos optan por el triunfo de una narratividad iluminadora, cuestionadora y desacralizadora por encima del conformismo de las verdades absolutas" (*De la Historia* 149). The strength and power of a critical narrative that interrogates received truths about the past, expressed through narrative structure, differentiates the works of Oses and Aguirre from many of the historical novels of the 1891 conflict that, while reflecting concerns about memory and lamenting the cost of the conflict, nevertheless do so through traditional narrative forms. The multiple perspectives and fragmented, yet generally chronological, narration of *Balmaceda* emphasizes competing ideologies of the conflict. Ultimately, this underlines the injustice of the conflict itself in an emotional appeal through Felipe's tragic death, at the same time preferring the truth-claims of the Balmaceda regime and its supporters. In *El viaducto* "se interesa por el pasado del presidente Balmaceda y la revolución del 91 solo en la medida en que el presente lo hace suyo" (Viu 173), and this influences the structure of the novel, as Maucho spirals toward madness by losing a sense of identity separate from his role, accentuated by the episodic nature of the narrative. However, elements beyond the narrative structure of these novels also contribute to an understanding of their historiographical orientation and its relationship to difference, violence, and social privilege as manifested in the Civil War. These elements include the role of historical figures and their characterizations, as well as explicit reflections on the archive that informs present-day knowledge of these events. As a result, the question of who gets to decide what story is told about the Civil War guides both narratives as they seek to make sense of the tragedy and pain of such a conflict.

In both novels, the characterization of historically extant individuals draws the attention of the reader to their presence and role in the narratives. This is particularly notable in the case of President Balmaceda, who becomes a synecdoche for the war. Felipe, a lovelorn survivor of the Lo Cañas massacre in Aguirre's novel, opens the text recounting his memory of Balmaceda, a man who carries himself elegantly in the style of a great man. "Con su melena crecida y su aire romántico, su estampa era más de un poeta que de un político" (Aguirre 8). This characterization resonates with Felipe's quotation of Rubén Darío's esteem for President Balmaceda. Even Balmaceda's political opponents see in his suicide the creation of a martyr (18). In *El Viaducto*, Balmaceda is, per the director of the soap opera, one of the most twisted and solitary characters of history (132), while a stranger remarks during an event that "Balmaceda es el único personaje de nuestra historia que tiene verdadera potencia dramática" (227). Unlike his phantasmal presence in Aguirre's novel, in *El Viaducto* Balmaceda—or rather, a 1970s interpretation of him—walks through the chapters of the book. Maucho becomes Balmaceda, mixing up the past and the present as he becomes ever less able to distinguish between historical empathy and his own perspectives. Early on, he recognizes a difference between his own emotions and Balmaceda's, speculating that he should feel a particular way (47), but by the end he abandons the distinction. The first time he goes into period hair and makeup, the rest of the cast obeys his directives without question; by the close of the novel, he marches around roadblocks to get to the viaduct over the Malleco River as if he were the state's chief executive. This reproduction of one of Balmaceda's triumphant political moments, however, is undermined by the weather and bad acting. Traditional historical fiction elides the protagonism of historical figures, and postmodern historical fiction often emphasizes it. Taken together, these novels underscore the role that Balmaceda plays in representing the conflict of the Civil War of 1891, as well as the strife leading to the military coup in 1973.[5] Balmaceda's figure shapes perspectives on the war, and his use in both novels reflects the synecdochic relationship between it and his person.

The archive, that is, the historical materials that provide evidence for historians to interpret, surfaces explicitly in both novels. In *Balmaceda*, the women who remain at home during the war receive letters from their family members describing the terrible savagery of battle, and through those archival documents, even characters who supported the war against Balmaceda and his partisans begin to question the purpose of the conflict.[6] One of Aguirre's narrative voices, don Luis Antonio, refers to the production of texts that become the archive on which contemporary historiography is based, such as when Balmaceda, from within his refuge at the Argentine embassy, plans to ask Julio Bañados to write an authoritative history of his government. His narration also uses Balmaceda's words themselves: "hay que salvar al país de las desgracias que lo afligen y poner un término patriótico y decoroso a esta contienda" (Aguirre 9). An avowed Balmaceda partisan, don Luis Antonio desires that future readers understand the justice of the position that animates all of his narrative interventions. However, as he is but one of many narrative voices, this push to vindicate Balmaceda is emotionally outweighed by the tragic losses conveyed by many other voices.

This sincere emotional impact contrasts with the parodic tone of Maucho's declamations of Balmaceda's speeches in *El viaducto*. These speeches are peppered throughout the novel and their reception mirrors Maucho's descent to madness. His ability to "turn on" Balmaceda ensures him the role and respect of his fellow cast, but by the time he is visiting the Malleco Viaduct as the dream of the democratic Chilean path to socialism crumbles around him, he struggles to remember the speech in the pouring rain. He finally recalls it, but delivers it all run together as the final text of the novel:

> Si nuestra bandera, encarnación del gobierno del pueblo verdaderamente republicano, ha caído ensangrentada en los campos de batalla, será levantada de nuevo, en tiempo no lejano, y con defensores numerosos y más afortunados, flameará un día para honra de las instituciones chilenas y para dicha de mi patria a la cual he amado sobre todas las cosas de la vida. (282)

The resonance between these last words and other famous presidential last words—Allende's final radio broadcast[7]—uses the archive not to vindicate Balmaceda's view but to draw a direct parallel between the Civil War and the end of the Popular Unity government, contributing to what Moreno identifies as a "fenómeno de fusión . . . resulta casi imposible distanciarse y no pueden sino desenvolverse simultáneamente en dos ámbitos, vivir al mismo tiempo dos existencias" (*De la Historia* 154). This fusion reaches its peak when the program films at La Moneda Palace, and Maucho as Balmaceda faces his own marble bust: "es como si se mirara en un espejo que insiste en devolverle una imagen falsa, impecable, puesta por encima del tiempo" (240). President Allende's arrival and conversation with Maucho-Balmaceda, on camera, underlines the import of this moment of fractured reflection. However, the serious tone that one might infer from such a momentous occasion is undermined by musings about the location of the physical film used that day: the archive of these encounters remains lost. Thus the notion of the archive in *El viaducto* wavers back and forth between the parodic reproduction of the textual archive and the absence and loss of key evidence.[8]

Historians use the archive to construct arguments and stories about the past, but memory often shapes popular understandings of the past more than an archive. What legacy comes from the Civil War? *Balmaceda* remembers the war as a lament, while *El viaducto* focuses more on regret, particularly given the way the text filters memories related to the 1890s through the lens of the early 1970s with a clear expectation that the reader is familiar with the military dictatorship and its consequences. In lament—"tuneful, texted weeping" that is "a means for grappling with loss" (Wilce 1)[9]—one grieves for what was and what no longer is, while feelings of sadness and disappointment characterize regret. Two of Aguirre's narrative voices raise the theme of remembrance in several of their chapters, though one more clearly expresses lament for the war. The chapters narrated by Abuela Eulalia, mother to one of the main opposition leaders and sympathetic to Balmaceda's government, present the consensus historiographical view of events even as she presents them as her own reflections on the recent past. She critiques both sides but not without repeatedly coming down against the choices political leaders made that led to the war in the first place. She laments that politicians did not use elections to resolve their differences, choosing instead a bloody conflict (Aguirre 36). For her, the war is "funesto," and she decries it as a violent armed conquest (54). Even as she grieves that the war is an event worthy of remembrance, she ponders how the future will interpret the past in a way that some today might find controversial: "A Balmaceda, ¿cuánto tardarán en erigirle una estatua? Y, ¿las habrá para aquellos que desataron la contienda civil?" (Aguirre 65). Memory matters in *Balmaceda*, and the reflections of this narrative emphasize that history is a process that constantly revisits and revises narratives of the past.

Part of history as a process involves the question of who gets to decide what story will be told. Aguirre's approach to history highlights many voices and perspectives while weaving strong threads through them. This effect imparts to the reader the appearance of balance, though by the close of the novel a clear editorial perspective emerges. Hope for the future exists alongside the lament of the war.[10] Felipe asserts the following to his domineering father:

¿Quiénes son los que tiemblan y dan la orden de encarcelar a los que defienden a los desposeídos? ¿O echan del país a los que hablan alto de

> justicia y de igualdad? . . . tal vez yo soy uno de esos ilusos. No me creo gran cosa, pero he descubierto que el hombre tiene la posibilidad de ser mejor. De hacer que las cosas cambien, de enderezar un poco esta torcida civilización. (Aguirre 141)

However, this dramatic declamation is shortly followed by Felipe's tragic death from a stray bullet. One might read this juxtaposition—a clear sense of calling for a better and more inclusive world with the meaningless death of the one who articulated it—as a mark against the hope that Felipe conveys. Nevertheless, its presence in the novel and the impact of Felipe's death on the other characters and narrative voices offer an opportunity to see it through a more hopeful lens: the war shows us the ugliness of humanity, but even within that, individuals dream and work toward a better future.

Aguirre's text, through its narrative structure and thematic connections to historiography, archives, and memory, plays with the notion of hope as an antidote to tragedy, even as lament for that which has been needlessly suffered sets the tone for the text. A late chapter in *El viaducto* offers another reading of the relationship between hope and tragedy. The production of *En medio de la muerte* has the opportunity to film at La Moneda Palace, and, by chance, President Salvador Allende arrives while they are still filming in the hallway. Allende speaks with Maucho, saying:

> yo soy protagonista . . . o más bien agonista, de esta otra historia, que a lo mejor es la misma, porque el imperialismo y la plutocracia siguen siendo los mismos, y la lucha contra sus poderes continua, y a lo mejor a usted y a mí nos vuelven a matar (241)

But rather than ending with their deaths, Allende concludes that their stubbornness means they will resurrect however many times are necessary to reach their goals. Even as the absurdity of Maucho's role as Balmaceda reaches its zenith, Allende's words resonate with the reader, offering hope for the future that is not dependent on one person, one president, one leader to fight against injustice and social exclusion. The tragic ends with which both Balmaceda and Allende met, as well as the unrealized consequences of their political projects for greater inclusion in Chilean society, are tempered with these narratives that offer limited hope. This "future" orientation hinges on the ways that these novels craft narratives of the past.

All in the Family?

The Civil War has been portrayed as the result of a political conflict among a small group of elite families. At the start of the nineteenth century, the so-called Santiago bourgeoisie elite was formed by

> cuarenta familias-no más de doce apellidos-que, dado el estrecho emparentamiento por sucesivos matrimonios entre sí y su residencia en Santiago, no tenía el carácter de nacional, sino, el oligárquico de una sola y extensa familia opulenta que acaparó para sus miembros el poder, los honores y los empleos públicos. (Alvear Ravanal 134n18)

The family bonds among the elite led to the perception that political conflict, such as happened in 1891, can be reduced to "rencillas histéricas entre familias oligarcas" (Salazar 109). The tendency to see certain families as indivisible from the nation has, however, diminished in recent historiographical literature. Nevertheless,

> Histories of elite families were portrayed as inseparable from the history of the Chilean nation-state; indeed, in such renderings, it is difficult to discern where the history of *las grandes familias* ends and that of the state begins . . . elites' own self-narratives situate kinship at the center of both collective identity and the birth of the nation. (Milanich 108)

Both *Balmaceda* and *El viaducto* probe the connection between certain families and Chilean history. Both writers also portray varying attitudes toward violence, often shaped by familial relationships, and explore the limits of how those families reflect the larger structure of Chilean society and politics. In examining violence's frame in these texts, we can understand how lament functions as an ideological move to critique past choices by trying to come to terms with the shifting representations of us, them, and how those two groupings reflect difference in Chile.

In Aguirre's novel, the Lo Cañas massacre is a watershed moment in the representation of violence. While other narrative voices reflect on its political function and consequences, Felipe, our romantic hero, recalls his own lived experience of the massacre. He is not a participant on either side and only goes to warn his cousins of the danger they face. He is too late, however, and witnesses the unnecessary cruelty (7) of the massacre of aristocratic youth by government forces. In hiding after the massacre, Felipe opens up to Corina, one of the servants in his home. The hesitancy with which he finally reveals what has happened underlines the episode's savagery, since he struggles to communicate that which still causes him such anguish (29). Rather than a straightforward narrative of events, Felipe's revelation is halting, broken up by pauses and responses from Corina. While the emotional responses of the narrative are predominantly Corina's, as Felipe tells his story, his own expressions become more emotionally charged. Corina uses "los "benaiga," los "Jesús" y "Virgen Santa . . . Ay niño, por Dios . . . ¡Cómo pudo ser! ¡Virgen Santísima!" (30), which leads Felipe to ask rhetorically, "¿Cómo pudieron convertirse en monstruos?" (31) As Felipe begins to share his experience, Corina worries and trembles, but when Felipe does not continue, she urges him on. He finally reveals that, having tried to go warn his cousins of the danger in which they placed themselves, he was caught and shot in the ankle. With the gunfire, his horse threw him and he wound up in a ditch and was considered dead. In the ditch, he bore witness to a hellish scene (31) in which the youths were hunted down and killed, even after having surrendered themselves to the Army. The soldiers became savage beasts (31), as the injured Felipe remained in the ditch for hours. The contrast between exclamation and silence invites the reader into the relational intimacy of Felipe and Corina reliving their roles as child and caregiver. The novel does not dwell on the embodied experience of violence. Indeed, Felipe's horror at the deaths of others, and its scale of violence, outweighs his own injury and physical suffering. His survival functions as a window for the narrative to share a firsthand account, even as that firsthand account remains distanced by political disaffection and a self-denying focus on others.

Felipe's role as sole survivor underscores a theme running throughout Aguirre's novel: toxic masculinity. Many of the narrative voices, especially Felipe's grandmother, lament the violence and dominance tied to notions of masculinity and power that they see behind much of the Civil War. When Felipe's cousins try to recruit him into the group of young aristocratic saboteurs, they respond to his distancing by trying to pass the proposal off as a joke. Felipe keeps to himself that "me habían llamado mariquita que tocaba el piano como las mujeres y que mientras el país se iba mucho a la mierda, me lo pasaba en tertulias de poetas" (30). His musical and artistic talents are taken as a sign of deficient manhood. If we understand toxic masculinity to be "the constellation of socially regressive male traits that serve to foster domination, the devaluation of women, homophobia, and wanton violence" (Kupers 714), Felipe's cousins inhabit this ugly notion. The slur against Felipe indicates their homophobia. They confidently affirm that violence is the only possible solution to political disagreement, which is evident even when they dismiss insults as jokes.

Felipe's father, don Alberto, also exhibits qualities of toxic masculinity. His inner monologue shows consideration of others in ways his actions do not, whether that takes the form of his ironclad opposition to Balmaceda and the discomfort he experiences at news of his suicide or his critique of Balmaceda's authoritarianism, offset by his realization of treating his wife and son the same way. By the end of the novel, the connection between toxic masculinity and the family becomes clear. Rosario, don Alberto's wife, does not agree with his political views or the methods by which he ensures their ascendancy. This breaks their domestic tranquility, and in a rare moment of calm at the opera, don Alberto admits to Rosario that he is tired of the role he is expected to play. It is

> El rol para el que nos preparan desde la infancia. Eso de los hombres no lloran, no debes mostrar cobardía. Y lo que sigue: debes cuidar el buen nombre de la familia, sobre todo el del rango que hemos mantenido desde hace un siglo. Y cuando te cases debes adquirir una mansión de dos pisos, fachada de mampostería, carruaje importado, un buen tronco de caballos ... y, por supuesto, abono a la ópera, palco propio, militancia en el partido de tu padre y de tu abuelo, escalar posiciones en los círculos sociales y políticos. ¡Y ya estás en la cúpula del poder! (120–21)

Don Alberto goes on to compare this expectation to a vice: one can't imagine a world in which his actions, his political success, do not determine the future of not only himself or his family but also his entire country. He bought into this practice after all. But after a lifetime of living this vision of masculinity, he is tired. Against the backdrop of a deteriorating marriage and a senseless war, this confessional moment highlights the harm of this form of masculinity—not only for the individual living it but also, implicitly, for the whole of a society in which he participates. With these examples of the practice and effect of toxic masculinity, we also observe an echo of the notion of Chilean history paralleling the history of aristocratic families. These men imagine that the country rides on their shoulders; a significant stream of historiographical narrative obliged them.

An element of toxic masculinity is the weight it places on violence as a mode of social interaction and dominance. In Aguirre's novel, Felipe's grandmother, Eulalia, identifies the disconnection between rhetorical postures and actual practice as the most terrible part of the Civil War: "su meta no era la defensa de la patria, sino la conquista del poder por las armas" (Aguirre 54). In the same reflection, she indicts people as hypocrites whose acts are steeped in cruelty, yet who believe themselves kind, just, and good.[11] In *El viaducto*, the consequences of violence are even more glaring than in Aguirre's novel because Oses, not without cause, pairs violence with absurdity. In the soap opera, Beatriz, a young woman whose family supports Congress, envisions herself defending her family and their shared political commitment by distracting the Army leader assigned to their property. At one point, she kisses the red-bearded officer, but when he continues to flirt with her, she treats him badly: "¿Qué clase de hombre es usted? . . . Un hombre de verdad hace las cosas, no las declama. ¿No se da cuenta de lo ridículo que se ve?" (188). Beatriz trades on the expectations of a masculine practice that values dominance and possession of others as the measure of manhood. The very public nature of their interactions also ensures that societal expectations weigh on the soldier—and that, be assured, is a calculated move through which Beatriz signifies her resistance to the brutality that inheres in the occupation of her family's property. The narrative inverts the expected story of an occupying soldier violently assaulting an aristocratic woman; instead, it portrays a love-struck soldier confused by the manipulations and insults of the object of his affections. This inversion of expectations underlines the carnivalesque tendencies of the novel, reminding the reader of the constructed nature of historical narrative and interrogating its role in memory and access to knowledge of the past. The novel presents historical referents as labyrinths without an apparent exit (Moreno *De la Historia* 160). It is a novel in which "the show must go on," even as the world crumbles around it, which results in violence functioning as a critique built into any representation of the past.

Many fictional texts allude to the Civil War's status as the bloodiest conflict in Chilean history while eliding the corporeality of violence's effects. This violence, in addition to being lived out through gendered family roles, also brings conflict of a less physical nature to families as a microcosm of the national conflict. On the eve of the coup in 1973 as the production prepares to travel to Temuco to film the famous viaduct speech, Maucho perceives polarization while Marta, a television producer, accuses the elite of paralyzing the country (245). Women's perceptions of violence and family conflict dominate Aguirre's novel. Felipe's grandmother Eulalia watches her grandchildren take different sides, try to save one another, and fail. Don Alberto's wife, Rosario, considers her frustration and horror at the war as the source of conflict in her marriage. She does not know how to make her spouse understand that his active participation in the war is the root of her discontent (86). These perspectives are not limited to the aristocratic women who supported Balmaceda. Doña Martina Barros de Orrego[12] describes a conversation with her husband Augusto during the war:

> Una vez desatada la violencia, poco cuenta la justicia. Le preguntaba hoy por la mañana a mi marido Augusto si no somos todos un poco responsables por lo que ocurre en el país. Se burló, diciendo que era una frase de filosofía barata. Pero nadie me quita la idea de que pudimos evitar este conflicto. Es más, tengo la certeza de que toda guerra puede evitarse. (44)

Through Barros de Orrego, Aguirre expands the lament so palpable in Eulalia's reflections. What other paths could have been taken besides armed conflict? The women of these aristocratic families, no matter which side they support, question the methods of conflict and lament its consequences for their families and larger society.

Who, then, is included in this society? *El viaducto*'s protagonist comes from a privileged background even as his own political perspectives do not align with his family's. Per her own family, his wife, Ana María, suffers because of her "marido izquierdista, bueno para nada; hija igual de loca que su padre, arrejuntada con un dirigente del MIR; nieta criada en el campamento Fidel-Ernesto; tías ricas, primas bien y un hijo de su primer matrimonio que la compadecen a ella, la parienta pobre" (12). Maucho's somewhat desultory commitment to left politics and to lifting up class consciousness outweighs the expectations of his upbringing. It is, however, that upbringing and background that make him attractive to the producers and writers of *En Medio de la Muerte*. Despite projecting a revolutionary and pro-Balmaceda perspective, one of the younger actors critiques the program as nothing but the oligarchy's empty pleasures (96). The "us" making the decisions—during the Civil War, in the soap opera production, and, by implication, during the Popular Unity government—is not the "us" that is sent to fight, or even the "us" that subscribes to a particular political position. Nacho Vattier, Maucho's friend, who, besides getting him involved in the series, also calls him out on his classism, looks forward to the day when "Chile va a volver a ser el país de siempre, en que las cosas se resuelven conversando frente a una buena comida y a un botellón" (220). Vattier laments the loss of this image of the past and dreams of a Chile where a small "us"—perhaps not the same "us" opposed to the Popular Unity government—negotiates disagreements for the benefit of the elite's interests. In this vision, democracy and justice do not matter, only the perception of those in power of civility and peace.

Gente Bien: Civil War and Social Class

While both novels gesture toward the impact of the conflict on individuals in all social classes, the protagonists and narrative perspectives privilege those of the Chilean upper classes. Maucho is viewed as a class traitor for his support of the socialist government, and this notion of betrayal permeates the riotous and somewhat ridiculous atmosphere of *El viaducto*. Aguirre's novel focuses on women's lives, and while women of various social classes are portrayed, the narrative viewpoint all characters seem to have internalized is upper class. That said, *El viaducto* uses the war and its relationship to social class in Chile to paint a pessimistic vision for greater social inclusion; *Balmaceda*, in comparison, interrogates the notion of disparate impact as it relates to the events of the war.

A major antagonist in *El viaducto* never appears: John Thomas North. He figures prominently in the historiography of the Civil War, especially within the stream that seeks economic explanations for the conflict. North, an English businessman, invested heavily in nitrates in northern Chile and undertook a countrywide public relations tour in 1889. Balmaceda's public works and development projects were not necessarily in line with the desires of foreign investors, who sought cheap labor with few protections, and little government involvement, that is, few regulations, taxes, or tariffs, on their businesses. In *En medio de la muerte*, the character Arturo Echaurren sneaks around, bribes, and extorts others to acquire power, and he then uses that power to fulfill his desires with women. As a scion of an aristocratic family fallen on hard times, he is North's— "ese gringo sinvergüenza" (Oses 120)—agent, corrupting politicians to enable the Englishman's consolidation of saltpeter and power. Echaurren's success— the writers find him to be more interesting to write, so he gets increasingly more screen time—mocks the ideological purpose of the program. His presence and actions drive the series, from blackmailing one character to seeking to sleep with another. He judges those around him constantly, concluding that "no se puede vivir en este país donde la gente es hostigada, perseguida, donde mandan los siúticos y gobiernan los recién aparecidos" (177). For Echaurren, the proper order of things is the class structure that affords him his privileges. He dies in a fight in a bordello.

Echaurren's ignominious end is one of the few examples in *El viaducto* of a character receiving their just desserts. The class-based statements he makes, however, are not unique. The tension between Chilean class structures and political programs, animated by a desire to change them, are both warp and weft of the 1970s and 1890s. After all, "lo que cuenta en este país es la posición social" (88). The dominant viewpoint remains that of the privileged upper class, who many of the soap-opera characters view as the whole world. The character Vicente, who previously advocated education for all regardless of class, has decided to go north to fight for the congressional forces. He reflects that everyone is leaving, concluding that "los demás no tienen mucho que hacer cuando se trata de decidir el destino del país" (191). The only people who matter are the decision makers, who happen to be from the social circles into which he was born. This is bound up in the political dealmaking behind the soap opera itself. We have, then, not only a character who chooses privilege and class loyalty over justice but also a character whose actor was falsely assumed to be a political infiltrator and treated accordingly.

Even though the upper-class disdain for any would-be parvenus is unvarnished in *El viaducto*, the novel also portrays negative attitudes toward Balmaceda's (and, by extension, Allende's) political projects from the perspective of the proletariat. Marta muses that the *pobladores* struggle to "tolerar que haya gente de su mismo medio que estudie y quiera subir de pelo . . . conozco a otros muchachos que han tenido problemas pero han sabido manejarlos, qué sé yo, esconden los libros, o conversan y explican que estudian para levantarlos a todos" (63). It is not simply the upper class that keeps everyone else under its boot. The majority of the population has bought into the class system and resents anyone who would try to live outside its strictures. The novel, however, filters these perspectives through the prejudices and understandings of those in power.

The power of the limiting structures and the perception of failure of Chile's socialist project in 1973 lead to the conversations between Marta and Maucho at the close of the novel. Marta loses hope in revolutionary projects, mourning the necessity to postpone the dream, since collective joy and stability belong to a future they may never experience (236). They then have to pretend to be deeply and passionately involved in one another to avoid the danger of a right-wing patrol. Despite the obvious chaos around them, Maucho persists in his blind hope. As he says earlier to others at a meeting, "a lo mejor el socialismo está perdido . . . pero yo no podría vivir sin tener por delante el sueño del socialismo" (230). But which attitude is the greater betrayal of hope for change: Marta's despair or Maucho's blindness? This tension between lament and a dogged faith in what is not coming to pass underscores that things are not changing. The structures remain in place, and the suffering and injustice they cause merely languish.

Where, then, *El viaducto* highlights class narratives and the failure to undermine them, *Balmaceda* laments the suffering of the Civil War has broadcast and highlights the disparate impacts of that suffering. It does so through centering women's lives and the question of who suffers in war. The novel features aristocratic women as narrative voices, but through Corina, the housekeeper, it also includes the perspective of a woman from a less privileged social class. Corina exclaims: "¡en la que casi todos los muertos eran gente humilde, ignorante, los soldados que mandaban los ricos a la pelea!" (Aguirre 14). The notion that the people, as opposed to the ruling class, suffered the most negative consequence for the war runs through the reflections of characters in the novel. This also runs counter to the prevailing narratives in historiography and fiction in which the concerns of the upper classes dominate interpretive frames for the Civil War. Even as Corina's charge, Felipe, suffers from his witness of the Lo Cañas massacre, she critiques the public reaction to that massacre contrasted against the many casualties in the previous eight months of war. "¿No ve que todos eran jóvenes de apellido? Si muere el pobre ¡nadita que se alarman!" (15). Corina's exclamations are the most direct critique of the class-based point of view for understanding the impact of the war. The reader understands that the stories we hear and tell about Balmaceda and the war are but a fraction of its lived experiences. Through this candor, Aguirre outlines the shadows of the stories outside the frame.

The impact of the war on less traditional groups—the working classes and women of all classes—distinguishes Aguirre's novel from the others texts on 1891. Younger women suffer social opprobrium for progressive views and practices. Rosario distinguishes the changing role of society women and the discomfort that it causes their husbands. As a result, she observes that many husbands heap praise on their wives to try to keep them home and out of politics, to the extent they are treated as the queens of their homes (38). Rosario's political disagreements with her husband and her incisive observations about the structures and practices of elite Chilean society set her apart from others of her class. The ideal of womanhood for late nineteenth-century Chile remained the European angel of the house, a woman reduced to the appearance of domestic tranquility. This woman's "special privilege and function [were orchestrated] to create and sustain the psychic space of the home and the emotional closeness that was now being marketed as the sign of the ideal marriage and family" (Jagoe 20). While this model transcends social class, Rosario's outspokenness in disagreement functions due to her class privilege, even as the public face of her marriage remains unified.

Rosario does not restrict her reflections to her own social sphere or to explicitly gendered concerns. She shows her husband that they speak different languages when they look at the world around them. While Rosario sees people who die as people who die and people who kill as those who kill, Alberto distinguishes between the unworthy and worthy dead, between a murderer and a heroic patriot soldier (96). Don Alberto's worldview accordingly limits the humanity and dignity of those around him based on their role; whereas Rosario dreams of a world that breaks free of such strictures. She longs for a world in which politicians resolve their conflicts themselves, rather than pay to have people fight in their stead (86). Rosario imagines a better and more inclusive future while her husband labors to maintain both the status quo and his own political power even as he ignores the damage that a masculinity built on a cracked foundation creates. Their paths have diverged, yet they are brought back together at the close of the novel—only because of grief.

Grief and lament shape remembrances of the Civil War in both Oses's and Aguirre's novels. Chilean class structures and their limitations shape the lives of the characters and narrative voices of both texts. Both novels lament the strictures of social class, how it shapes the conflict, and whose lives matter in the grand narrative of conflict. Historical fiction as represented by *Balmaceda* and *El viaducto* stresses the foundations on which our stories of the past rest, pointing out the voids we might not have noticed and gesturing toward different ways of conceiving the conflict in the light of the present day.

Conclusion

Hope and lament live side by side in recent representations of the Civil War of 1891. Texts allude to violence without representing its horror directly. This is not in and of itself unusual, as representation allows the creator to select certain elements and omit others. Violence's function—its absence, its exaggeration, its consequences—varies throughout narratives of the Civil War, and none of them can reproduce the lived experience of those who suffered in the conflict. This elision repeats itself in Chilean history and narrative. Present-day Chilean society remains unable to reckon with violence. "The country has struggled to construct public memory and deal with the ugly dimensions of its recent history . . . silences, injustices, discrimination, and rampant socioeconomic inequality still exist" (Lazzara *Civil* 3–4). Like the dictatorship, the Civil War represents a discontinuity in how Chile's normative political narrative progresses. The stakes of these political conflicts appear to be out of proportion to the human cost of their violence. Historical fiction of the Civil War cannot avoid resonating with memories of the dictatorship even as the stories focus on romance or propaganda. The works of Isidora Aguirre and Darío Oses draw clear lines between past, present, and future, as their narratives reveal that the Chilean family is not as caring or expansive as some might have believed. Closing with a meaningless death and a ridiculous reenactment, one might expect these novels to leave the reader with a sense of cynicism. However, in telling these stories, historical fiction warns its readers that, if the same path is followed, they, too, will experience the hope in lament.

CONCLUSION
Chile Awakens?

AT ONE POINT, 2010 felt a natural end for a period of the democratic transition in Chile. For the first time since Pinochet left the office in 1989, right-wing political parties gained the power of the presidency. Sebastián Piñera's administration was filled with those who had governed during the dictatorship, as well as those who had profited from it, but they had gained power through elections rather than a violent coup. Perhaps Chile's transition from dictatorship to democracy was complete. Certainly, in his 2018 inaugural address, Piñera lauds how, with unity, faith, and hope, "los chilenos realizamos con notable éxito la primera transición, la que nos permitió avanzar hacia una sociedad con libertad y con democracia." He continues by arguing for a new transition in which Chile would become a well-developed country with no poverty. Over a decade after the end of the Concertación government, however, it is clear that the right's return to executive power in Chile, first from 2010 to 2014, and then again from 2018 to 2022, did not mark the beginning of a flourishing and diverse democratic system, nor has poverty been eliminated. We are not all Chile.

The period during which the works studied here were published, 1990–2010, was democratic "as much as possible," *a la medida de lo posible*, and possibility was defined by those who constructed and benefitted from the authoritarian political and economic systems of the dictatorship. Recall that Pinochet remained head of the military until 1998 and died in 2006 without having been found legally culpable of any of the crimes of which he was accused. Recall that the constitution of 1980, installed by the dictatorship, remained in full force during this period. Recall that the security and terrorism laws, vastly expanded during the dictatorship, remain on the books and are applied disproportionately. Recall that limited constitutional reforms in 2005 included the elimination of senators-for-life and affirmed that the entire government, not only the armed forces, are the guarantors of institutionality. Recall that the binominal system for elections, which helped to ensure that supporters of the dictatorship would remain part of the government systems, was not changed until 2015 after long debate and more than twenty-five attempts to do so. Recall that supermajorities of varying stripes were required for most reforms. The political imagination of Chile has been trapped inside arbitrary borders that preserve authoritarian practices and contribute to injustice and inequality.

In 2006, over 100,000 high school students across the country went on strike and protested against the education system. The concerted effort led to changes in national education policy, the reawakening of youth organizing, and protest movements. Students returned to the streets in 2008. In 2011, student organizations led massive countrywide protests sparked by the quality of education at all levels, as well as an economic system within which high-quality education was limited to those families of means. Leaders of those protests—among them Gabriel Boric, president of Chile since 2022—became leaders in political parties, serving as legislators for various constituencies and in ministerial roles in government.

The presidential election in 2017 led to the return of the conservative coalition to executive power, under the promise of "Better Times." However, those better times never came. On 18 October 2019, Chilean society woke up after thirty years of so-called democracy, countless corruption scandals, hypocrisy, and desperation within a system that dehumanizes and disenfranchises the masses while the very wealthy gain even more. The government's response stuck to the dictatorship playbook: call the military into the streets, declare a curfew, and use violence against peaceful protesters. Social media was alight with videos of protests, of military and police violence, with requests for images or videos of particular places at particular times, of requests for information about people who had not been found. Amnesty International observed that the levels of state violence occurring from 18 October did not have any precedent during democracy in Chile (*Ojos* 4). Over thirty people were killed in the protests,[1] those detained were often tortured, and hundreds of people have damaged eyesight caused by the rounds police had fired into them.[2] The image of Chile as the modern, civilized, successful twenty-first-century country was belied by the ugliness that has always lurked beneath the surface: inequality, injustice, exploitation, and violence.

Artists and authors were in the midst of the protests. They brought out their pots and spoons to make noise in the *cacerolazos*, penned op-eds, attended protests, participated in citizen *cabildos* to discuss what Chile should be like, and encouraged others to do likewise. A few publicly criticized the protests by appealing to an anachronistic sense of civil decorum in which most Chileans could never even get into the room, much less to the table. But most are like author, actor, and screenwriter Nona Fernández:

> ¿Por qué no explotamos antes? No lo sabemos. Pero ahora estamos aquí, lejos de esa vida e intentando otra mejor. Con la incertidumbre de no saber cómo calcular el futuro, pero con la certeza de haber despertado de un mal sueño al que no queremos regresar. La antigua normalidad no existe y es parte de un pasado pesadillesco. Tomarnos otra vez la pastilla sería el fracaso más absoluto.

At that point, no one was sure what the future would hold, but there was confidence that this was an inflection point. One way or another, Chile's path, as a country, as a society, and as a culture, is different now than what some might have predicted before the protests—though not as different as the many who protested had desired. On 25 October 2020, seventy-eight percent of the Chilean electorate voted to begin the process of writing a new constitution, one of the major demands of the protests in 2019. In May of 2021, voters overwhelming chose to place their trust in left-wing and independent candidates for a constitutional convention.[3] Chilean society had awakened, sick of being trampled by the cost of health care and education, unable to retire due to an ineffective pension system, concerned about environmental disasters from water access and pollution to air quality and a higher risk of wildfire, and fed up with inequality that was only made more visible by the COVID-19 pandemic.

The story of Chile's constitutional process, however, would not be so simply and triumphally structured. The 2022 constitutional reform process, driven primarily by left and grassroots political actors, failed spectacularly. "Citizens initially supported the process, the rules matched many of the recommendations made by global scholars and the proposal made by the Convention was supported by several international observers who praised its progressive nature," which sought to "advance a social rights agenda that the existing constitutional framework does not secure" (Verdugo and García Huidobro 157–58). The progressive proposal in 2022 offered a dream where, yes, everyone is part of Chile. And yet 61.86 percent of Chilean voters[4] rejected the proposed constitution. What followed that rejection was a second constitutional process dominated by the right and far-right actors who fashioned a draft constitution that reflected conservative, market-focused reform. It was rejected by 55.76% of voters.[5] Taking up this lead, the current Chilean government announced that it would not seek an additional referendum or convention; instead, it would pursue changes through the existing legislative processes. As of 2024, the constitution of 1980 remains in force. In the wake of it all, scholars and politicians continue to discuss the failures of constitutional reform in Chile.

Surely historical fiction will be written of these times, but it is too soon to predict what it might reveal. Perhaps one of the students who was out on the street is penning a novel about the state massacres of striking workers in the early twentieth century. Perhaps the grandparents who stood by their doors to hug passing protesters are working on a story about Manuel Rodríguez and Chile's independence. The images beamed around the world over the weeks and months of massive protest recall the images and stories that emerged from Chile during the dictatorship, often accompanied by the hashtags #ChileDespertó, #ChileViolaALosDDHH, and #RenunciaPiñera. Many shared and commented on photographs of injuries, of peaceful multigenerational protest interrupted by water cannons and tear gas, and of generalized and mindless destruction. One image widely circulated on social media features heavily armed police standing guard outside a women's clothing store. The image is of note due to the store's name: "Privilege." The English name and the tony area of its location juxtaposed with the power of the state defending it from unseen adversaries summarizes much of the public sentiment about why Chile woke up, even as that awakening has not borne the fruit many had hoped for.

If Chile woke up in 2019, might we say that it was asleep, or dozing, or napping for decades? Historical narrative in the first twenty years postdictatorship tried to imagine a Chile where everyone mattered. Many novels tried to tell new stories and spotlight new characters. Many critiqued the authoritarian tendencies of Chilean society. After the initial protests, many public voices in Chile asked, why didn't we see this coming? *La Tercera's* Sunday magazine on 20 October featured a photograph of a burned-out Metro station with the headline, "La crisis que nadie previó," "The crisis that no one foresaw," in the lower right-hand corner. The image of destruction dominates the page. However, some journalists and many academics have argued that experts did warn that something like this could happen. Time and again in Chile, when those with power ignore the demands of the people, the people rise up. Time and again in Chile, though, the efforts to change are hobbled and fail to deliver on the promise they offered.

Historical narrative, fictional or not, matters. In the recent social upheaval in Chile, a sense of historical injustice lives alongside the day-to-day concerns reflected in social movements. In the first twenty-five years of the transition postdictatorship, historical fiction predominated, and since 2015, historical nonfiction has captured the reading public. Complementing the appetite for historical fiction is another, a hunger for historical narratives that allow Chileans to see themselves in the story. Historical narratives provide symbolic space for people to imagine a better future for their families and loved ones. While these narratives alone cannot change the material conditions in which people live, they can awaken hope for the future that can inspire change. Without this hope, it is not possible that all could be Chile. Instead, Chile will remain an outpost for those with money and power.

NOTES

Introduction

1. In February 2022, at the conclusion of Piñera's second term, various public policy surveys estimated his leadership approval between 15 percent (Leighton) and 24 percent (Informe Especial CADEM). Contrast this with a near 50 percent approval at the beginning of his first term in 2018 and his 21 percent approval immediately prior to the crisis of the *estallido social* in October 2019 (Chevalier Naranjo).

2. In the twenty-first century, exceptionalism is most often associated with the United States or China.

3. A number of texts were published around the centennial in 2007, the most well-known of which is Hernán Rivera Letelier's *Santa María de las flores negras*.

4. The Inka Empire at its height extended throughout the Andes from southern Colombia to the southern boundary at the Maule River in Chile.

5. By *criollo* (creole), I mean a social class of persons of European (generally Spanish) descent born in the Americas.

6. For more detail on these issues from a Chilean context, consult Tomás Moulián's *Chile actual*. Luis Cárcamo-Huechante addresses many of the economic policies in the introduction to *Tramas del mercado*.

7. The 1980 constitution is still in force in Chile, with limited reforms having been carried out under the auspices of various governments.

8. For more detail, see Nelly Richard, *Cultural Residues* and Patricia Richards, *Race and the Chilean Miracle*.

9. This consensus is particularly well articulated in the work of Macarena Gómez-Barris and Steve Stern.

10. Many of these works engage in an explicit political project to recuperate voices silenced by the authoritarianism of the dictatorship. Choosing either democratic transition or postdictatorship implies a political position. Democratic transition tends to be preferred by those involved in the political projects of the *Concertación* coalition of parties; although postdictatorship can be used by those same groups, it is the preferred term of those who position themselves outside the mainstream of Chilean political culture.

11. One might also consider this to be the *Concertación* period, given that 2010

marked the election of the first conservative president since the dictatorship and the corresponding electoral defeat and eventual dissolution of the *Concertación por la democracia* that governed for twenty years. A shift from the years of the Concertación was particularly notable due to the 2011 student protest movement that has launched political careers and shifted political dialogue in such a way that reforms thought impossible in 2009 were major platform planks for a new center-left coalition, the *Nueva Mayoría* (New Majority), in 2013 elections. For more on the student movements and the shift in political discourse and civic engagement, see Donoso, Mayol and Azócar, and Webb and Radcliffe.

12. For an excellent review of recent work involving historical memory, see the introduction of Kristin Sorensen's *Media, Memory, and Human Rights in Chile*.

13. Anderson's formulation of the imagined community has been very influential and often critiqued, especially in clearly defined historical and geographical cases. One example of the critique of Anderson's concept of nationalism is available in *Beyond Imagined Communities* (2003).

14. An example of this gesture is the anthology *McOndo* (1998) in which the nation is not the limit of the identity category but, instead, a postnational regional group that shares certain globalized and urban ideas and practices.

15. Writers and critics may appeal to cosmopolitanism in different ways; thus, it functions contingently. Mariano Siskind observes that for Latin American writers, cosmopolitanism is an "attempt to undo the antagonistic structures of a world literary field organized around the notions of cultural difference that Latin American cosmopolitan writers perceive to be the source of their marginality, in order to stake a claim on Literature with a capital L" (6).

16. Early work in the late twentieth century on historical fiction in Latin America argues that the production of historical fiction (New Historical novel or something else) in Chile is insignificant. This omission is understandable given that many of these critical studies were published circa 1992. Any examination of twentieth-century historical fiction in Chile evinces several chronological pulses when publications are clustered: the 1930s–1940s, the 1960s, and then post-1990s. Works from these earlier waves are studied in several chapters of this study.

17. This refers to White's use of the term "emplotment," that is, "the encodation of the facts contained in the chronicle as components of specific kinds of plot structures" (*Tropics* 83).

18. Pons emphasizes that, while she will impose less draconian restrictions on the way she writes about history and fiction than other intellectuals working on similar topics, those limitations can be nebulous in theoretical terms, particularly due to the thought that "el concepto de Historia, elemento esencial del género, no es un concepto estable y unívoco, como tampoco es muy claro en qué medida y de qué manera debe darse la presencia de la Historia en la ficción como para que consideremos a una novela como histórica" (34–35).

19. In addition to the romantic historical novel (though he saw Scott as a realist), Lukács writes of the historical novel within realism and what he terms "the new

humanism," that is, anti-Fascist work being done in Nazi-occupied areas. Amado Alonso considers *modernismo* in the historical novel through a study of Enrique Larreta's *La gloria de don Ramiro*. María Cristina Pons also anchors her study of the historical novel in an examination of the different literary currents within the subgenre.

20. Many of the studies of the historical novel that do not focus explicitly on its manifestation in the Hispanic world tend to omit those examples. I include these Eurocentric theories fully conscious of the fact that they don't necessarily map clearly onto phenomena in Spanish America.

21. See Richard Walter's 1987 article.

22. In addition to the tensions and fruitful exchanges between historical fiction and academic history, the popularity and influence of historical nonfiction for a popular audience complicates the context in which historical knowledge is produced and consumed. Popular historical nonfiction attracts attention for its commercial success, yet remains less frequently analyzed than historiography or fiction. These points of contact remain an area for further study, especially in the Chilean context when from 2010–2019 historical nonfiction reached unprecedented audiences of the Chilean reading public at the same time it attracted public critiques from certain quarters of the academic historical establishment.

23. These intentionalities are: (a) didactic; (b) parodical; (c) poetic; (d) allegorical; (e) metadiscursive; and (f) mythic.

24. Viu distills her categorizations and their differing relationships with historical representation (Insignia, Memorial, Inscription, Tableau, Biographical Sketch, and Vignette) along several axes, which include revisionism and historiography; homage to irreverence faced through past events; verisimilitude in representation to caricature; chronology to achronology; melodrama to postmodern novel; and narrative to poetry.

25. Doris Sommer's important *Foundational Fictions* (1993) observes that national novels of the nineteenth century are all love stories; novels of the Chilean conquest are more of a twentieth- and twenty-first century phenomenon.

26. After the publication of *La isla bajo el mar* (2009), Allende shifted away from historical novels in her writing. In an interview, she noted that "I have been writing a lot of historical novels, and they require huge research and to be so careful with every detail . . . . Four years of research about slavery, the worst possible subject. I got sick with it" (Allende "Novelist"). However, since *Largo pétalo del mar* (2019), she has returned to the genre.

Chapter One

1. In 2023 the city government announced that the statue of Valdivia would be repaired and returned to the central plaza of the city, with a projected completion date for restoration in October 2024.

2. Most studies of historical fiction about the conquest focus on a handful of novels dealing with Spanish conquistadors, usually those in Mexico and the Caribbean. Although the majority of works feature men's experiences, Kimberle López notes that a

number of works seek to recuperate "some significant female figures" (11) such as Lucía Miranda, a Spanish woman who is supposed to have been part of the sixteenth-century conquest of the Río de la Plata.

3. Representations of the nineteenth-century Occupation of Araucanía are the topic of chapter 4.

4. This follows the pattern in which the majority-culture seeks to define indigenous and to fix what it perceives to be problems for indigenous life. Historical fiction usually follows this pattern as well, with majority-culture writers interpreting indigenous cultures for a majority-culture public.

5. Women historians write on the colonial period, but their work focuses on the period after the general establishment of the colony, usually beginning around the governorship of García Hurtado de Mendoza (1535–1609). Cecilia Salinas's work, as well as the essays in the collection *Historia de la vida privada en Chile*, focus on the latter half of the sixteenth century through the early nineteenth century.

6. The characterization of Inés Suárez and the *criollas* of Chile as manly women—or in Spanish, *mujeres varoniles*—resonates with sixteenth- and seventeenth-century representations in Spanish theatre.

7. Diego Portales was a minister in the government of José Joaquín Prieto (1831–1841), and he is associated with the idea of authoritarian government and the subjection of civil society to the authoritarian regime. Novels set during this period, such as Marta Blanco's *La emperrada* (2002) and Jorge Guzmán's *La ley del gallinero* (1999), have been amply studied by Chilean critics of historical fiction.

8. For more detail see chapter 2.

9. While Villalobos has won the National History Prize in Chile and has been well-regarded in the academy during his long and prolific career, he has become a controversial figure due to his work regarding indigenous groups. Mapuche historians view his work as Eurocentric and criticize how it reflects and perpetuates racist understandings of indigenous peoples, particularly the Mapuche, and their history.

10. Romance is a fuzzy term when applied to literature. It is one of the four archetypal plot structures that Hayden White identifies in his theory of emplotment in historiography. "The Romance is fundamentally a drama of self-identification symbolized by the hero's transcendence of the world of experience, his victory over it, and his final liberation from it . . . it is a drama of the triumph of good over evil, of virtue over vice, of light over darkness" (8–9). This notion of a romance—a story that pulls more from the imagination than from a realistic depiction of observed life—is distinct from the popular sense that associates a romance with love, passion, and sex. What the love romance plot shares with the literary fiction romance is the end of a romance emplotment: a drama of victory and triumph.

11. Romance (love) novels have been the subject of feminist criticism since the benchmark studies of Janice Radway and Tania Modleski affirmed the value of the romance novel as a subject for academic study, as well as a more complex form of literary expression than what simple affirmations of the patriarchal oppression of women would have.

12. We recall that this term is suggested by José de Piérola as a concept that elucidates

the way in which the reader understands historical references in the context of historical fiction.

13. Ann K. Nauman's biography of Inés Suárez, the only monograph dedicated exclusively to this figure, sources much material from May's novel.

14. Rodrigo Díaz de Vivar lived in the eleventh century and was a soldier and leader whose myth has become one of the foundational heroic stories of Spain.

15. Allende describes herself as Chilean (Cerda) and in late 2009 was recognized by a plurality of Chileans as their favorite Chilean writer ("Queremos"). Despite (or because of) her popularity, however, some literary critics and a number of writers, among them Roberto Bolaño, have accused her of being a bad writer of no real literary import. These debates were brought to the forefront during the press coverage surrounding the 2010 National Literary Prize awarded to Allende.

16. In previous work, I argue that the first-person narration of *Inés del alma mía* contributes to the relationship between Suárez and Santiago and, in so doing, underlines Suárez's maternal function and the gendering of the city itself (Karr-Cornejo "Imagined").

17. The common pot is a tradition of community nourishment and sustenance that continues throughout the region today. For example, during pandemic lockdowns, community organizers in Chile managed massive *ollas comunes* to ensure that folks had food: the United Nations FAO reports that for the period from 2020–2022, 18.2 percent of the Chilean population experienced moderate or severe food insecurity (*State of Food Security* 156).

18. Suárez uses a cooking implement—a frying pan—as a weapon of self-defense on several occasions. She first uses it to prevent her husband from physically abusing her. She again uses it as a blunt instrument on one occasion when Sebastián Romero tries to rape her.

Chapter Two

1. A number of different television stations were said to be preparing soap operas centered on Quintrala as part of the bicentennial celebrations in 2010, though none was ultimately produced. However, in 2011–2012, *La Doña*, a *teleserie nocturna*, which is generally more violent and sexually explicit than traditional melodramatic programming, was produced for Chilevisión, directed by Vicente Sabatini and starring Claudia Di Girólamo in the title role.

2. Victor Maturana raises the related issue of the bias of Vicuña Mackenna's primary documents as a defensive move in his 1904 history of the Augustinian order in Chile: "Si todos esos hechos á cual más grotescos estuvieran esparcidos en varios volúmenes, no habría quizás motivo para desconfiar de su relator, pero están tomados de una misma carta en que abundan otros del mismo jaez . . . hechos todos son estos que sólo han existido en la imaginación del vulgo, y que ni la historia, ni la ciencia jamás pudieron comprobar" (305). However, Vicuña Mackenna's accounts were generally accepted as containing kernels of truth.

3. Current criticism on historiography and fiction dealing with the early seventeenth century in Chile, and particularly those individuals and events related to the Lisperguer family, widely accepts that Vicuña Mackenna and later writers, filmmakers, and journalists unconsciously collaborated in the making and remaking of a myth contributing to national considerations of gender and race. No contemporary portrait, if any had been painted, has survived. As Rebecca Lee notes, Vicuña Mackenna's "trope of the treacherous and contaminating *mestiza* woman suggested that colonial decadence was a result of a corrupt and racially mixed aristocratic society and championed an alternative understanding of Chilean national identity based on a white Europeanizing ideal" (104), an important distinction as the Chilean state expanded, through conquests in the War of the Pacific (1879–1884) and the Occupation of Araucanía (the subject of chapter 4).

4. Vicuña Mackenna also connects Quintrala's depravity to alleged crimes committed by female relatives, most notably her mother and aunt, who are also referred to as Messalinas. Of note, it is only the women of the family who are characterized in such strongly negative terms.

5. For more detail on the relationships between the Spanish Inquisition in the sixteenth and seventeenth centuries and women, see the works of Lisa Vollendorf, Mary E. Giles, and Georgina Dopico Black. Vollendorf collects the stories of individual women in Spain, including Elena/o de Céspedes and various nuns, while offering preliminary evidence for a history of women's education in Spain. Giles collects essays by various scholars focusing on recuperating the life stories of women processed by the Inquisition from a variety of walks of life during the period in question. Dopico Black reads conduct manuals and honor plays to elaborate a framework for understanding the theological and pragmatic implications of sexual practice.

6. A theatrical version of the novel, adapted by Petit, was published in 1935.

7. Marjorie Agosín notes that "lo inusitado, raro, extraño, y el laberinto de lo diabólico, constituyen el tema principal que Petit emplea para recrear vívidamente a la Quintrala. Es precisamente ese elemento popular el vehículo esencial para novelar y exponer una realidad íntima y personal que se ha convertido a través de la historia en un mito de realidad colectiva" (32).

8. Edgerton's work studies the United States and as such should not be unthinkingly applied to the case of Chile. However, his assertions with regard to the role that television plays in public perceptions of a collective self find analogues through various countries and cultures.

9. Alicia Muñoz discusses the use of the confessional mode in her dissertation chapter on Quintrala; Cecilia Ojeda also addresses this narrative strategy.

10. Gustavo Frías notes on his blog that "si bien *El inquisidor* es una novela independiente, podría ser parte de la saga *Tres nombres para Catalina*, que incluye *Catrala* y *La doña de Campofrío*. A diferencia de las otras dos obras donde Catalina de los Ríos y Lisperguer es la protagonista, en *El inquisidor* la Quintrala es una poderosa sombra entre bastidores, una presencia que lo domina todo y que aun en vida es una leyenda en el reino."

11. In a closing author's note, Valdivieso comments that "un atrevimiento fue meterse con doña Catalina de los Ríos y Lisperguer, Quintrala de la leyenda, esa única mujer que

la historia del siglo XVII menta y que menta para mal, para que las Catalinas no se repitan. En tal atrevimiento participaron amigos con quienes hablé de la doña y quienes me ayudaron a recuperarla a nuestro tiempo, desde un pasado de tres siglos" (143).

12. "No os asombréis, si al paso que vamos, estamos construyendo una nación de mestizos brujos que hasta se van a olvidar de los pueblos originarios y día llega que don Alonso de Ribera, creador del ejército profesional y permanente para exterminar y doblegar a los naturales, será considerado el organizador del ejército chileno. ¿Cómo sabéis si antes de cuatrocientos años no aparece un autoasignado capitán general que considere a su propio ejército como "la continuidad de la hueste indiana"? —profetiza don Joan Canudos" (74).

13. Scholars use the term Picunche (people of the north) to refer to Mapudungun-speaking residents of the central valley at the time of the conquest that acculturated to the invaders.

14. The connection between memory and identity-group belonging has been characterized by Lessie Jo Frazier as that which "determines who becomes included and excluded under the rubric of the nation, and consequently to whom the state responds. It also determines the place of particular nation-states in regional and global arenas" (54).

15. Much of the canon of colonial Latin American women's writing is spiritual autobiography. Frías therefore inscribes Catalina within the literary history of her place and time.

16. Readers of the novel may be familiar with this figure due to its presence in José Donoso's *El obsceno pájaro de la noche* (1970).

17. "So God created humankind in his image, in the image of God he created them; male and female he created them" (NSRV).

18. It is of note that during the course of most of *Catrala* and all of *La doña de Campofrío* Catalina is pregnant, expecting De Britto's child, while engaged to marry Alonso de Campofrío.

19. Frías reproduces and alters the confessional verse at the end of Mercedes Valdivieso's novel when he writes a song that is sung repeatedly during Catalina's *Día más largo* and forms part of the sacramental practice of the people of Toda el Agua, including Catalina: "*Esta soy yo, Mamalluca / la hija de Llanka Curiqueo / que es hija de Elvira de Talagante / que es hija de Agueda Flores / que es hija de Catalina / que es mi madre / que soy yo. / Todas hijas de Dios / todas creadoras de linaje / todas caciques de esta tierra*" (*La doña* 189).

20. In *Catrala*, Catalina invites a man she is in love with, the Italian Esteban de Britto, to share her bed for the evening. However, her slave, whom she had experimented with sexually in her youth, is consumed by jealousy and stabs de Britto in the back while he is with Catalina.

21. Francisco Maldonado de Silva (1592–1639) was a *marrano* physician practicing in Chile who was discovered and judged guilty of Judaizing by the Inquisition (imprisoned 1627; executed 1639). Frías's use of Maldonado, who reportedly practiced in Concepción, along with Catalina de Erauso, the lieutenant nun, (1592–1650), plays with chronologies while connecting Catalina to popularly known figures of early seventeenth-century Chile. It is of note that both Maldonado and Erauso have been the subject of historical novels

in the past twenty years; *Camisa limpia* (1989) by Fernando Blanco, *La gesta del marrano* (1991) by Marcos Aguinis, *Catalina, mi padre* (2004) by Gloria Durán, and *Confesiones, la verdadera historia de Catalina de Erauso* (2005) by Juanita Gallardo.

22. She does have both heterosexual and homosexual relationships, though the only scene in which she is sexually intimate with a woman is with her father's lover who is also her future business partner; however, the focus of Catalina's sexual expression is generally with men, despite the fluidity of her gender practice.

23. This can be observed in *Flandes indiano* by Diego de Rosales (written 1674) and *Descripción Histórico-Geográfica del Reino de Chile* by Vicente Carvallo Goyeneche (composed late in the eighteenth century).

24. For more information on slavery as it was practiced in seventeenth century Chile, see Hanisch.

25. The Society of Jesus arrived in Chile in 1593 and signified a new European force that focused on evangelization, learning languages, and teaching; this departed from previous conquering practices in Mapuche territory that focused on violence, exploitation, and destruction.

26. Isidora Aguirre's extensive body of work includes novels and over thirty plays. A critique of the effects of capitalism runs thematically through it.

Chapter Three

1. Bárbara Silva warns that "uno de los peligros propios de situaciones conmemorativas de esta magnitud, es el llegar a repetir tanto una palabra, que ésta tiende a perder su significado" (179); the sheer quantity of projects, official and not, make *Bicentenario* mean many things at once and nothing at all.

2. "Joaquín Toesca fue una de las personalidades más destacadas del período colonial" ("Joaquín Toesca").

3. She carried on a series of affairs with his students; attempted to kill Toesca and escape her marriage by poisoning his asparagus; and was confined to a series of convents that had little effect on her behavior. However, in the last years of Toesca's life, they reconciled. For more detail on their marriage and Fernández de Rebolledo's life, see Albornoz Vásquez, Guarda, and "Toesca."

4. "Place is security; space is freedom" (Tuan 3); Yi-Fu Tuan's understanding of space and place as dependent on experience and perspective informs my use of the terms. Place can define a space; the terms are not mutually exclusive.

5. Kelly Donahue-Wallace observes that during the late eighteenth century, the architectural style practiced by Toesca, among other architects, functioned multivalently in Spanish America. "While crown administrators may have viewed the neoclassical style as evidence of American loyalty to Spain, many Latin Americans, particularly the elite criollo populations, may not have agreed. Independence-minded colonists may have associated neoclassicism with the art of France and the United States of America, whose late eighteenth-century revolutions soon inspired Latin Americans to pursue freedom. The

style that arrived to draw the viceroyalties into the centralized fold of the Spanish state became instead the art of independence and of new republics" (240). France's revolution began in 1789, and the American Revolution occurred between 1776 and 1783; Toesca arrived in Chile in 1780.

6. The reader observes this tendency in Vicente Carvallo y Goyeneche, *Descripción histórico-geográfica del Reyno de Chile*; Aurelio Díaz Meza, *Leyendas y episodios chilenos*; Claudio Gay, *Historia física y política de Chile*; and Felipe Gómez de Vidaurre, *Historia geográfica, natural y civil del Reino de Chile*; among others.

7. Toesca appears, often in a positive light, in Diego Barros Arana's *Historia General de Chile*; Francisco Encina's *Historia De Chile Desde La Prehistoria Hasta 1891*; Jaime Eyzaguirre's *Historia de Chile*; Gabriel Guarda's, *El arquitecto de La Moneda. Joaquín Toesca. 1752–1799. Una imagen del imperio español en América*; Alfredo Jocelyn-Holt's *Historia general de Chile*; Eugenio Pereira Salas's *La historia del arte en el reino de Chile*; and Benjamín Vicuña Mackenna's *Historia crítica y social de la ciudad de Santiago: desde su fundación hasta nuestros*.

8. A number of monographs have studied different aspects of Jorge Edwards's oeuvre. Bernard Schulz Cruz's study, published before the release of *El sueño*, focuses on the way that Edwards portrays authoritarianism. Adrián Santini, Roberto Ampuero, and María del Pilar Vila published monographs in 2006 that studied *El sueño* alongside other novels written by Edwards. Antonia Viu emphasizes *El sueño* in a study of the contemporary historical novel in Chile.

9. Reyes studies the use of language in the novel to elucidate the function of anachronism. Viu argues that colonial language crystallizes the relationship between words and societal attitudes. Schulz Cruz identifies a particular colloquial language as a marker of parody and the absurd in Edwards's novels, which brings the narrative voice close to hope and power without effecting change in cultural structures. Ignacio reflects on the power of colonial language's ambiguity (Edwards 31), which embodies the principle of obedience without compliance.

10. While the Plaza de Armas, the southern edge of which is the Portal Fernández Concha, was the center of life in Santiago during the colonial period, patterns of urban development and economic segregation provoke one to question whether it would, indeed, be considered the heart of the city in the twenty-first century, as the upper classes move progressively further east.

11. However, Fernández de Rebolledo was able to carve out space for resistance in her "inability to accommodate herself to societal norms, privileging her own desires above the rigidity and maintenance of her society's system" (Karr-Cornejo "Imagined" 11).

12. Although some of these threats, such as those rooted in the War of Arauco, are specific to Chilean experience, the instability of various locations within the Americas necessitated the abandonment of settlements (as in the case of the Roanoke colony in the late sixteenth century), or their refoundation and reconstruction. "Sometimes it was a hurricane which caused the relocation of a city (as in the case of the first Santo Domingo), or an earthquake (as in the case of Guatemala City), or poor site location with regard to transportation networks (like Buenos Aires), or a pestilential climate (as with Vera Cruz)" (Kinsbrunner 9).

13. After multiple infidelities and attempts to reform Manuela's behavior, they eventually abandoned their annulment proceedings. Having officially reconciled, Toesca, on his death bed, is thought to have forgiven his wife.

14. Although various periods in Chile's history as an independent nation-state participate in these operations, the work of Diego Portales during José Joaquín Prieto's presidency (1831–1841) and its parallels with Augusto Pinochet's military dictatorship have garnered particular attention. For more detail, see Alfredo Jocelyn-Holt's *El peso de la noche. Nuestra frágil fortaleza histórica* (1999); the titular phrase, taken from one of Portales's letters, is also the title of Jorge Edwards's first novel, the award-winning *El peso de la noche* (1965).

15. María del Pilar Vila observes that in the novel "los silencios, los murmullos, el toque de queda y las últimas señales de la dictadura son la argamasa de la opresión y de control, trasfondo sombrío de la decadencia y el olvido como otra perspectiva del fracaso y de la pérdida de las ilusiones" (204).

16. A *cacerolazo* is a form of protest in which citizenry bang on pots and pans to express their discontent with governmental actions. While in some cases this is done publicly, as was the case with this kind of protest during the Allende government, an advantage of a *cacerolazo* is that the protesters may remain anonymous, creating noise from within their personal dwellings. This remains a potent protest tactic in Chile.

17. This is not uncommon in novels of the democratic transition. As an example, Alberto Fuguet's topography of Santiago, as seen in *Mala onda, Por favor, rebobinar*, and other works, appears to have a western limit of Plaza Italia and a southern limit of the municipality of Ñuñoa (both restricted to majority upper middle- and upper-class spaces), which, given the relationship between class and race in Chile, are also racially segregated from a darker population whose indigenous heritage is more physically obvious. One must also consider that the social landscape of the city is not static and that today's slums were classed differently in the not-so-distant past (Palacios 2010).

18. Although the consensus currently posits that Allende committed suicide, in May 2011 judge Mario Carroza ordered the exhumation of the president's body as part of a larger investigation into officially unresolved cases of death and disappearance during the military dictatorship. The study performed by the *Servicio Médico Legal* was completed in July 2011 and concluded that the president had committed suicide.

19. That is not to say that continual memory work is not being performed on the site of the palace; for example, in 2003, and as part of the commemorations of the thirtieth anniversary of the military coup, the door at Morandé 80, through which President Allende's body was removed from the palace, was "reopened" by President Ricardo Lagos after its having been covered over during the dictatorship. That door was not part of Toesca's design for the building, but rather part of early twentieth-century modifications.

20. "Toesca's mint embodied the state's authority. Manufacturing coins bearing the likeness of the king, the building reinforced Santiago's colonial relationship to the metropolis. Its currency guaranteed an economic lingua franca, as all Spanish subjects employed identical weights and measures in the marketplace. Hence the building stood as a monument to the unity of the vast Spanish empire. Its neoclassical style evoked the

same aura of governmental authority inherited from Roman antiquity that informed contemporary monuments in Europe and the Americas. The classical forms and their associated meaning undoubtedly inspired Chilean politicians to use Toesca's structure as a mint, government office building, and now, presidential palace" (Donahue-Wallace 238–39)

21. Although the images related to the bombing of La Moneda Palace and the suicide of President Allende are gripping and have been widely disseminated, I do not mean to suggest that La Moneda Palace is the only place through which these processes of monumentalization and reconciliation are taking place, though this process is further elaborated in an unpublished dissertation by Mary Grace Strasma. Katherine Hite has examined the National Stadium's role as alternately a place for entertainment and the execution of state terrorism, as well as the contemporary attempts to reconcile these roles. For more analysis of these processes, see the work of Macarena Gómez-Barris and Steve Stern.

22. For details of the development of this area of Santiago, see Alberto Gurovich's study. Gurovich's explanation of the various modes of interpretation of this area of the city are of particular interest to the reader of *El sueño*.

23. La Moneda Palace "debía ostentar un maravilloso escudo de piedra tallada, con las armas reales de España, y una reja no menos artística que por "godas" no fueron jamás colocadas, y se admiran actualmente en el cerro de Santa Lucía" (Peña Otaegui 130).

24. Roberto Ampuero elaborates on this structural parallelism.

25. *El sueño* is unusual in its focus on the late eighteenth century; Chilean historical fiction features a gap for historical referents between roughly 1650 and 1810, with few exceptions.

26. An accounting of the different government-funded projects can be found in Sebastián Piñera "Bicentenario." This is not to imply that the bicentennial celebrations are limited to government projects.

27. Throughout this chapter, I refer to the historical figure by her last name, or if there is need to avoid confusion with her brothers, both her first name and first surname.

28. Per Michel-Rolph Trouillot, "the production of traces is always also the creation of silences" (29) in historical narratives.

29. Manuel Rodríguez completes a sort of trinity of Chilean independence heroes; while he supported independence, he is most remembered for his work against the Spanish during the period of the Reconquest between 1813 and 1817. He also worked with and was used by both Carrera and O'Higgins, though Rodríguez cannot be associated clearly with either camp; he collaborated with the liberating army led by José de San Martín as well. He was assassinated in 1818 after years of struggle as a guerrilla fighter and remains a popular rogue figure. Many texts about Rodríguez (see Guajardo) exist, though narrative fiction is relatively rare, Alberto Blest Gana's *Durante la Reconquista* (1897) notwithstanding. The only text I have been able to locate primarily featuring Rodríguez published between 1990 and 2010 is a biography by Ana María Larraín, *Manuel Rodríguez: flecha ardiente y fugaz*. However, greater interest in his story surfaces alongside the popularity of historical nonfiction in the 2010s. Given his in-between role and the lack of a chronologically appropriate text telling his stories, I have excluded him from this section.

30. The Chilean independence movement is commonly studied and understood

as a three-part process taking place between 1810 and 1823. The first portion, known as the *Patria Vieja*, may debatably be periodized beginning with the Cabildo declaration of 18 September 1810, that, rather than declaring definitive independence from Spain, recognized the lack of central authority produced by Napoleon's invasion and responded by creating mechanisms for local administration. In 1814, the battle of Rancagua sealed the defeat of the patriot forces, many of whom fled to Mendoza in the aftermath of the battle. This period, in which Spanish control was reestablished in the territory, is known as the Reconquista. In 1817, and with the support of José de San Martín and other figures in Argentina, the Ejército de los Andes defeated the Spanish royalist forces and Bernardo O'Higgins was installed as supreme director; he also declared independence from Spain in February of 1817. His time in power as supreme director, an office he held until 1823, is known as the *Patria Nueva*.

31. Graham is by far the best-known of these travelers, but the accounts of Basil Hall, Samuel Haigh, John Miers, and William Bennet Stevenson also describe the characters of the Chilean independence movements.

32. There are novels in both English and Spanish, a movie, and an opera about Sáenz, in addition to her appearances in both historical films and television programs.

33. Javiera Carrera, alongside figures such as Paula Jaraquemada (1768–1851) and Inés Suárez, is presented by right-wing women as a model for women's civic participation, as observed in the work of Margaret Power. Also, despite narratives that privilege men's contributions to independence struggles, women throughout the region were instrumental. In many cases their actions, regarded as extraordinary, were widespread. For more information on women's roles in independence struggles throughout Latin America, see the work of Claire Brewster.

34. This concern about women's possible contamination of the noble ideals of independence is not unique to Chile. Manuela Sáenz, the mistress of Simón Bolívar, has also been presented in such a way. For a study of the way in which historiography constructed Manuela Sáenz throughout the twentieth century, see the work of Pamela Murray.

35. This is particularly notable in contrast with Sady Zañartu's *Xaviera Carrera* (1940), a novel that pursues such contorted means to maintain the metaphorical birth of a nation that it results in an awkwardly obscene figuring of Javiera and her brothers as progenitors who masturbate to avoid incest.

36. Gallardo's novels function as recuperative documents that seek to refinish the images of figures from the past: the female ancestors of Catalina de los Ríos y Lisperguer; Catalina de Erauso, the Lieutenant Nun; Rosario Puga and Bernardo O'Higgins; and José Manuel Balmaceda.

37. A historical overview of women's activities during the struggle for independence can be found in Peña González.

38. Each section also features an epigraph, many of which come from the poetry of Gabriela Mistral—especially, "A Javiera Carrera."

39. Class does not disappear within the convent; indeed, social class as imposed by the world outside the convent walls operates and controls the relationships between the women enclosed within its space. For more information about convents in the Chilean

context, see the essay by René Millar and Carmen Gloria Duhart in *Historia de la vida privada en Chile*.

40. The metaphorical configuration of the nation as a family homogenizes its diversity, though it is a political philosophy with roots from Aristotle to Confucius. Carrera's symbolic motherhood recalls the role of Inés Suárez, as discussed in chapter 1.

41. Salinas explains that "en la sociedad tradicional el matrimonio cristiano no fue la única forma de unión estable y «honesta» a que aspiró la gente. Otras formas—como el concubinato—también fueron practicadas masivamente. Estas «uniones de hecho» iban desde una convivencia con la pareja «amada» hasta la unión de un hombre con una mujer libre cuyo único patrimonio era su cuerpo (lindante con la prostitución). El tipo de unión conocida como «amancebamiento» se practicó masivamente y con un alto grado de tolerancia social, aun cuando numerosos casos fueron el resultado de la imposibilidad que tuvieron muchos solteros para superar las barreras legales, económicas y espaciales que exigía el matrimonio" (23). The debate about "uniones de hecho," common law marriage, remains pertinent to twenty-first-century Chilean politics.

42. The Jaime Eyzaguirre to whom Gallardo refers is the twentieth-century historian, not a fictional figure.

Chapter Four

1. These include *El lento silbido de los sables* (2010) by Patricio Manns, *Casas en el agua* (1997) by Guido Eytel, and *Vientos de silencio* (1999) by J. J. Faundes. Manns's novel tells a story of violence and exploitation from the perspective of a decadent and grotesque Chilean military leader. Eytel's text recounts the foundation of the fictional town San Estanislao de Rucaco in the mode of a chronicle of conquest. *Vientos de silencio* focuses on Francisco de Paula Frías (1847–1889) and the creation of independent press in southern Chile. For a reading of these texts, see Karr-Cornejo "Aspects."

2. "La plurinacionalidad es, primero, un proyecto político: se trata del reconocimiento de que al interior de un solo Estado conviven diversos pueblos y naciones indígenas, los cuales participan en la vida política en cuanto colectivos con derecho a determinar sus propias prioridades de desarrollo, de acuerdo a sus formas diversas de ver y entender el mundo. No es un estándar internacional por sí mismo; no existe tratado internacional que se refiera a la plurinacionalidad (como sí es el caso de la libre determinación). Es, más bien, una forma distinta de entender la igualdad, la democracia y la composición del Estado" (#Constitucionalista).

3. An excellent example of this trend is *Y así nació la Frontera* by Ricardo Ferrando.

4. This is much more common than the use of "la frontera"; in recent texts the term *frontera* is used less often and when present often refers to previous historiographical postures that exclusively privilege pro-state civilizing discourses. Those privileging "relaciones fronterizas" have been roundly criticized by Mapuche intellectuals and their allies due to the racist undertones of their epistemology and the direct discriminatory statements of one of its most prominent adherents.

5. Some indigenous activists critique the term Araucanía as an imposition of the colonizing state and instead prefer Wallmapu, Mapudungun for the universe.

6. Tomás Guevara's *Ocupación de Araucanía* exemplifies this pattern.

7. See Joanna Crow's *The Mapuche in Modern Chile*, Jorge Pinto Rodríguez's *La formación del estado y la nación, y el pueblo mapuche: de la inclusión a la exclusión*, Patricia Richards's *Race and the Chilean Miracle*, and José Bengoa's *Historia del pueblo mapuche*.

8. For example, certain *lonkos* (Mapuche tribal authorities) led their people to fight for Spain during the independence conflict (1810–1818); allied with the royalist Pincheira brothers (1810–1832); and fought against the state in rebellions in 1851 and 1859.

9. These reservations made up a tiny proportion of the land they had previously occupied. Nearly a third of the survivors of the Occupation, moreover, received nothing. (Richards 40–41).

10. Detailed in the work of both Pinto and Bottinelli in the context of the Occupation. His role in the solidification of the Quintrala myth is detailed both in the second chapter of this book and in Rebecca Lee's article.

11. Tounens made it to Chilean territory in 1869 but was forced to leave again in 1871 due to lack of financial resources. His third attempt to get to Chilean territory failed; he died in France in 1878.

12. For details of current work, see *Le Royaume D'Araucanie et de Patagonie* (www.araucanie.com) and *Mapuche International Link* (www.mapuche-nation.org).

13. Quilapán was son of a prominent cacique Juan Mangin Hueno. On his father's death in 1866, he became the head of the rebelling Mapuche west of the Andes. He was the last unifying leader of the *arribanos*, also known as the Wenteche or people of the plains. (Bengoa 86–91)

14. Pinto Rodríguez reviews the state of relevant Chilean historiography in the twentieth century and analyzes the connection, or lack thereof, with pedagogical materials used to teach Chilean history to children and adolescents (251–59).

15. Fictional texts (including biographies) cited include the works of Armando Braun Menéndez, Víctor Domingo Silva, and Jean Raspail, several of which are also studied later in this chapter.

16. Monomania was understood to be an obsession with one particular idea in such a way as to deform the individual's perception of reality.

17. For example, he notes that one of the elements that contributed to Mapuche acceptance of Tounens "fue la innegable necesidad de centralización política que se venía dando en la sociedad mapuche" (Bengoa 190).

18. Some of the texts excluded include *Yo, Antoine de Tounens, Rey de la Patagonia* (1981) by the conservative French royalist Jean Raspail and the more recent Argentine text *El rey de la Patagonia* (1999) by Claudio Morales Gorleri.

19. Alejandro de Vivar, or Ñamku (1635–1660), was the son of Kurivilú and a Spanish captive, Isabel de Vivar y Castro. He was raised in the Mapuche community until he was five, at which time his father was murdered and he and his mother returned to the settlements. There, he entered the Spanish military but was unable to move up the ranks due to his racial background. He abandoned the Spanish and returned to the Mapuche, where

he became a military leader before being murdered by his Mapuche wives after he took a Spanish captive as a concubine.

20. The word used is *luzbeliano*, that is, Luciferesque.

21. Fernando Zúñiga notes that linguists of European extraction highly value Mapudungun as a language.

22. See José Luis Alonso Marchante, *Menéndez Rey de la Patagonia* (2014) on the family's role in Patagonian history, particularly related to economic consolidation and the extermination of the Selk'nam.

23. As seen in the portrayal of figures such as Lautaro, discussed briefly in chapter 1, narratives construct living indigenous peoples as barbaric and uncivilized, but, when vanquished and dead, they are heroic and worthy opponents to the conquerors.

24. Ellingson examines the history of the noble savage as a discursive construct, concluding that the construct obfuscates and that it, in a way, tricks us into affirming an essentialist definition of a people as savage (373).

25. This belief calls to mind the Western tradition of the Arthurian romance.

26. See Muñoz Román for a study of mainstream newspaper coverage of the "conflicto mapuche." See Merino and Mellor for a study of discriminatory and racist language-use against Mapuche subjects.

27. While Staiger's novel is often listed in studies of historical fiction in Chile, close readings of the text have not been published. Pedro Staiger has also written other historical novels, such as *Las tres muertes de Vicente Benavides* (2010).

28. In 2016, Mapuche scholar Elisa Loncón reflected on the necessity of teaching indigenous languages to indigenous youth: "We are human because we have language. Without that, our culture is silenced" (UC).

29. Sebastián Castro and Guido "Kid" Salinas have collaborated to create a DC/Marvel style comic series, *Guardianes del sur*, featuring four sixteenth-century Mapuche heroes: Galvarino, Caupolicán, Janequeo, and Lautaro. The "Mapuverso" was published as an omnibus collection in 2022. Prior to the 2019 uprising, the comic was picked up by Netflix.

30. For details on the armed conflict, see William Sater's *Andean Tragedy*.

31. However, the consequences of this victory are ongoing for Chilean foreign policy. Although military hostilities ceased in 1884, border treaties were not signed until 1904, and the fates of Tacna and Arica were not decided until 1929. Disputes over ocean access and maritime borders have been ongoing for a century. The International Court of Justice ruled in 2018 that Chile does not have a legal obligation to negotiate with Bolivia for ocean access.

32. The main Chilean fictional text dealing with these events is Jorge Inostroza's *Adiós al séptimo de línea* (1955), which was also dramatized as a television program. It is of note that there is significant literary production set during and reflecting on the events of the War of the Pacific from Peruvian and Bolivian perspectives. One would be remiss not to mention Alcides Arguedas's *Pisagua* (Bolivia, 1903), Joaquín Aguirre's *Guano maldito* (Bolivia, 1976), or the four novels by Guillermo Thorndike (Peru) also published in the late 1970s: *1879*, *El viaje de Prado*, *Vienen los chilenos*, and *La batalla de Lima*. However,

recent literary interest in these events remains relatively low, other than the lone exception of Ignacio López-Merino's novel *Sangre de hermanos* (Peru, 2008).

33. The episode relating to the *Quintrala*, discussed in chapter 2, merits more minutes.

34. While this patriotic image and a brief discussion about the process of Prat's mythification close one episode, in the next the atrocities committed by occupying Chilean troops in Peru are clearly explained and condemned.

35. Images of the solitary flag remain symbolically potent, as can be observed by the popularity of a photograph taken in the aftermath of the February 2010 earthquake; in that photo, a man stands in the foreground of a tsunami-destroyed landscape, holding a muddy Chilean flag (Candia).

36. Prat is described by William Sater as a secular saint and key to understanding the heroic image in Chile. He is subject of many popular biographies and many public spatial commemorations (statues) throughout Chilean territory.

Chapter Five

1. These categories, pulled from the index of the article, include the following: "antecedentes económicos; antecedentes políticos; Balmaceda; causas; cultura y sociedad; discursos y proclamas; decretos y leyes/documentos oficiales; enfrentamientos militares; el conflicto en el extranjero; participación de la iglesia; historiografía; persecuciones, crimines y saqueos; relatos y memorias; teatro, novela y música" (123–24).

2. While José Manuel Balmaceda and his wife, Emilia Toro y Herrera, had six children, Dolores is an invented character.

3. Juan of God is the most directly connected to religious stories, as he ends up a herder. Juan the Evangelist is a gardener, connected to the beloved disciple who both authored one of the Gospels and tried to stay awake with Jesus at the garden of Gethsemane. Juan of Carmen's full name alludes to the patron saint of Chile, Our Lady of Mount Carmel.

4. This structure is very visual, using metanarrative, irony, and critique of failure, in a manner similar to comedy films such as Carlos Sorín's *La película del rey* (1986), referenced in chapter 4, and Jorge Alí Triana's *Bolívar soy yo* (2002).

5. For a brief overview of the Popular Unity government (1970–1973), see "El gobierno de la Unidad Popular (1970–1973)" in Spanish and "Milestones in the History of U.S. Foreign Relations" in English.

6. Letters and diaries are a key primary source document in historiographical work. "The historical value of reading diaries and letters involves understanding the significance of how individual writers employed, experimented with, or altered the conventional forms alive in their time. Perhaps more than any other kind of historical text, the personal writing we are considering reveals how people both embraced and resisted the time and place in which they lived. Their personal motives for employing either form—the emotional and intellectual energy infusing the form with life each time it is written with

a new subjectivity—suggest much about how people in the past made their cultures, but made them from the materials at hand." (Stowe 3)

7. Today it is easy to listen to the recording of Salvador Allende's final speech on 11 September broadcast on radio Magallanes. The most cited lines conclude the broadcast, when he says "Trabajadores de mi patria: tengo fe en Chile y su destino. Superarán otros hombres este momento gris y amargo, donde la traición pretende imponerse. Sigan ustedes sabiendo que, mucho más temprano que tarde, de nuevo abrirán las grandes alamedas por donde pase el hombre libre para construir una sociedad mejor. ¡Viva Chile! ¡Viva el pueblo! ¡Vivan los trabajadores! Éstas son mis últimas palabras y tengo la certeza de que mi sacrificio no será en vano. Tengo la certeza de que, por lo menos, habrá una lección moral que castigará la felonía, la cobardía y la traición." (Allende Gossens)

8. This calls to mind stories of how images and film documenting the abuses of Pincohet's dictatorship were censored or destroyed, or of how the footage that became Patricio Guzmán's *La batalla de Chile* was smuggled out of the country.

9. Wilce defines lament as "a discursive and musical genre linked with crying and with funerary observances, but also used in other contexts" (25).

10. Lament "stems from an acute experience of pain, be it physical, emotional or spiritual" (Harasta and Brock 1). Lament does not simply regret pain but rather implies a hope for the future despite the experience of suffering.

11. Eulalia observes that this cruelty also becomes evident in armed conflicts outside of national boundaries, as well as how the myth of the civilized Chilean can be maintained when such violence is enacted outside national territory (54).

12. A number of the characters in Aguirre's novel are fictional inventions, such as Felipe and the members of his family. Others are not. Martina Barros Borgoño de Orrego (1850–1944) is known today as a writer and feminist precursor in Chile, publishing the first translation of John Stuart Mill's *The Subjection of Women* in 1872–73. The spouse with whom she argues, Augusto Orrego Luco (1849–1933), was a distinguished author, doctor, and politician.

Conclusion

1. The UN Human Rights mission to Chile in late 2019 reported that, through 22 November, twenty-six people had been killed (*Report* 10); as of 2024, the number of those killed varies between thirty and forty people.

2. This number is documented by the Chilean Instituto Nacional de Derechos Humanos (*Información* 6). In 2023, the INDH noted that 220 people were part of cases they brought relating to ocular trauma (Pino).

3. "Protesters demanded the protection of a heterogeneous set of rights. The demands ranged from public transportation prizes to social security, from the gender agenda to the healthcare system's problems, and from the highly unequal educational system to environmental demands. Faced with increased pressure, the political parties organized a constitution-making process to channel those demands and simultaneously

end the Pinochet-era Constitution. Most scholars true to the process, including non-Chilean comparative constitutional scholars, were excited about the prospect of replacing the 1980 Constitution. The Chilean process that was opening was supposed to become a beacon for a popular but post-sovereign approach that could have avoided the democratically risky neo-Bolivarian path that other Latin American countries had experienced." (Verdugo and García-Huidobro 160)

4. "Voters" refers to ballots that indicated either approve or reject; for the 2022 draft, two percent of the total number of people voting (not included in the percentages of valid ballots) turned in invalid or blank ballots.

5. For the 2023 draft, five percent of the total number of people voting (not included in the percentages of valid ballots) turned in invalid or blank ballots.

WORKS CITED

Agosín, Marjorie. *Las hacedoras: mujer, imagen, escritura*. Cuarto Propio, 1993.
Aguirre, Isidora. *Balmaceda: diálogos de amor y muerte*. Uqbar Editores, 2008.
———. *Guerreros del sur*. Uqbar, 2011.
Aínsa, Fernando. "Invención literaria y 'reconstrucción' histórica en la nueva narrativa latinoamericana." *La invención del pasado. La novela histórica en el marco de la posmodernidad*, edited by Karl Kohut. Vervuert Iberoamericana, 1997, pp. 111–21.
Alalef, Alejandro. "Crítica de cine: La Esmeralda, 1879." *La Tercera*, 24 May 2010, https://www.latercera.com/noticia/critica-de-cine-la-esmeralda-1879/.
Albornoz Vásquez, María Eugenia. "Desencuentro de afectos y de poderes." *Nuevo Mundo Mundos Nuevos*, 2007, https://doi.org/10.4000/nuevomundo.12752.
Alfieri, Carlos. "Jorge Edwards, la ficción de la memoria." *Cuadernos Hispanoamericanos*, vol. 571, 1998, pp. 122–38.
Allende, Isabel. *Inés del alma mía*. Sudamericana, 2006.
———. "Novelist Isabel Allende on Her Literary Career and Memories of Chile During the CIA-Backed Coup." Interview by Amy Goodman. *Democracy Now!*, 28 Nov. 2014, http://www.democracynow.org/2014/11/28/novelist_isabel_allende_on_her_literary.
Allende Gossens, Salvador. *Discurso del presidente Salvador Allende en la radio Magallanes, 11 de septiembre de 1973*. Audio, 11 Sept. 1973, https://www.bibliotecanacionaldigital.gob.cl/visor/BND:82594. Biblioteca Nacional de Chile.
Alonso, Amado. *Ensayo sobre la novela histórica. El modernismo en La gloria de don Ramiro*. Facultad de Filosofía y Letras de la Universidad de Buenos Aires, 1942.
Alonso Marchante, José Luis. *Menéndez Rey de la Patagonia*. Catalonia, 2014.
Álvarez, Ignacio. "El Rey de Araucanía y la Endemoniada de Santiago: aportes para una historia de la locura en el Chile del siglo XIX." *Persona y Sociedad*, vol. 20, no. 1, 2006, pp. 105–24, https://repositorio.uc.cl/handle/11534/47860.
Alvear Ravanal, Julio. "El proceso de Reforma Agraria en Chile: un análisis crítico de la revolución." *Derecho Público Iberoamericano*, no. 11, Oct. 2017, pp. 129–51, https://revistas.udd.cl/index.php/RDPI/article/view/84.
Ampuero, Roberto. *La historia como conjetura. Reflexiones sobre la narrativa de Jorge Edwards*. Edwards Bello, 2006.

Amunátegui, Miguel Luis. *Descubrimiento i conquista de Chile.* Leipzig, 1885.
———. *La dictadura de O'Higgins.* Santiago, 1914.
———. *El terremoto del 13 de mayo de 1647.* Santiago, 1882.
Anderson, Benedict. *Imagined Communities: Reflections on the Origin and Spread of Nationalism.* Verso, 1991.
Anderson Imbert, Enrique. "Notas sobre la novela histórica en el siglo XIX." *La novela iberoamericana.* Edited by Arturo Torres-Rioseco. U of New Mexico P, 1952, pp. 1–24.
Araya, Juan Gabriel. *1891: Entre el fulgor y la agonía.* Universitaria, 1991.
Avelar, Idelber. *The Untimely Present: Postdictatorial Latin American Fiction and the Task of Mourning.* Duke UP, 1999.
"Balmaceda y El Fin de La Guerra." *Algo Habrán Hecho Por La Historia de Chile,* directed by Nicolás Acuña, episode 7, Televisión Nacional de Chile, 29 Aug. 2010.
Barr-Melej, Patrick. *Reforming Chile. Cultural Politics, Nationalism, and the Rise of the Middle Class.* U of North Carolina P, 2001.
Barrientos, Juan José. *Ficción-historia. La nueva novela histórica hispanoamericana.* UNAM, 2001.
Barros Arana, Diego. *Historia General de Chile.* Universitaria, 1999. 16 vols.
———. *Proceso de Pedro de Valdiva i otros documentos ineditos concernientes a este conquistador.* Santiago, 1873.
Behar, Ruth. "Sexual Witchcraft, Colonialism, and Women's Powers: Views from the Mexican Inquisition." *Sexuality and Marriage in Colonial Latin America,* edited by Asunción Lavrín, Uof Nebraska P, 1989, pp. 178–206.
Bengoa, José. *Historia del pueblo mapuche (Siglo XIX y XX).* Ediciones Sur, 1985.
Benhabib, Seyla. *The Claims of Culture. Equality and Diversity in the Global Era.* Princeton UP, 2002.
Berlant, Lauren. *The Anatomy of National Fantasy. Hawthorne, Utopia, and Everyday Life.* U of Chicago P, 1991.
Bhabha, Homi. *The Location of Culture.* Routledge, 2004.
Blakemore, Harold. "The Chilean Revolution of 1891 and Its Historiography." *Hispanic American Historical Review,* vol. 45, no. 3, 1965, pp. 393–421, https://doi.org/10.1215/00182168-45.3.393.
Block, Melissa. "Allende Reimagines Life of Conquistador 'Ines'." *All Things Considered.* NPR. 6 Nov. 2006.
Boric, Gabriel. "Presidente de la República, Gabriel Boric Font, se dirige al país con motivo del sensible fallecimiento del ex Presidente Sebastián Piñera Echenique." *Prensa Presidencia,* 6 Feb. 2024, http://prensa.presidencia.cl/comunicado.aspx?id=280626.
Bottinelli, Alejandra. "'El oro y la sangre que vamos a prodigar.' Benjamín Vicuña Mackenna, la ocupación de la Araucanía y la inscripción del imperativo civilizador en el discurso público chileno." *Historias de racismo y discriminación en Chile,* Uqbar Editores, 2009, pp. 107–25.
Bravo Díaz, Pablo. "La Guerra Civil 1891 Fichero Bibliográfico." *Dimensión Histórica de Chile,* vol. 8, 1991, pp. 121–40.

Brennan, Niall. "Representing National Culture, Values and Identity in the Brazilian Television Miniseries." *Networking Knowledge: Journal of the MeCCSA Postgraduate Network*, vol. 2, no. 1, 2009, pp. 1–21.
Brennan, Teresa. *The Transmission of Affect*. Cornell UP, 2004.
Brewster, Claire. "Women and the Spanish-American Wars of Independence: An Overview." *Feminist Review*, vol. 79, 2005, pp. 20–35. *JSTOR*, https://www.jstor.org/stable/3874426.
Butler, Judith. *Gender Trouble: Feminism and Subversion of Identity*. Routledge, 1990.
Cádiz Ávila, Ilda. *La pequeña Quintrala de Joaquín Toesca*. Editorial Aníbal Pinto, 1993.
Calhoun, Craig. "Social Solidarity as a Problem for Cosmopolitan Democracy." *Identities, Affiliations, and Allegiances*, edited by Seyla Benhabib, Ian Shapiro, and Danilo Petranović, Cambridge UP, 2007, pp. 285–302.
Camp, Charles. *American Foodways: What, When, Why, and How We Eat in America*. August House, 1989.
Candia, Roberto. *27 de Febrero de 2010. Pelluhue*. Photograph, 29 Feb. 2010, https://www.robertocandia.com/index/G0000TAq5I3BNXdU/I0000u7UdnHzPK28.
Cano Roldán, Imelda. *La mujer en el Reyno de Chile*. Municipalidad de Santiago, 1981.
Cánovas, Rodrigo. *Novela chilena. Nuevas generaciones. El abordaje de los huérfanos*. Ediciones Universidad Católica de Chile, 1997.
Cárcamo-Huechante, Luis. *Tramas de mercado: imaginación económica, cultura pública y literatura en el Chile de fines del siglo veinte*. Cuarto Propio, 2007.
Carvallo y Goyeneche, Vicente de. *Descripción histórico-geográfica del Reyno de Chile*. Santiago, 1875.
Castillo Sandoval, Roberto. "'¿Una misma cosa con la vuestra'?: Ercilla, Pedro de Oña y la apropiación post-colonial de la patria araucana." *Revista iberoamericana*, vol. 61, no. 170–71, 1995, pp. 231–47, https://doi.org/10.5195/reviberoamer.1995.6406.
Castro, Sebastian, and Guido Salinas. *Guardianes del sur*. Integral, Planeta Cómic, 2022.
Castro-Klarén, Sara and John Charles Chasteen. *Beyond Imagined Communities: Reading and Writing the Nation in Nineteenth-century Latin America*. Johns Hopkins UP, 2003.
Chevalier Naranjo, Stéphanie. "Infografía: La aprobación de Piñera se desploma en Chile." *Statista Daily Data*, 23 Oct. 2019, https://es.statista.com/grafico/19740/tasa-de-aprobacion-de-la-gestion-del-presidente-pinera-en-chile.
"Chile celebra el Bicentenario y enfrenta un futuro promisorio." *La Tercera*, 18 Sept. 2010, www.latercera.com/noticia/opinion/editorial/2010/09/894-292769-9-chile-celebra-el-bicentenario-y-enfrenta-un-futuro-promisorio.shtml.
Choay, Françoise. *The Invention of the Historic Monument*, translated by Lauren M. O'Connell, Cambridge UP, 2001.
"Cines abrirán sus puertas para que escolares vean la película 'La Esmeralda 1879.'" *La Tercera*, 20 May 2010, https://www.latercera.com/noticia/cines-abriran-sus-puertas-para-que-escolares-vean-la-pelicula-la-esmeralda-1879/
Cisternas, Cristián. "Ay, Mama Inés, de Jorge Guzmán: La madre y el deseo como historia." *Revista Chilena de Literatura*, vol. 46, 1994, pp. 97–100.
Clemence, Stella R. "Review." *Hispanic American Historical Review*, vol. 13, no. 4, 1933, p. 484.

Clissold, Stephen. *Bernardo O'Higgins and the Independence of Chile*. Frederick A. Praeger, 1969.

Collins, Patricia Hill. "Toward a New Vision: Race, Class and Gender as Categories of Analysis and Connection." *Social Class and Stratification: Classic Statements and Theoretical Debates*, edited by Rhonda F. Levine, Rowan & Littlefield, 2006, pp. 219–33.

"Concepción colonial—Memoria Chilena." *Memoria Chilena: Portal*, https://www.memoriachilena.gob.cl/602/w3-article-573.html. Accessed 26 May 2024.

#Constitucionalista. "(17) Estado plurinacional: qué es y qué cambia." *CIPER Chile*, 11 July 2022, https://www.ciperchile.cl/2022/07/11/17-estado-plurinacional/.

Contardo, Óscar. *Siútico. Arribismo, abajismo y vida social en Chile*. Ediciones B, 2008.

@Coordinadora8M. "AHORA—EL METRO DE SANTIAGO SE VUELVE FEMINISTA Las líneas y estaciones de metro de Santiago han amanecido diferentes hoy, se viene la huelga feminista! #SuperLunesFeminista" *Twitter*, 4 Mar. 2019, 3:20 a.m., twitter.com/Coordinadora8m/status/1102529212815237122.

Correa Morandé, María. *Inés . . . y las raíces en la tierra*. Zig-zag, 1964.

Crow, Joanna. *The Mapuche in Modern Chile. A Cultural History*. UP of Florida, 2013.

Cumplido, María José. *Chilenas rebeldes*. Montena, 2018.

Délano, Luis Enrique. *JM Balmaceda*. Ediciones Nuevas, 1944.

Dhamoon, Rita. *Identity/Difference Politics: How Difference is Produced and Why It Matters*. U British Columbia P, 2009.

Discurso de la Presidenta de la República al anunciar el proceso constituyente. 13 Oct. 2015, http://www.gob.cl/2015/10/13/discurso-de-la-presidenta-de-la-republica-al-anunciar-el-proceso-constituyente/.

Domingo Silva, Víctor. *El rey de la Araucanía*. Zig-zag, 1937.

Donahue-Wallace, Kelly. *Art and Architecture of Viceregal Latin America, 1521–1821*. U of New Mexico P, 2008.

Donoso, Sofia. "Dynamics of Change in Chile: Explaining the Emergence of the 2006 Pingüino Movement." *Journal of Latin American Studies*, vol. 45, no.1, 2013, pp. 1–29.

Dopico Black, Georgina. *Perfect Wives, Other Women: Adultery and Inquisition in Early Modern Spain*. Duke UP, 2001.

Edgerton, Gary R. "Television as Historian. A Different Kind of History Altogether." *Television Histories. Shaping Collective Memory in the Media Age*, edited by Gary R. Edgerton and Peter C. Rollins, UP of Kentucky, 2001, pp. 1–16.

Edwards, Jorge. "Mito, historia, y novela." Editorial Universitaria, 1980.

———. *El sueño de la historia*. Tusquets, 2000.

Edwards Bello, Joaquín. *La Quintrala, Portales y algo más*. Universitaria, 1969.

Ellingson, Terry Jay. *The Myth of the Noble Savage*. U of California P, 2001.

Encina, Francisco A. *Historia De Chile Desde La Prehistoria Hasta 1891*. Nascimento, 1948–1956.

Ercilla, Alonso de. *La Araucana*. Salamanca, 1574.

Errázuriz, Crescente. *Pedro de Valdivia*. Imprenta Cervantes, 1911–1912.

La Esmeralda 1879, directed by Elías Llanos, Azul Producciones, 2010.
Eyzaguirre, Jaime. *Fisonomía histórica de Chile*. Fondo de Cultura Económica, 1948.
———. *Historia de Chile*. Zig-zag, 1973.
———. *O'Higgins*. Zig-zag, 1960.
———. *Ventura de Pedro de Valdivia*. Universitaria, 1986.
———. *Viejas imágenes*. Universitaria, 1978.
Fernández, Nona. "No era depresión, era capitalismo." *El periodista*, 31 Oct. 2019, https://www.elperiodista.cl/nona-fernandez-no-era-depresion-era-capitalismo/.
Ferrando Keun, Ricardo. *Y así nació la Frontera . . . Conquista, Guerra, Ocupación, Pacificación 1550–1900*. 1986. Univerisdad Católica de Temuco, 2012.
Flores, Norberto. "La Quintrala: The Rejection of History as a Patriarchal Legitimizing Discourse in Mercedes Valdivieso's *Maldita yo entre las mujeres*." *Symposium: A Quarterly Journal in Modern Literatures*, vol. 48, no. 4, 1995, pp. 277–84.
Frazier, Lessie Jo. *Salt in the Sand. Memory, Violence, and the Nation-State in Chile, 1890 to the Present*. Duke UP, 2007.
Frías, Gustavo. *El inquisidor*. Alfaguara, 2008.
———. "El Inquisidor. Nueva novela." *Gustavo Frías, escritor chileno*, 2008.
———. *Tres nombres para Catalina. Catrala*. Alfaguara, 2008.
———. *Tres nombres para Catalina. La doña de Campofrío*. Alfaguara, 2003.
———. "Un comienzo para la Quintrala." *El Mercurio*, by Jennifer Abate, 10 Aug. 2008.
Gallardo, Juanita. *Déjame que te cuente*. Planeta, 1997.
Gallardo, Juanita and Luis Vitale. *Balmaceda: sus últimos días*. ChileAmérica, CESOC, 1991.
García, Gabriela. "Publican *Guerreros del Sur*, la obra póstuma de Isidora Aguirre." *La Tercera* 22 Sept., 2011, p. 39.
García Canclini, Néstor. *Consumers and Citizens: Globalization and Multicultural Conflicts*, translated by George Yúdice, U of Minnesota P, 2001.
García-Corales, Guillermo. *Dieciséis entrevistas con autores chilenos contemporáneos. La emergencia de una nueva narrativa*. Edwin Mellon P, 2005.
Garibotto, Verónica. *Crisis y reemergencia. El siglo XIX en la ficción contemporánea de Argentina, Chile y Uruguay (1980–2001)*. Purdue UP, 2015.
Gasca, Pedro. "Documentos relativos al licenciado Pedro Gasca sobre la comisión que le dio Cárlos V en 1545 para ir á pacificar el Perú, sublevado por Gonzalo Pizarro y los suyos." *Colección de documentos inéditos para la historia de España. Tomo XLIX*. Los señores marques de Miraflores y d. Miguel Salva, individuos de la Academia de la Historia, compiladores. Madrid, 1866.
Gay, Claudio. *Historia de la Independencia Chilena*. Paris, 1856.
———. *Historia física y política de Chile*. Santiago, 1844–1854.
Gay Gigante. (gaygigante). "Un amigo en tu privilegio." *Instagram*, 7 Nov. 2019, https://www.instagram.com/p/B4jw9PoAkAw/.
Giddens, Anthony. *The Consequences of Modernity*. Stanford UP, 1991.
Giles, Mary E. *Women in the Inquisition: Spain and the New World*. Johns Hopkins UP, 1999.

"El gobierno de la Unidad Popular (1970–1973)—Memoria Chilena." Memoria Chilena: Portal, https://www.memoriachilena.gob.cl/602/w3-article-31433.html. Accessed 27 May 2024.

Gómez-Barris, Macarena. *Where Memory Dwells. Culture and State Violence in Chile*. U of California P, 2009.

Góngora de Marmolejo, Alonso. *Historia de Chile desde su descubrimiento hasta el año de 1575*. Santiago, 1862.

González de Nájera, Alonso. *Desengaño y reparo de la guerra del Reino de Chile*. Santiago, 1889.

Grau, Olga. "El mito de la Quintrala en el imaginario cultural chileno." *L'hybride/Lo híbrido: Cultures et littératures hispanoamericaines*, 2005, pp. 257–72.

Greenblatt, Stephen. *Marvelous Possessions. The Wonder of the New World*. U of Chicago P, 1991.

Guajardo, Ernesto. *Manuel Rodriguez Historia y Leyenda*. RIL, 2010.

Guarda, Gabriel. *El arquitecto de La Moneda. Joaquín Toesca. 1752–1799. Una imagen del imperio español en América*. Universidad Católica de Chile, 1997.

Guerra, Lucía. "'Maldita yo entre las mujeres' de Mercedes Valdivieso: Resemantización de la Quintrala, figura del mal y del exceso para la chilenidad apolínea." *Revista Chilena de Literatura*, vol. 53, 1998, pp. 47–65.

Guerrero, Elisabeth. *Confronting History and Modernity in Mexican Narrative*. Palgrave Macmillan, 2008.

Guerrero, Gustavo. "Literatura, nación, y globalización en Hispanoamérica: explorando el horizonte post-nacional." *Revista de estudios hispánicos*, vol. 46, no. 1, 2012, pp. 73–81.

Guevara, Tomas. *Ocupación de la Araucanía*. Andújar, 1998.

Gurovich Weisman, Alberto. "La solitaria estrella: en torno a la realización del Barrio Cívico de Santiago de Chile, 1846–1946." *Revista de urbanismo*, vol. 7, 2003, https://doi.org/10.5354/0717-5051.2003.6214.

Guzmán, Jorge. *Ay mama Inés*. Andrés Bello, 1993.

———. *Deus machi*. LOM, 2010.

Harasta, Eva, and Brian Brock. *Evoking Lament: A Theological Discussion*. T & T Clark, 2009.

Hayden, Dolores. *The Power of Place*. MIT P, 1995.

Héroes: La gloria tiene su precio. Corporación de Televisión de la Universidad Católica de Chile and Siglo XXII, 2007–2008.

Herrera y Tordesillas, Antonio de. *Historia General de los hechos de los castellanos en las Islas y tierra firme del mar Océano*. Madrid, 1598.

Hite, Katherine. "Chile's National Stadium. As monument, as memorial." *ReVista: Harvard Review of Latin America*, vol. 3, no. 3, Spring 2004, pp. 58–61. https://revista.drclas.harvard.edu/chiles-national-stadium/.

Hughes-Hallett, Lucy. *Heroes*. Knopf, 2004.

Hutcheon, Linda. *A Poetics of Postmodernism: History, Theory, Fiction*. Routledge, 1988.

Huyssen, Andreas. *Present Pasts. Urban Palimpsests and the Politics of Memory*. Stanford UP, 2003.

Información constatada por el INDH al 31–01–2020. Instituto Nacional de Derechos Humanos, 31 Jan. 2020, https://www.indh.cl/bb/wp-content/uploads/2020/02/Reporte-31-enero-2020.pdf. Accessed 13 Feb. 2020.

"Informe Especial Cadem: Sebastián Piñera Cierra Su Mandato Con 71% de Desaprobación y 24% de Aprobación." *Sitio Web Cadem,* https://cadem.cl/estudios/informe-especial-cadem-sebastian-pinera-cierra-su-mandato-con-71-de-desaprobacion-y-24-de-aprobacion/. Accessed 29 May 2024.

Izquierdo Fernández, Gonzalo. *Historia de Chile.* Andrés Bello, 1989.

Jagoe, Catherine. *Ambiguous Angels. Gender in the Novels of Galdós.* U of California P, 1994.

Jara, Álvaro. *Guerra y sociedad en Chile; La transformación de la Guerra De Arauco y la esclavitud de los indios.* Universitaria, 1971.

Jelin, Elizabeth. *State Repression and the Labors of Memory,* translated by Judy Rein and Marcial Godoy-Anativia, U of Minnesota P, 2003.

Jenkins, Keith. *On "What is History?" From Carr and Elton to Rorty and White.* Routledge, 2005.

Jitrik, Noé. *Historia e imaginación literaria. Las posibilidades de un género.* Biblos, 1995.

"Joaquín Toesca (1752–1799)—Memoria Chilena." *Memoria Chilena: Portal,* https://www.memoriachilena.gob.cl/602/w3-article-658.html.

Jocelyn-Holt, Alfredo. *Historia General de Chile. Tomo II: Los césares perdidos.* Sudamericana, 2004.

———. *Historia general de Chile. Tomo III. Amos, Señores y Patricios.* Sudamericana, 2008.

———. "La Quintrala en un hilo." Prologue of *Los Lisperguer y la Quintrala. Doña Catalina de los Ríos* by Benjamín Vicuña Mackenna. Sudamericana, 2001.

Kaminsky, Amy. *After Exile. Writing the Latin American Diaspora.* U of Minnesota P, 1999.

Karr-Cornejo, Katherine. "Aspects of Social Justice Ally Work in Chilean Historical Fiction: The Case of the Pacification of Araucanía (1860–1883)." *Hispanic Studies Review,* vol. 3, no. 1, 2018, pp. 151–63, https://hispanicstudiesreview.cofc.edu/section/2895-vol-3-issue-1–2018.

———. "Imagined Worlds and the Gendered City in Chilean Historical Fiction." *Cincinnati Romance Review,* vol. 44, spring 2018, pp. 1–18.

Kinsbruner, Jay. *The Colonial Spanish-American City: Urban Life in the Age of Atlantic Capitalism.* U of Texas P, 2006.

Kupers, Terry A. "Toxic Masculinity as a Barrier to Mental Health Treatment in Prison." *Journal of Clinical Psychology,* vol. 61, no. 6, June 2005, pp. 713–24, https://doi.org/10.1002/jclp.20105.

LaCapra, Dominick. *History, Politics, and the Novel.* Cornell UP, 1987.

Landsberg, Alison. *Prosthetic Memory: The Transformation of American Remembrance in the Age of Mass Culture.* Columbia UP, 2004.

Lara, Horacio. *Crónica de la Araucania: descubrimiento i conquista, pacificacion definitiva i campaña de Villa-Rica (leyenda heroico de tres siglos).* Santiago, 1889. Archive.org.

Larner, Christina. "Was Witch-Hunting Woman-Hunting?" *The Witchcraft Reader,* edited by Darren Oldridge, Routledge, 2001, pp. 273–75.

Larraín, Jorge. *Identidad chilena.* LOM, 2001.

Larrea, María Isabel. "Heteroglosia y metaficción en *Déjame que te cuente* de Juanita Gallardo." *Documentos Lingüísticos y Literarios*, vol. 29, 2006.

Lastarria, José Victorino. "Investigaciones sobre la influencia social de la conquista y del sistema colonial de los espanoles en Chile." *Historia jeneral de la República de Chile desde su independencia hasta nuestros días*. Santiago, 1882.

Lazzara, Michael. *Chile in Transition. The Poetics and Politics of Memory*. U of Florida P, 2006.

———. *Civil Obedience. Complicity and Complacency in Chile since Pinochet*. U of Wisconsin P, 2018.

Lee, Rebecca. "Iconic Womanhood, Liberal Discourse and National Identity: Mercedes Valdivieso's *Maldita yo entre las mujeres* (1991) and Benjamín Vicuña Mackenna's *Los Lisperguer y la Quintrala* (1877)." *Latin American Literary Review*, vol. 35, no. 69, 2007, pp. 104–19. *JSTOR*, https://www.jstor.org/stable/20119990.

Leighton, Cristian. "¿El peor gobierno de la historia? Estudio revela que aprobación del segundo período del Presidente Piñera es más baja que la dictadura de Pinochet." *El Mostrador*, 18 Feb. 2022, https://www.elmostrador.cl/destacado/2022/02/18/el-peor-gobierno-de-la-historia-estudio-revela-que-aprobacion-del-segundo-periodo-del-presidente-pinera-es-mas-baja-que-la-dictadura-de-pinochet/.

Linares, José Agustín. *El ultimo clarín*. Andrés Bello, 1991.

López, Kimberle S. *Latin American Novels of the Conquest: Reinventing the New World*. U of Missouri P, 2002.

Lukács, György. *The Historical Novel*, translated by Hannah and Stanley Mitchell, Humanities P, 1978.

Mansilla, Luis Alberto. "Las mujeres chilenas en el encaje colonial." *Las chilenas de la colonia: virtud sumisa, amor rebelde*, edited by Cecilia Salinas, LOM, 1994, pp. 7–12.

Mapuche International Link. www.mapuche-nation.org.

Mariño de Lobera, Pedro. "Crónica del reino de Chile." *Colección de historiadores de Chile y de documentos relativos a la historia nacional. Tomo 6*. Santiago, 1861.

Martínez, Renato. "Ay Mama Inés, de Jorge Guzmán: Entre la crónica y el testimonio." *Revista Chilena de Literatura*, vol. 50, 1997, pp. 21–37.

Maturana, Victor. *Historia de los agustinos en Chile*. Valparaiso de Federico T. Lathrop, 1904.

May, Stella Burke. *The Conqueror's Lady*. Farrar & Rinehart, 1930.

Mayol, Alberto and Carla Azócar. "Politización del malestar, movilización social y transformación ideológica: el caso 'Chile 2011.'" *Polis (Santiago)*, vol. 10, no. 30, 2011, pp. 163–84.

Meacham, Cherie. "Resisting Romance: Isabel Allende's Transformation of the Popular Romance Formula in *Hija de la Fortuna*." *Latin American Literary Review*, vol. 35, no. 69, 2007, pp. 29–45.

Méndez, Cecilia. *The Plebeian Republic. The Huanta Rebellion and the Making of the Peruvian State, 1820–1850*. Duke UP, 2005.

Menton, Seymour. *Latin America's New Historical Novel*. U of Texas P, 1993.

Merino, María Eugenia and David John Mellor. "Perceived discrimination in Mapuche discourse: contemporary racism in Chilean society." *Critical Discourse Studies*, vol. 6, no. 3, 2009, pp. 215–26. https://doi.org/10.1080/17405900902974902.

"El mestizaje, la Quintrala y el poder de los jesuitas." *Algo Habrán Hecho por Chile*, directed by Nicolás Acuña, episode 2, Televisión Nacional de Chile, 25 July 2010.

Metzger, Scott Alan. "Pedagogy and the Historical Feature Film: Toward Historical Literacy." *Film and History*, vol. 37, no. 2, 2007, pp. 67–74, https://doi.org/10.1353/flm.2007.0058.

Milanich, Nara B. *Children of Fate. Childhood, Class, and the State in Chile, 1850–1930*. Duke UP, 2009.

Milestones in the History of U.S. Foreign Relations—Office of the Historian. https://history.state.gov/milestones/1969–1976/allende. Accessed 27 May 2024.

Millar, Rene and Carmen Gloria Duhart. "La vida en los claustros. Monjas y frailes, disciplinas y devociones." *Historia de la vida privada en Chile. El Chile tradicional. De la Conquista a 1840*, edited by Cristián Gazmuri and Rafael Sagredo, Aguilar, 2005, pp. 125–59.

Miranda, Rodrigo. "Isidora Aguirre regresa a la novela con el suicidio de Balmaceda." *La Tercera*, 16 Dec. 2008. *LaTercera.com*, http://www.latercera.com/noticia/isidora-aguirre-regresa-a-la-novela-con-el-suicidio-de-balmaceda/.

Molina, Abate Juan Ignacio. *Compendio de la historia geográfica, natural y civil del Reyno de Chile*, translated by Domingo Joseph. Madrid, 1788.

Montaldo, Graciela. "La desigualdad de las partes." *A contracorriente*, vol. 7, no 1., Fall 2009, pp. 14–44.

Montanari, Massimo. *Food is Culture*, translated by Albert Sonnenfeld, Columbia U P, 2006.

Montecino, Sonia. *Madres y huachos: alegorías del mestizaje chileno*. Sudamericana, 1996.

"Montt y Mackenna." *Algo Habrán Hecho Por La Historia de Chile*, directed by Nicolás Acuña, episode 6, Televisión Nacional de Chile, 22 Aug. 2010.

Morales Piña, Eddie. "Brevísima Relación de la Nueva Novela Histórica en Chile." *Notas históricas y geográficas*, no. 12, 2001, pp. 177–90.

Moreno, Fernando. "De la Historia a la novela (en torno a *El viaducto* de Darío Oses)." *1898–1998; fines de siglos; historia y literatura hispanoamericanas*, edited by Jacques Joset, Library Droz, 2000, pp. 147–61.

———. "Novelar y revelar la Historia." *Literatura y Lingüística. Homenaje al Instituto Pedagógico de la Universidad de Chile Sede Valparaíso*, 2003, pp. 9–16.

Moulián, Tomás. *Chile actual. La anatomía de un mito*. LOM, 2002.

Muñoz Román, Ricardo. "Discurso informativo y luchas por el reconocimiento. El 'conflicto mapuche' en El Mercurio y La Segunda (Chile, 2008–2009)." *Perspectivas de la Comunicación*, vol. 3, no. 2, 2010, pp. 29–47, https://www.perspectivasdelacomunicacion.cl/ojs/index.php/perspectivas/article/view/94.

Murray, Pamela. *For Glory and Bolívar: the Remarkable Life of Manuela Sáenz, 1797–1856*. U of Texas P, 2008.

Nelson, Robert S. and Margaret Olin. *Monuments and Memory, Made and Unmade*. U of Chicago P, 2003.

Nicoletti, María Andrea. "Los misioneros salesianos y la polémica sobre la extinción de los selk'nam de Tierra del Fuego." *Anthropológica*, vol. 24, no. 24, 2006, pp. 153-77, http://www.scielo.org.pe/scielo.php?script=sci_arttext&pid=S0254-92122006000100007.

Nussbaum, Martha. "Cultivating Humanity in Legal Education." *University of Chicago Law Review*, vol. 70, no. 1, 2003, pp. 265-79, https://chicagounbound.uchicago.edu/uclrev/vol70/iss1/18.

OECD. *Does Inequality Matter?: How People Perceive Economic Disparities and Social Mobility*. OECD, 2021. DOI.org *(Crossref)*, https://doi.org/10.1787/3023ed40-en.

Ojos sobre Chile: Violencia policial y responsabilidad de mando durante el estallido social. Amnistía Internacional, Oct. 2020, https://www.amnesty.org/es/documents/amr22/3133/2020/es/.

Olivares, Miguel de. *Historia militar, civil y sagrada de Chile*. Santiago, 1864.

Oña, Pedro de. *Arauco Domado*. Universitaria, 1917.

Ondarza, Antonio. *Javiera Carrera V. Heroína de la Patria Vieja*. Neupert, 1967.

Orrego Vicuña, Eugenio. *O'Higgins. Vida y Tiempo*. Losada, 1957.

Ortega, Manuel. *Inés de Suárez en defensa de Santiago*. 1897, Museo Histórico Nacional, Santiago.

Oses, Darío. *El viaducto*. Planeta, 1994.

Ovalle, Alonso de. *Histórica relación del Reyno de Chile y de las missiones y ministerios que exercita en el la Compañia de Jesus*. Rome, 1646.

Palacios, Carlos. "¿Cómo migró la clase alta en estos 100 años?" *La Tercera*, 12 Sept. 2010, p. 52.

La película del rey, directed by Carlos Sorín, Motion Pictures, 1986.

Peña González, Patricia. "Y las mujeres, ¿dónde estuvieron?: mujeres en el proceso independentista chileno." *Anuario de postgrado/Universidad de Chile, Facultad de Filosofía y Humanidades, Escuela de Postgrado*. LOM, Oct. 1997, pp. 235-42.

Peña Otaegui, Carlos. *Santiago de siglo en siglo: comentario histórico e iconográfico de su formación y evolución en los cuatro siglos de su existencia*. Zig-zag, 1944.

Pereira Salas, Eugenio. *Apuntes para la historia de la cocina chilena*. Universitaria, 1977.

Pérez García, José Antonio. *Historia de Chile*. Santiago, 1900.

Pérez Rosales, Vicente. *Recuerdos del pasado: 1814–1860*. Santiago, 1886.

Perkowska, Magdalena. *Historias híbridas. La nueva novela histórica latinoamericana (1985–2000) ante las teorías posmodernas de la historia*. Vervuert Iberoamericana, 2008.

Petit, Magdalena. *La Quintrala*. Zig-Zag, 1966.

Piérola, José de. "At the Edge of History: Notes for a Theory for the Historical Novel in Latin America." *Romance Studies*, vol. 26, no. 2, 2008, pp. 151-62. https://doi.org/10.1179/174581508x287446.

Pilcher, Jeffrey. *Food in World History*. Routledge, 2006.

Piñera, Sebastián. "Bicentenario: Juntos por Chile." *Gobierno de Chile*. 23 June 2010.

———. "'Chile somos todos y debemos soñarlo, dibujarlo y construirlo entre todos'; el primer discurso del Presidente Piñera en el Palacio de La Moneda." *Prensa Presidencia*, 11 Mar. 2018, http://prensa.presidencia.cl/comunicado.aspx?id=71719.

Pino, Patricio. "INDH presentó cifras a cuatro años de crisis social de 2019: de 3.216

querellas, sólo en 33 de ellas existen sentencias condenatorias." *INDH*, 18 Oct. 2023, https://www.indh.cl/indh-presento-cifras-a-cuatro-anos-de-crisis-social-de-2019-de-3–216-querellas-solo-en-34-de-ellas-existen-sentencias-condenatorias/.

Pinto Rodríguez, Jorge. *La formación del estado y la nación, y el pueblo mapuche: de la inclusión a la exclusión*. DIBAM, Centro de Investigaciones Diego Barros Arana, 2003. *Memoria chilena*. http://www.memoriachilena.gob.cl/602/w3-article-9268.html.

Pons, María Cristina. *Memorias del olvido. Del Paso, García Márquez, Saer y la novela histórica de fines del siglo XX*. Siglo Veintiuno, 1996.

Power, Margaret. *Right-Wing Women in Chile: Feminine Power and the Struggle Against Allende, 1964–1973*. Pennsylvania State UP, 2002.

"Quince minutos duró el bombardeo a La Moneda." *La Tercera*, 13 Sept. 1973, p. 7.

La Quintrala—Memoria Chilena, Biblioteca Nacional de Chile. https://www.memoriachilena.gob.cl/602/w3-article-96785.html. Accessed 2 June 2021.

Rabine, Leslie W. *Reading the Romantic Heroine. Text, History, Ideology*. U of Michigan P, 1985.

Radway, Janice. *Reading the Romance: Women, Patriarchy, and Popular Literature*. U of North Carolina P, 1984.

Ramos Collado, Lilliana. "Sueños patrimoniales: Chile reinventa su historia ante la UNESCO." *Romanitas: Lenguas y literaturas romances*, vol. 3, no. 1, 2008, n.p.

Raspail, Jean. *Yo, Antoine de Tounens, Rey de La Patagonia*. Emecé Editores, 1983.

Report of the Mission to Chile 30 October–22 November 2019. United Nations Human Rights, 13 Dec. 2019, https://www.ohchr.org/Documents/Countries/CL/Report_Chile_2019_ EN.pdf. Accessed 13 Feb. 2020.

Reyes, Germán. "Jorge Edwards y el viaje inmóvil de la escritura crítica." *Anales de literatura chilena*, vol. 7, no. 7, 2006, pp. 173–85, https://doi.org/10.7764/ANALESLITCHI.07.11.

Richard, Nelly. *Cultural Residues: Chile in Transition*, translated by Alan West-Durán y Theodore Quester, U of Minnesota P, 2004.

——. "Introducción." *Pensar en/la postdictadura*, edited by Nelly Richard and Alberto Moreiras, Cuarto Propio, 2001, pp. 9–20.

Richards, Patricia. *Race and the Chilean Miracle*. U of Pittsburgh P, 2013.

Ricoeur, Paul. *Memory, History, Forgetting*, translated by Kathleen Blamey and Davild Pellauer, U of Chicago P, 2004.

——. *The Reality of the Historical Past*. Marquette UP, 1984.

Rivera Letelier, Hernán. *Santa María de las flores negras*. Seix Barral, 2002.

Rodden, John, editor. *Conversations with Isabel Allende*. U of Texas P, 1999.

Rosales, Diego de. *Historia general del reino de Chile. Flandes indiano*. Santiago, 1877–1878.

Le Royaume D'Araucanie et de Patagonie. www.araucanie.com.

Sabato, Hilda. "On Political Citizenship in Nineteenth-Century Latin America." *American Historical Review*, vol. 106, no. 4, 2001, pp. 1290–1315, https://doi.org/10.1086/ahr/106.4.1290.

Sagredo, Rafael. "Prólogo." *1891: Entre el fulgor y la agonía*, by Juan Gabriel Araya, Universitaria, 1991, pp. 9–11.

———. *Vapor al norte, tren al sur. El viaje presidencial como práctica política en Chile. Siglo XIX*. DIBAM, Centro de Investigaciones Diego Barros Arana, 2001.
Salazar Vergara, Gabriel. *Conversaciones con Carlos Altamirano: memorias críticas*. Debate, 2011.
Salinas, Cecilia. *Las chilenas de la colonia: virtud sumisa, amor rebelde*. LOM, 1994.
Salinas, Maximiliano. "Población, habitación e intimidad en el Chile tradicional." *Historia de la vida privada en Chile. El Chile tradicional. De la Conquista a 1840*, edited by Cristián Gazmuri and Rafael Sagredo, Aguilar, 2005, pp. 11–47.
San José Vázquez, Eduardo. *La memoria posible. El Sueño de la Historia, de Jorge Edwards: Ilustración y transición democrática en Chile*. Universidad de Oviedo, Departamento de Filología Española, 2007.
Santini, Adrián. *La vulnerable ostentación del orden. La parodia en tres novelas de Jorge Edwards*. Catalonia, 2006.
Sater, William. *Andean Tragedy: Fighting the War of the Pacific, 1879–1884*. U of Nebraska P, 2007.
Schulz Cruz, Bernard. *Las inquisiciones de Jorge Edwards*. Pliegos, 1994.
Scott, Joan Wallach. *Gender and the Politics of History*. Columbia UP, 1999.
Silva A., Bárbara. *Identidad y nación entre dos siglos. Patria Vieja, Centenario y Bicentenario*. LOM, 2008.
Síntesis de Resultados. Censo 2017. Instituto Nacional de Estadísticas, June 2018, https://www.ine.gob.cl/docs/default-source/censo-de-poblacion-y-vivienda/publicaciones-y-anuarios/2017/publicaci%C3%B3n-de-resultados/sintesis-de-resultados-censo2017.pdf?sfvrsn=1b2dfb06_6.
Sommer, Doris. *Foundational Fictions: The National Romances of Latin America*. U of California P, 1993.
Sorensen, Kristin. *Media, Memory, and Human Rights in Chile*. Palgrave Macmillan, 2009.
Staiger, Pedro. *La corona de Araucanía*. Planeta, 1998.
The State of Food Security and Nutrition in the World 2023. Food and Agriculture Organization of the United Nations (FAO), the International Fund for Agricultural Development (IFAD), the United Nations Children's Fund (UNICEF), the World Food Programme (WFP), the World Health Organization (WHO), 2023, https://doi.org/10.4060/cc3017en.
Stern, Steve. *Reckoning with Pinochet. The Memory Question in Democratic Chile, 1989–2006*. Duke UP, 2010.
Stocker, Margarita. *Judith, Sexual Warrior. Women and Power in Western Culture*. Yale UP, 1998.
Stowe, Steven. "Making Sense of Letters and Diaries." *History Matters: The U.S. Survey Course on the Web*, 2002, http://historymatters.gmu.edu/mse/letters/.
Strasma, Mary Grace. "Histories in its Walls: La Moneda, Memory and Reconciliation in Post-Authoritarian Chile." U of Minnesota, 2010.
Stringer-O'Keefe, Susan. "Inés Suárez, "Primera Dama" del Reyno de Chile (o la mujer en la conquista de Chile)." *ALPHA*, vol. 15, 1999, pp. 53–67.
Sturken, Marita. *Tangled Memories: The Vietnam War, the AIDS Epidemic, and the Politics of Remembering*. U of California P, 1997.

Subercaseaux, Bernardo. "El 91 y la literatura." *Revista chilena de literatura*, no. 45, 1994, pp. 121–25.

———. *Historia de las ideas y de la cultura en Chile. Tomo II. Fin de siglo: La época de Balmaceda*. Universitaria, 1997.

Super, John C. *Food, Conquest, and Colonization in Sixteenth-Century Spanish America*. U of New Mexico P, 1988.

Suthrell, Charlotte. *Unzipping Gender: Sex, Cross-Dressing and Culture*. Berg, 2004.

Sutton, Imogen. "'De gente que a ningún rey obedecen': Republicanism and Empire in Alonso de Ercilla's *La Araucana*." *Bulletin of Hispanic Studies*, vol. 91, no. 4, 2014, pp. 417–35, https://doi.org/10.3828/bhs.2014.27.

Tabbush, Berta de. *El Intruso*. Selectas, 1967.

Tally, Robert T., Jr. "On Literary Cartography: Narrative as a Spatially Symbolic Act." *New American Notes Online*, 2011, https://nanocrit.com/index.php/issues/issue1/literary-cartography-narrative-spatially-symbolic-act.

Telles, Edward and René Flores. "Not Just Color: Whiteness, Nation, and Status in Latin America." *Hispanic American Historical Review*, vol. 93, no. 3, 2013, pp. 411–49, https://doi.org/10.1215/00182168-2210858.

La Tercera Domingo. 20 Oct. 2019, p. 1.

Thayer Ojeda, Tomás and Carlos J. Larraín. *Valdivia y sus compañeros*. Universitaria, 1950.

"Toesca, Manolita y sus amasios o las inenarrables desventuras de Joaquín Toesca en Chile." *Revista Patrimonio Cultural*, vol. 9, no. 30, 2004.

Tounens, Antoine de. *Orllie-Antoine I Rey de Araucania y de Patagonia. Su asunción al trono y su cautiverio en Chile. Relato escrito por el mismo*, translated by Loreto Camilo, Valente Editores, 2005.

Trouillot, Michel-Rolph. *Silencing the Past: Power and the Production of History*. Beacon Press, 1995.

Tuan, Yi-Fu. *Space and Place. The Perspective of Experience*: U of Minnesota P, 1977.

Turner, Joseph W. "The Kinds of Historical Fiction: An Essay in Definition and Methodology." *Genre*, vol. 12, no. 3, 1979, pp. 333–55.

UC, Digital Direction-Provost Office. "Elisa Loncón: The Decolonization of Language." *Pontificia Universidad Católica de Chile*, http://www.uc.cl/en/news/elisa-loncon-the-decolonization-of-language/.

Valdivia, Pedro de. *Cartas de Pedro de Valdivia: que tratan del descubrimiento y conquista de Chile*. Establecimiento Tipográfico de M. Carmona, 1929.

Valdivieso, Mercedes. *Maldita yo entre las mujeres*. Planeta, 1991.

Verdugo, Sergio, and Luis Eugenio García-Huidobro. "How Do Constitution-Making Processes Fail? The Case of Chile's Constitutional Convention (2021–22)." *Global Constitutionalism*, vol. 13, no. 1, 2024, pp. 154–67. Cambridge UP, https://doi.org/10.1017/S204538172300031X.

Vicuña, Alejandro. *Inés de Suárez*. Nascimiento, 1941.

Vicuña Mackenna, Benjamín. *Doña Javiera de Carrera: rasgo biográfico: leído en el Círculo de Amigos de las Letras*. Guillermo E Miranda, 1904.

———. *Historia crítica y social de la ciudad de Santiago: desde su fundación hasta nuestros días (1541–1888)*. Santiago, 1869.

———. *Lautaro y sus tres campañas contra Santiago, 1553–1557: estudio biográfico según nuevos documentos*. Santiago, 1876.

———. *Los Lisperguer y la Quintrala. (Doña Catalina de los Ríos). Episodio histórico-social con numerosos documentos inéditos*. Santiago, 1877.

———. *El ostracismo de los Carrera*. Santiago, 1857.

Vidal, Virginia. *Javiera Carrera, Madre de la Patria*. Sudamericana, 2000.

———. *Oro veneno puñal*. Bronquil, 2002.

Vila, María del Pilar. *Las máscaras de la decadencia*. Beatriz Viterbo, 2006.

Villalobos, Sergio. *Historia de los chilenos*. Taurus, 2006.

Viu, Antonia. *Imaginar el pasado, decir el presente. La novela histórica chilena (1985–2003)*. RIL, 2007.

Vivar, Jerónimo de. *Crónica y relación copiosa y verdadera de los reinos de Chile. Tomo 2*. Fondo Histórico y Bibliográfico José Toribio Medina, 1966.

Vollendorf, Lisa. *The Lives of Women: A New History of Inquisitional Spain*. Vanderbilt UP, 2005.

Waisberg, Myriam. *Joaquín Toesca; arquitecto y maestro*. Facultad de Arquitectura y Urbanismo, Universidad de Chile, 1975.

Waldman, Gilda. "Chile: indígenas y mestizos negados." *Política y cultura*, vol. 21, 2004, pp. 97–110.

———. "La 'cultura de la memoria': problemas y reflexiones." *Política y cultura*, vol. 26, 2006, pp. 11–34.

Walter, Richard J. "Literature and History in Contemporary Latin America." *Latin American Literary Review*, vol. 15, no. 29, 1987, pp. 173–82.

Ward, Rhonda. "A Colonial Woman in a Republican's History: Benjamin Vicuña Mackenna and La Quintrala." *Journal of Women's History*, vol. 13, no. 1, 2001, pp. 83–107, https://doi.org/10.1353/jowh.2001.0036.

Webb, Andrew and Sarah Radcliffe. "Mapuche Demands during Educational Reform, the Penguin Revolution and the Chilean Winter of Discontent." *Studies in Ethnicity and Nationalism*, vol. 13, no. 3, 2013, pp. 319–41, https://doi.org/10.1111/sena.12046.

Weisman, Leslie Kanes. *Discrimination by Design. A Feminist Critique of the Man-Made Environment*. U of Illinois P, 1992.

White, Hayden. *Metahistory: The Historical Imagination in Nineteenth-Century Europe*. Johns Hopkins UP, 1975.

———. *The Tropics of Discourse. Essays in Cultural Criticism*. Johns Hopkins U P, 1978.

Yeager, Gertrude. "Barros Arana, Vicuña Mackenna, Amunátegui: The Historian as National Educator." *Journal of Interamerican Studies and World Affairs*, vol. 19, no. 2, 1977, pp. 173–200.

Zúñiga, Fernando. *Mapudungun. El habla mapuche*. Centro de Estudios Públicos, 2006.

INDEX

Aguirre, Isidora, 88-91, 169–70, 171–77, 180–87
Allende, Isabel, 20, 26, 42–55
Allende, Salvador, 6, 174, 176
architecture and building practices, 4, 95–96, 100–102. *See also* Santiago architecture
archival sources, 14–15, 34, 172–75
authority, narrative, 42–44, 72–74, 119–20, 124–26, 137

Balmaceda, José Manuel, 5; history, 159–60; as mythical figure 164–66; characterization 168–69, 172–73
bicentennial celebrations, 93–94, 113, 205n26

Carrera, Javiera, 4; history 114–15; as national cypher 115–16, 118; as mother figure 118, 120; as communicator 119–20
citizenship, 10–12
Civil War of 1891, 159–60; brutality, 181–83; historiography 162–64
class: identity, 161–62, 177; importance of, 177, 182–84
colonialism, 43, 78–79, 88–91
Concepción, 23, 89
conquest, 24, 32, 44, 71–72, 77–78
constitutional reform of 2022, 191–92
Correa Morandé, Maria, 37–39
Coup d'etat of 11 September 1973, 6, 93, 105, 107

cultural memory, 7–9, 73–74

democratic transition, 6, 127, 129–30, 149–50, 189, 204n17
difference, 10–12
domesticity, 30, 116, 121, 185

Edwards Bello, Joaquín, 67–68
Edwards, Jorge, 95–96, 97–104, 111–12
empanadas, delicious, 52–54

feminism, 48, 96–97
foodways, 50–52, 123, 142
Frías, Gustavo, 69, 73–83, 85–86

Gallardo, Juanita, 113, 120–26, 168–69

historical competence, 17–18, 121–23
historical novel, 12–19
history in film, 67–68, 129, 157–58, 209n32
historiographical metafiction, 29, 168–72

identity: collective, 78, 102, 107; national, 42, 66, 68, 94, 113
independence from Spain, 98, 113–15, 205–6n30
indigenous perspective: erasure of, 5, 138–39, 152–53; in government, contemporary, 149–50
inquisition, 79

La Moneda Palace, 104–12

Lagos, Ricardo, 6, 204n19
language as culture, 44, 142, 155, 158, 185–86
Lientur, 88–91
Lisperguer, Catalina de los Ríos, 4; embodiment of racial mixing, 80–83; history, 57–58; as mythical figure, 60–61, 64, 69, 75, 85–87; as violent actor, 83–85; as witch, 67, 70–71
Lo Cañas massacre, 170, 178–79

Mapuche: history, 131–32; rebellion, 88–90; representation, 145–46, 148–49, 153–54; reservations, 5; resistance, 21, 49
masculinization of historical women, 26, 32–33, 35, 45, 82–83, 115–16
memory, 66, 73–74, 86, 102, 175–76; place memory, 105–6
mestizaje, 41–43, 48–50, 61, 68, 75–76, 91
military dictatorship, 2, 6
monuments, 23–24, 105–12

Naval Battle of Iquique, 157
national character as represented by woman, 36, 37
neoliberalism, 6, 110–11, 121
New Historical novel, 16, 19–20, 39–40, 69–70
North, John Thomas, 183

O'Higgins, Bernardo, 112, 113–15, 117, 118, 120–26; as father figure, 122
Occupation of Araucanía, 129–32, 135–38, 140–41, 155–56, 158
Oses, Darío, 160–72, 180–86

philosophy of history, 9, 14–15
picunche, 76–77, 201n13
pigmentocracy, 161–62
Piñera, Sebastián, 189
Pinochet, Augusto, 2, 6, 71, 98, 189–90

place memory, 105–6
plurinationality, 130, 207n2
political protest of 2019, 23, 103, 190–91
power, 9–12, 39–41, 59–62, 78–83, 96–102, 107–11, 116–17, 140, 182–86
Puga, Rosario, 4, 115, 117; history, 120–21; as everyday woman, 124–26

Quintrala, 71–72. See also Lisperguer, Catalina de los Ríos

race and ethnicity. See mestizaje; class
representation of historical women, 27, 31–33, 185
romance literature, 33–34, 38–39, 41–42, 198n10

Santiago, 30, 96, 99; founding of, 31–32; naming, 112–13; urban landscape, 99–100, 102–4
Selk'nam genocide, 144
sex, 25–27, 45–48, 53, 64–65, 75–76, 85–86, 117
silence and absence, historical, 58, 205n28
Staiger, Pedro, 22, 150–55
Suárez, Inés, 4, 26–27, 43–44, 49–50; characterization, 32, 34–37, 38, 45; history, 24; as mother figure, 26, 30, 36, 41; as sexual being, 44–47; as violent actor, 26, 28, 31, 41
syncretic religion, 74–75, 81

television, 66-68, 113, 157–58
Toesca, Joaquín, 4, 95–96, 98–99, 109
Tounens, Orélie-Antoine, 5; history, 132–35; in fiction, 141–42, 144–47, 150–54; as public figure, 136–39
toxic masculinity, 178–80

Valdivia, Pedro de, 4, 27; history, 24; relationship with Inés Suárez, 31–32, 33–34, 38–41, 43, 45
Valdivieso, Mercedes, 69–70, 74–75

Vicuña Mackenna, Benjamín: anti-indigenous rhetoric, 132; on Catalina de los Ríos Lisperguer, 63–65, 67–69; on Inés Suárez, 25, 29–30, 36; on Javiera Carrera, 115–17; Ur-Narrative of Quintrala, 59–62

Vidal, Virginia, 19, 71–73, 83–86, 95, 113, 118–20, 126–27, 168–69

violence, 83–86, 180–81

War of Arauco, 3, 5, 21. *See also* Occupation of Araucanía

War of the Pacific, 21, 130, 156–58

witchcraft, 61–62

www.ingramcontent.com/pod-product-compliance
Lightning Source LLC
Chambersburg PA
CBHW030648230426
43665CB00011B/999